Contemporary Russia

Second Edition

Edwin Bacon

First edition 2006
Second edition 2010

Published by
PALGRAVE MACMILLAN

Palgrave Macmillan in the UK is an imprint of Macmillan Publishers Limited, registered in England, company number 785998, of Houndmills, Basingstoke, Hampshire RG21 6XS.

Palgrave Macmillan in the US is a division of St Martin's Press LLC, 175 Fifth Avenue, New York, NY 10010.

Palgrave Macmillan is the global academic imprint of the above companies and has companies and representatives throughout the world.

Palgrave® and Macmillan® are registered trademarks in the United States, the United Kingdom, Europe and other countries.

ISBN 978–0–230–22370–7   hardback
ISBN 978–0–230–22371–4   paperback

This book is printed on paper suitable for recycling and made from fully managed and sustained forest sources. Logging, pulping and manufacturing processes are expected to conform to the environmental regulations of the country of origin.

A catalogue record for this book is available from the British Library.

A catalog record for this book is available from the Library of Congress.

10 9 8 7 6 5 4 3 2 1
19 18 17 16 15 14 13 12 11 10

Printed and bound in China

Contents

List of Illustrations, Maps, Figures, Tables and Boxes

Acknowledgements to the Second Edition

As with the first edition of *Contemporary Russia*, this second edition owes much to the insights of colleagues working in the range of specialist fields covered in its chapters. I am particularly grateful to Mark Sandle, Erica Richardson, Jon Oldfield, Cathy Shaw, David White and an anonymous reviewer for their helpful comments. I am grateful too to the Department of Politics at Birkbeck, University of London, for providing support, both intellectually and, more practically, by facilitating trips to Russia in order to gather material.

The second edition is substantially revised in all areas where developments in Russia have necessitated such revision. This does not just mean the inclusion of new facts, such as the election of Dmitrii Medvedev as president, or the economic difficulties of 2008 and beyond, but also changes in interpretation. Discussions with colleagues and friends too numerous to mention, from various areas of activity relating to Russia, have contributed to the ongoing process of seeking to understand this fascinating country. If I mention fruitful conversations in London, Birmingham, Rome and Moscow, then I probably won't miss out too many interlocutors. They have my gratitude.

What has not changed between editions is the gratitude I owe to my family. Invaluable support and succour has come from my wife Deborah, and our daughters Eleanor, Charlotte, Emily and Joanna. They have my love and thanks as always.

EDWIN BACON

List of Abbreviations

BBC	British Broadcasting Corporation
CEO	chief executive officer
CIS	Commonwealth of Independent States
CSTO	Collective Security Treaty Organization
FIDE	World Chess Federation
FDI	foreign direct investment
FSB	Russian security service
GDP	gross domestic product
GUAM	semi-official grouping of states of Georgia, Ukraine, Azerbaijan and Moldova
IMF	International Monetary Fund
KGB	national security agency of the USSR
LDPR	Liberal Democratic Party of Russia
MDR-TB	multi-drug-resistant tuberculosis
MFA	Ministry of Foreign Affairs (Russia)
NGO	non-governmental organization
OECD	Organisation for Economic Co-operation and Development
OSCE	Organization for Security and Cooperation in Europe
PJC	Permanent Joint Council (consultation forum between Russia and NATO)
POW	prisoner of war
R&D	research and development
RSFSR	Russian Soviet Federative Socialist Republic
SCO	Shanghai Cooperation Organization
UNDP	United Nations Development Programme
UNICEF	United Nations Children's Fund (formerly United Nations International Children's Emergency Fund)
USSR	Union of Soviet Socialist Republics
WHO	World Health Organization
WTO	World Trade Organization

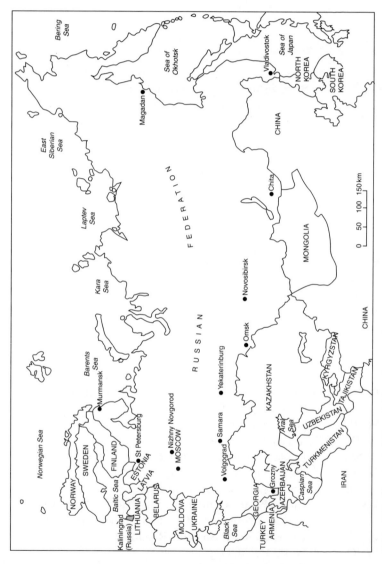

Map 0.1 Russia and its neighbouring states

Introduction

Russia has re-emerged on to the world stage in the first decade of the twenty-first century. In the 1990s, the superpower that was the Soviet Union collapsed and a Russian state much reduced in power, strength and influence came into being. Its president, Boris Yeltsin, was a sick man given to bouts of heavy drinking, and he seemed to encapsulate symbolically the state of which he was head. On Millennium Eve 1999, Yeltsin resigned. This step can be seen as symbolizing a new era in Russia's development. Under the presidencies of Vladimir Putin and Dmitrii Medvedev, Russia since 2000 has appeared revital-ized – more confident, stronger and richer. From Yeltsin, through Putin, to Medvedev there has been a rapid generational change in leadership. Yeltsin spent his adult life among the Communist elite of the Soviet regime. Putin, having served in the KGB in the latter years of the Soviet Union's existence, did not enter politics until he joined the democratic movement in the early 1990s. President Medvedev was only in his mid-twenties when the Soviet collapse occurred, and his entire working life – as a lawyer and politician – has been in the post-Soviet era.

Contemporary Russia is much argued over by Western observers. There is no general consensus about its political aims or its position in the world. Many revert to conceptualizations familiar from the Cold War years – an undemocratic Russia governed by a narrow and self-perpetuating elite, using violence, imprisonment and censorship to keep its domestic opponents in check, and pursuing an expansion-ist and destabilizing foreign policy opposed to the interests of the West. Others argue that, twenty years after the Cold War ended, such an approach to Russia takes insufficient account of the difference between that era and today. There is no great ideologically-based systemic divide between Russia and the West. While not to be condoned, the use of violence, imprisonment and censorship by the government of Russia today is on nothing like the same scale in terms of prevalence, method and clear-cut state involvement as that seen in

1

the Soviet years. Most markedly, the notions of 'East' and 'West' are not so self-evident as they once were. Russia is a member of the G8 (though its membership has been called into question in recent years) and has a formally close relationship with NATO. Russian business interests are global in scope. The closed world of Soviet Russia has given way to a time when Russians, like so many other people, interact across the world by means of technology and travel.

This book explores these conflicting conceptualizations of contemporary Russia. It details developments in Russian politics, analyses the strengths and weaknesses of Russia's economy, considers the nature of Russian society today, assesses the rights and freedoms of the Russian people, explores the key ideas informing contemporary Russia's political and cultural life, and evaluates Russia's place in the world in the light of recent international events. Its analysis of contemporary Russia builds on the foundation of chapters on Russia's history and ethno-geographical make-up.

No overview of Russia today can, or should, avoid the consideration of the Soviet era as a contextualizing factor. However, it is the contention of this volume that it is no longer appropriate, almost two decades after the collapse of the Soviet Union, to remain fixated on the notion of post-Communism. In looking for immediate historical influences on and explanations for the way that contemporary Russia is developing, it is the transition years of the 1990s that are the most influential. Out of this era emerged the giant companies that dominate Russia's economy; the political developments of the Putin–Medvedev years are most commonly explained in Russia as a reaction to the relative chaos of the Yeltsin years; and, as President Medvedev exemplifies, it is the generation who came to adulthood as the Soviet Union disappeared who are now beginning to come to the fore in Russia.

However, as this book makes clear, the immediate history of contemporary Russia, though immensely influential, is only part of what makes Russia what it is today. There are two other key themes that recur time and again in the book. First is the deep-seated Russian national identity. Both Communism and, since 1991, Western liberalism can to some extent be portrayed accurately as a veneer applied over more influential and longer-lasting features of Russian life. Under Presidents Putin and Medvedev, Russia's government has actively sought to recreate a Russian national identity, based on a particular narrative emphasizing Russia's distinctiveness among European nations.

Whatever the regime, there are elements of 'Russian-ness' that recur repeatedly:

- An ambivalent relationship between the state and the people – the alleged desire of the Russian people for a 'strong hand' to lead them, and yet at the same time a deep distrust of those who operate on behalf of the authorities, and a deep cynicism about the political process. At times it can appear as if there is a recurrent cycle of reform and reaction in Russian life, of the gaining of individual liberties and the reeling back in of the same by the state.
- A self-identity that often defines Russian-ness in relation to the West. For many centuries, Russian history has developed through cycles of embracing and deriding Europe and 'the West' more generally, torn between adopting many of the West's advances in prosperity and technology, but at the same time believing in the inherent uniqueness of Russia and its superiority over the materialist, decadent West. Russia is – geographically and demographically, culturally and spiritually – both European and Asiatic. To understand Russia it is essential to recognize this fact.

The second theme that occurs repeatedly throughout this book stands at odds to some extent with what this introduction has so far outlined. That theme is change, and the inevitability of a new generation shaping Russia in the globalized world of the twenty-first century. To gain a good understanding of what characterizes contemporary Russia, it is important not to buy too readily into the clichés of Russian history. One can recognize the importance and influence of history without being blind to the inevitability of change.

Despite the predictions of some observers as the Putin regime strengthened the Russian state in the early years of the twenty-first century, Russia cannot go back to what it was in the Communist era. Russia is not locked into an unbreakable imperialist impulse, or on an inevitable path back to an all-powerful authoritarian state. At least as influential as history are today's circumstances and today's Russians.

Contemporary Russia is a country replete with tensions and problems:

- The gap between the growing affluent middle class and the fifth of the population living below the poverty line is widening.
- More Russians travel and live abroad than ever before, and yet at home Russian nationalism and xenophobia are growing political forces.

- Russia's leaders have emphasized the nation's uniqueness and sovereignty, but continued economic growth depends on closer international co-operation.
- During the early years of the twenty-first century, the Russian economy has grown impressively, largely on the back of oil and gas production, but the actions of the state in overtly controlling such production fly in the face of a commitment to the free market.
- Russia is facing a demographic crisis during the decades to come, with a declining and ageing population, which will create serious difficulties for economic development.
- Despite having a democratic constitution since 1993, five parliamentary elections and four presidential elections have still not seen a democratic change of regime in Russia.
- The formal structures and rules in place in relation to the state's engagement with the people are frequently supplemented or undermined by informal practices, corruption and political interference.

These issues and many others are examined in this book, presenting an introduction to Russia today – to its society, politics, economy, and culture. Chapter 1 provides the historical background, covering briefly the Tsarist period, the Communist years, the collapse of the Soviet Union, and the presidencies of Boris Yeltsin and Vladimir Putin. It ends with President Medvedev's rise to power. Throughout the chapter, key elements of Russia's history are drawn out, notably the role of the state and Russia's relationship with 'the West', and the interaction of these issues with questions of modernization and national identity.

Chapter 2 introduces the Russian land and peoples. The first part deals with Russia's physical setting, environmental issues, borders, cities, the impact of Russia's geostrategic location on its development and history, and an outline of its demographic development and current demographic crisis. The second part discusses the identity of the inhabitants of Russia, focusing particularly on the multi-ethnic nature of the Russian Federation. It considers too the notion of national values. This chapter also focuses on Russia's regions, outlining development of the federal structure of Russia in recent years and the centralizing policies of Putin and Medvedev.

Chapter 3 looks at Russian society today. In particular, it covers four areas of great significance to the inhabitants of Russia: namely, living standards; demographic and health issues; judicial policy; and education. The chapter supplies key data about mortality and birth

Table 0.1   Quick facts about Russia

Official name	Russia, or the Russian Federation
Capital	Moscow
Area	17,075,200 sq km (6,592,800 sq miles)
Population (2007)	142.2 million
Population density (2007)	8.3 per sq km (21.6 per sq mile)
Population growth rate (2007)	-0.17%
Languages	Russian, and other minority ethnic languages
Religions	Predominantly Russian Orthodox, with a significant Muslim minority. Christianity, Islam, Buddhism and Judaism officially acknowledged as Russia's historical religions
GDP (2007)	$1.289 trillion
Per capita GDP (2007)	$9,064
Distribution of GDP (2007)	56% services, 39% industry, 5% agriculture
Literacy	99%
Infant mortality	11 per 1,000 live births
Life expectancy	65.9 years
Government type	Federation with elected president and parliament
Administrative divisions	21 republics, 46 oblasts, 4 autonomous okrugs, 9 krais, 2 federal cities, 1 autonomous oblast
Executive	President, prime minister and government
Legislature	Bicameral Federal Assembly; Federation Council, two members appointed from each of the 83 regions, one by the regional legislature, one by the regional executive; State Duma, 450 members elected by party list
Party structure	Formally multi-party with United Russia dominating parliament (2007–11) and the other main parties being the Communists, the Liberal Democratic Party of Russia, and 'A Just Russia'
Judiciary	Constitutional Court, Supreme Court and Higher Court of Arbitration – judges appointed by the Federation Council on the recommendation of the president
Head of state	President Dmitrii Medvedev (2008–)

rates, and sets out contemporary policy responses such as the introduction of the National Projects in health, housing, rural development
and education. Discussion of the judiciary focuses on reforms. It also
considers the gap between the rhetoric of Putin and Medvedev about
the rule of law, and the practice of state interference in the legal
sphere.

Chapter 4 turns to the governance of Russia. It establishes the main
features of the Russian constitution and deals with the tensions inherent in Russia's decisions surrounding the form of democracy chosen
in the early 1990s. It then sets out the formal powers of the executive,
legislature and judiciary, and considers the changes in the political
process made in recent years, such as the introduction of a law on
political parties, an end to gubernatorial elections, the shift to a party
list system and a higher threshold for representation in parliamentary
elections, the move of Vladimir Putin from the presidency to the
prime-ministership, and the overall decline of formal democratic
procedures. Emphasis is also laid on the development of politics aside
from the formal structures – the reduction in the possibility of opposition, the rhetoric about a Russian path to democracy, and a public
and official opinion that values order and stability ahead of the unpre-
dictability of a more open democracy.

Chapter 5 focuses on the economic transition of Russia, from the
centrally planned command economy of the Soviet era, through the
economically catastrophic transition period of the 1990s to the relative prosperity of the early years of the twenty-first century, and on to
Russia's attempt to deal with the effects of the global economic crisis
that began in 2008. The structure of Russia's GDP is set out, alongside discussion on the relative importance and performance of different sectors of the economy. The benefits of high energy prices will be
placed in the context of the potential dangers of the rapid growth of
and over-reliance on income from gas and oil – including the question of developing other sectors, and investing to modernize the infrastructure and output portfolio. Substantial attention is also paid to
recent developments – notably the interaction between the state and
Russia's major companies, the use of energy as a foreign policy tool,
the difficulties faced by foreign investors in Russia, and moves by
Russian companies to invest abroad.

Chapter 6 deals with the subjects of rights, freedoms and civil
society. Having briefly noted the Soviet Union's poor record in this
area, and the constitutional commitment of Russia to human rights
and the existence of a healthy civil society, Chapter 6 sets out devel-

opments in these areas during the post-Soviet years. Media ownership is considered, particularly the increase in state control and its influence on content. The chapter then turns to the development of registration laws for religious organizations, political parties and non-governmental organizations since the late 1990s, paying particular attention to freedom of religion and the development of civil society in its various forms – including an assessment of the state of Russian trade unionism and workers' activism. Within the context of civil society, the role of the security services in Russian life is analysed, the difficulties faced by foreign religious groups and NGOs are highlighted, and the development of civil society groups supported by and supportive of the authorities is assessed.

Chapter 7 turns its attention to the less tangible aspects of Russian life – namely, ideas, culture and ideology. The 'Russian idea' is a distinctive, if partly mythical, aspect of national identity. This chapter draws out the provenance and central features of the Russian idea and explores the place of ideas and ideology in the national consciousness. It provides an account of official attempts to craft a national identity in recent years – noting the way that they draw on pre-Soviet events, public figures and leaders, and the deeply ambiguous way they deal with the Soviet era. Continuity in what might be seen as 'Soviet' attitudes and habits, and nostalgia for aspects of Soviet culture and everyday life are also touched on. The focus then turns to contemporary culture (both high and low) in Russia, discussing the state of music, architecture, literature and sport in today's Russia, and their increasingly significant place in the national psyche.

Chapter 8 turns its attention outwards, considering Russia's place in the world in the sphere of international relations. It traces the re-emergence of Russia as an independent sovereign great power in the twenty-first century, from the weakness of the 1990s, and investigates what lies behind Russia's current standing in the world. The cooling of relations between Russia and the USA in the Putin–Bush years, particularly during Putin's second term, is set out, and Medvedev's foreign policy line is considered. The Medvedev line is avowedly pro-European, but in practice this is undermined by Russia's insistence on a sphere of influence around its borders. Against this background, the relationship between Russia and the EU, as well as bilateral relations between Russia and European states, are of key significance. Other international questions covered include the growth in influence of the Shanghai Cooperation Organization, Russia's relations with Iran, and how Russia operates within key international organizations such as the United Nations, the Council of Europe, the OSCE, and the G8. Significant attention is also paid to Russia's policy with regard to the former Soviet states in general, and the Commonwealth of Independent States in particular.

The final chapter of the book deals with conceptualizations of contemporary Russia, drawing on the material in the preceding chapters. It assesses how Russia conceptualizes itself and presents competing narratives to explain contemporary Russia's current situation. The concluding section offers scenarios for Russia's likely path over the next decade or so.

1

The Historical Context

Russia is the world's biggest country, nearly twice the size of China and more than one and a half times the size of the United States. And yet the area it covers in the twenty-first century is smaller than at any time since the nineteenth century. At that time, the Russian Empire was engaged in a process of expansion that had begun more than 300 years earlier, and, interrupted only by world wars, was to continue until the invasion of Afghanistan by the Soviet army in 1979.

Twelve years later, in 1991, the Soviet Union – one of two global superpowers and to many critics merely the Russian Empire by another name – ceased to exist. Each of its fifteen constituent republics, including Russia itself, declared independence from the Soviet state. Expansion gave way to an immediate loss of lands that had been under Russian rule for well over a century, be it the rule of a Russian Tsar or a Communist Party Secretary. When Russia emerged from the Soviet Union in 1991, the territory ruled from Moscow reduced by a third.

This geopolitical introduction to contemporary Russia – or the Russian Federation, to use its other official name – serves to highlight a duality that is essential to our understanding of Russia today. There is a combination of decline and greatness which shapes much of what goes on in the various areas of activity considered in this book.

For most of the 1990s and into the twenty-first century, the socio-economic and political dividing lines in Russia ran through the question of how far this great nation should open itself up to the West in terms of economic policy, international allegiance, cultural identity, governance, and much more. The ancient question of whether Russia is a backward country trying to catch up with Europe, or a unique civilization carving out its own superior path through history still has a resonance in contemporary debate. During the second term in office of President Putin (2004–8), the emphasis shifted to a strong Russia that was confident in following its own lights into the future. However, the relationships between Russia and the West, between the past and the present, still remain nuanced and prominent in official discourse and wider public debate. One thing is clear, with Russia perhaps more so than with most other countries, that it is impossible to read the contemporary scene correctly without knowing what has gone before.

This chapter is about introducing the past to help us understand the present, and to that end the overview of Russia's history given here considers the development of ideas and moods in Russia's past within the framework of key events. We start our look at contemporary Russia with a *tour d'horizon* of its history over the past centuries, focusing most strongly on the tumultuous twentieth century and its aftermath. Box 1.1 provides a chronology of key events. This chapter then draws out the significant elements of Russian history in three phases: Russia before 1917; the Soviet period (1917–91); and the post-Soviet era.

Russia before 1917

The history of Russia is the history of a country on the edge of Europe. The 'semi-European-ness' of Russia is apparent in a number of key historical moments. First, there was the adoption of Eastern Orthodoxy as the religion of modern Russia's predecessor state, Kievan Rus, in the tenth century. Like the countries of Europe, Russia has been predominantly a 'Christian nation' throughout most of its existence. Unlike most of Europe, however, the form of Christianity that Russia adopted was Eastern, not Roman. After Constantinople fell to the Turks in 1453 and hegemony in the Orthodox world shifted to Muscovy, the uniqueness of Russian civilization was emphasized still further. The faithful would refer to Moscow as 'the third Rome'. According to this theory, ancient Rome fell because of heresy, and the 'Second Rome', Constantinople, was brought down by infidels. The 'Third Rome', Muscovy, would illuminate the world and never fall.

There is therefore an 'otherness' about Russia's cultural history, which was heightened by the fact that for most of the medieval era in Europe, from 1237 to 1480, the territories that make up contemporary Russia came under the control of the Asiatic Mongol Khanates, or

Box 1.1   Key events in Russian history

c. 882	Establishment of first Russian state with Kiev as its capital (Kievan Rus)
1237–1480	Mongol rule in Rus
1547	Ivan IV ('The Terrible') becomes first Tsar
1598–1613	'Time of Troubles' – civil war and foreign invasions, ends with founding of the Romanov dynasty
1682–1725	Reign of Peter the Great
1762–96	Reign of Catherine the Great
1812	Napoleon invades Russia and reaches Moscow before retreating
1861	Emancipation of the serfs, under the rule of reformist Tsar Alexander II
1905	'The 1905 revolution' – promise of limited parliamentary rights
March 1917	Tsar Nicholas abdicates in the face of popular demonstrations and mutinies
October 1917	Russian Revolution; Communists seize power under Lenin's leadership
1922	Formal establishment of the Soviet Union
1924	Death of Lenin
1928–9	Stalin's power consolidated.
1930s	Industrialization, collectivization of agriculture, and growth of labour camps
1937–8	The 'Great Terror' sees a wave of arrests and executions
1941	German invasion of the Soviet Union
1941–5	Soviet Union fights on the allied side in the Second World War
1945–8	Soviet Union consolidates control of Eastern Europe
1953	Death of Stalin; Khrushchev becomes leader of the Communist Party
1964	Khrushchev replaced by Brezhnev as Soviet leader
1982–5	Death of Brezhnev; successors Andropov and Chernenko each die in post
1985	Gorbachev becomes Soviet leader
1989	Countries of Eastern Europe leave the Soviet bloc
1991	Yeltsin elected president of Russia; collapse of Soviet Union
1993	Presidential–parliamentary conflict resolved in Yeltsin's favour by military means; new Russian Constitution adopted
1999	Yeltsin resigns on 31 December
2000	Putin elected president
2004	Putin re-elected president
2008	Medvedev elected president; Putin becomes prime minister

'hordes', of Ghengis Khan and his successors. So, as Europe moved into the Renaissance and Reformation of the sixteenth and seventeenth centuries, Russia, expanding from the principality of Muscovy, appeared on the European scene as a relative newcomer, undergoing the brutal and sadistic rule of Ivan the Terrible and the anarchic period of civil war and foreign invasion known as the 'Time of Troubles'.

The separation of Russia from the mainstream of European cultural developments and the imposition of Mongol forms of government have been seen by some historians as a key determinant of Russia's subsequent socio-political system. For those within and outside Russia who emphasize the nation's Euro-Asiatic identity, distinct from but linked to the European lands to the west, these two and a half centuries of Mongol rule followed by brutal autocracy and chaotic internecine war serve as a formative feature of Russian identity. Only in 1613, with the establishment of the Romanov dynasty, which was to last until the workers' revolution of 1917, did a degree of stability and 'normality' begin to appear. None the less, the perceived separation of Russia from the European mainstream continued to play a key part in historical developments.

Peter the Great

Peter the Great (Tsar of Russia, 1682–1725) oversaw a period in which the Russian state was modernized and increased its power through a mixture of discipline and administrative reform. This combination of approaches appears as a pattern throughout Russian history right up to the present day.

For Peter the Great, the humiliating defeat of Russian forces by the Swedes at Narva in 1700 can be seen as the trigger for fundamental reforms, which began by introducing foreign expertise and technology into the armed forces. Driven on by his main concern, the military, the Tsar sought reform in many areas – notably tax rises and a social reorganization that affected both peasantry and nobility, with lifetime conscription into the army for one peasant from every twenty households, and a strict 'table of ranks' for the nobility.

Nothing symbolized reform in Peter's reign more than the construction of a new capital city, St Petersburg, as a 'window on the West' (see Chapter 2, Box 2.3); nothing apart from perhaps his infamous tax on beards, whereby men who continued with the 'Slavic look', rather than adopting the clean-shaven Western fashion, would be singled out for the regime's fiscal disapproval. Alongside these symbolic representations of Peter's Westernizing intent, came the introduction to the Russian court and nobility of Enlightenment philosophies that were flourishing in Europe.

Catherine the Great

The influx of Western political thought continued throughout the eighteenth century and flourished in particular during the reign of Catherine the Great (1762–96). Intellectual life in Russia was transformed as knowledge of European languages grew and indicators such as the number of books published and number of students studying in universities showed a dramatic increase. However, there was a duality present in the attitude of the regime to the influence of Enlightenment thought. The desire to embrace the new ideas of European thinkers and to benefit from a closer relationship with Europe had to be kept in increasingly uncomfortable tension with the autocratic nature of the Russian state itself. Catherine's enthusiasm for Enlightenment philosophy waned after its contribution to the French Revolution and the subsequent anti-royalist terror in France.

Russia's history over the first half of the nineteenth century was dominated by military and diplomatic, as well as intellectual, engagement with Europe. As the French Empire spread across the continent, under the leadership of Napoleon Bonaparte, Russia – led by Alexander I – initially reached an accommodation with the French, which bought time. In 1812, however, Napoleon attempted to invade Russia. These efforts famously resulted in Napoleon's army reaching Moscow, which had been set on fire by the retreating Russians, before succumbing to the ferocity of the Russian winter. In the retreat from Moscow in 1812, Napoleon's renowned '*grande armée*' was destroyed, and by 1814 Russian troops following in their wake had entered Paris.

For many years, the Russian nobility had imported Western European ideas and customs into Russia without a great deal of experience of Western Europe itself. For many of those Russian officers who entered Paris in 1814, the firsthand experience was formative, and played a role in the debates that were to dominate Russia over the following decades. These debates can be summed up in two examples:

- Demands for the Tsar to cede some of his autocratic powers to representative bodies began to be put forward among the more liberal members of society's upper stratum. Most important, the Decembrist Revolt of 1825 entailed a group of military officers putting together a low-level, poorly organized revolt in support of a demand for some representation. While the actions of the Decembrists in themselves posed little danger to the Tsar's powers, their symbolic significance as the first liberal challenge to autocracy was seminal.

- The intellectual debate between the Slavophiles and the Westernizers flourished in the years after the Decembrist revolt. In short, it developed the arguments of the Slavophiles, who saw in Russia a unique, and superior, civilization, and the Westernizers, who preferred to pursue Western examples and ideals.

Alexander II

Not until the reign of Alexander II (1855–81) were further far-reaching reforms introduced in Russia. Alexander's natural reformist tendencies were given more urgency by the defeat of Russian forces in the Crimean War, coinciding with his accession to the throne in 1855. Military defeat highlighted the need for Russia to catch up with the West economically, technologically and socially. In simple terms, war was a huge burden to an already heavily indebted state, and the technological advances of a rapidly industrializing Europe were absent from a Russia whose social structure was still founded on serfdom. Alexander II gradually but radically reformed his realm, most notably overseeing the abolition of serfdom in 1861 (four years before the abolition of slavery in the United States). The Tsar, like Soviet leader Mikhail Gorbachev over a hundred years later, faced the difficulty of conducting fundamental changes without bringing down the regime. He succeeded in the short term, in that the Tsarist regime remained in place into the twentieth century, though he himself was assassinated by revolutionary terrorists in 1881.

Each of the reform periods noted above was accompanied by a discourse of reform which implicitly, and sometimes explicitly, sought to import values from the West.

The development of political thought, with its roots in Europe, can be seen throughout the nineteenth century in Russia. After victory against the French armies of Napoleon, Russian troops, with many members of the educated nobility among them, saw and experienced Western Europe, occupying Paris in 1814. By 1825, the Decembrist uprising sought the beginnings of constitutional reform and representation in Russia, only to be met by the determined autocracy of Tsar Nicholas I (1825–55). During the reign of Alexander II (1855–81) the liberal movement, with its basis in Enlightenment thought, saw a little progress with the creation of local representative bodies, *zemstva*, as the Tsar facilitated a widening of debate on policy, though he was not willing to concede actual decision-making powers.

The European Enlightenment did not, however, only give birth to a weak Russian liberalism, but also to a more robust and radical strain, the revolutionary socialist movements. In Russia there existed both a Marxist revolutionary movement with its roots in European political thought, out of which the Communists emerged to rule Russia for most of the twentieth century, and a revolutionary social-ist movement, the Populists, which looked to Russian traditions as opposed to Western European thought as a model for the future. The Populists saw the organization of the traditional Russian peasant *mir* (village) as a model for a democratic future, and the more radical Populists, from whose ranks came the terrorists who assassinated Alexander in 1881, explicitly counted among their heroes the leaders of past peasant revolts, such as Pugachev and Razin.

To summarize rather crudely, as Alexander II carried out his programme of reforms he was opposed by conservative members of the nobility and the land-owning class, who objected to the loss of their serfs as well as more subtly to the sense, so brilliantly portrayed in Chekhov's play *The Cherry Orchard* (1904), that the relatively privileged world which they knew was being changed irreparably. He was also opposed by the radical revolutionaries, who did not want to see reform of the system, but rather an entirely new system, in which there would be no role for the tsar and the nobility. Between the two sat the liberals, whose aim was evolutionary reform of the system in a more democratic and more representative direction.

The Soviet period, 1917–91

Russian history is for the most part dominated by a strong 'garrison' state. However, partly as a factor of the size of Russia, and partly stemming from the nebulous concept of an authoritarian political culture, the Russian state has repeatedly seemed profoundly insecure about itself and so constantly sought to expand its control over society. This insecurity is not ill-founded though, as there are regular episodes in Russian history where the authority and power of the state collapses and 'society' rises up. Such a perspective offers one approach to the advent of rule by revolutionaries in Russia in 1917.

The Bolshevik Party – later to become the Communist Party of the Soviet Union – came to power in October 1917. There had been a 'revolution' in Russia twelve years earlier in 1905, when largely uncoordinated unrest across the Russian Empire resulted in the Tsar, Nicholas II (1894–1917), agreeing to the creation of a parliament, or Duma, whose actual influence on policy was minimal to begin with and then faded further. However, the hardships and social upheaval of the First World War created fertile soil for revolutionary and reformist movements to flourish, and protest became increasingly frequent.

In February 1917, unrest in Petrograd – as the Tsarist capital St Petersburg was then known – developed into a revolution which forced the abdication of Tsar Nicholas and the creation of a Provisional Government, based on the largely liberal Duma. At the same time, the revolutionary movements re-created the Petrograd Workers' Council – or 'Soviet' – that had first existed in 1905, and similar Soviets came into being in other cities. A situation of 'dual power' existed, with the Provisional Government and the Soviets both claiming legitimacy. It is only a slight oversimplification to say that the elite and the masses were at loggerheads.

In October 1917, the Bolshevik Party staged a seizure of power in the name of the Soviets. In its implementation if not its effect, this event was more akin to a coup than a revolution. And in the immediate situation of Petrograd in 1917 it represented simply another twist in a year of violence and upheaval that had seen a workers' uprising, the abdication of the Tsar, the creation of a Provisional Government, a failed attempt by the revolutionaries to seize power in the 'July Days', a failed counter-revolutionary reaction led by former Tsarist General Kornilov in September, and now a seizure of power by the Bolsheviks, the most radical of a number of socialist parties, in October.

Earlier in 1917, Vladimir Lenin had said that he did not expect to see a revolution in his lifetime. The idea that a Bolshevik uprising in October might leave them in power for most of the century would have been greeted by many observers at the time as tenuous to say the least. The Communists' first few years in power were – like the 'Time of Troubles' over three centuries earlier – years of civil war, foreign intervention and economic uncertainty. Russian novelist Boris Pilnyak captured this chaos, and what he saw as the essence of Russia's elemental spirit, in his work *The Naked Year*. He portrayed the worst year of the civil war, 1919, as a year when the civilized Western clothes of Russia were stripped away to reveal beneath them the true Asiatic nature of the Russian masses. Such a force was more ready to be harnessed by the radical revolutionaries, be they urban Bolsheviks or rural Socialist Revolutionaries, than by the weak and sparse liberal elite. The tradition of peasant revolt against landowners was replayed again under the initially supportive gaze of Lenin and his government. By a combination of propaganda, populist measures, ruthlessness, military skill, and a strong minority of popular support, the Bolshevik regime survived and prospered.

By the late 1920s, with the rise to power of Josef Stalin, the state was ready once again to fully reassert control. Forced collectivization of agriculture, state-planned industrialization, centralization, state-induced famine, a vast labour camp network and political terror all combined in the 1930s to rebuild a state that was now not merely authoritarian, but totalitarian, seeking to dominate every aspect of its citizens' lives. During the Stalin years, millions of victims were incarcerated in the labour camps of the Gulag or were executed during the 'Great Terror', and all aspects of public life came under the dictatorial control of the regime.

Playing catch-up

As we have noted above, a clear pattern supports the discourse of a perennial need for Russia to catch up with Europe, and with 'the West' in general. From this point of view, the motivation for reform and accompanying upheaval in Russia has regularly been realistic self-interest, driven by a combination of economic decline and related security threats. Be it the perceived need to build a modern navy under Peter the Great, a modern army under Alexander II, or a more high-tech military industrial complex under Gorbachev in the 1980s, a realist motive lay behind these times of upheaval. The dictum that 'war is the locomotive of history' applies to Russia perhaps more than to anywhere.

We can add to these examples the defeat by Russia in war with Japan, which precipitated the revolution and constitutional reform of 1905, and the defeat of the Russian forces on the eastern front during the First World War, which served as a catalyst for the collapse of the Tsarist regime and the rise of the Communists in 1917. We can add too the industrialization of the 1930s under Stalin, who stated explicitly in 1931 that Russia had to catch up or be crushed, as war was coming within the next decade (the Stalin years will be considered in more detail below).

The statue of Alexander Pushkin (1799–1837) is flanked here by a temporary memorial erected to commemorate 'Victory Day', marking the end of the Second World War in Europe, 9 May 1945. This combination of nineteenth- and twentieth-century history, bringing together elements of the Tsarist and the Soviet, represents well the official discourse of twenty-first-century Russia.

Illustration 1.1   Pushkin Square, Moscow, May 2008

None the less, if we are adopting the catch-up approach to understanding the major features of Russian history – and this is certainly not the only approach possible, as we shall see later – then a more idealist, as opposed to realist, explanation for these periods of reformism can also be offered.

There are two main difficulties with the catch-up approach outlined above, and an awareness of these related problems is extremely helpful for our understanding of contemporary Russia:

- First, Russia has not spent its entire history in unsuccessful pursuit of a superior European ideal. While the periods discussed above provide examples of such a pursuit, the whole picture – both of Russia itself and even of those particular periods – is more complex. In particular, there was not always a concurrence in

Russian history of modernization and Westernization. Although Peter the Great, Alexander II and others all used selective borrowing from and imitation of the West, there were other periods, such as the reigns of Alexander III (1881–94) and Nicholas II, and the Stalin years, when overcoming backwardness was attempted within more traditional approaches, such as autarky and repression. In other words, there were strategies that sought to synthesize modernization and Russian-ness.

- The second difficulty with the catch-up approach is that the idea of a backward Russia is, understandably, not one that is held dear by most Russians. This has a resonance in Russia today, in the policies of the ruling regime and the opinions of the people. A sense of injured national pride, and of being patronized by the West in the post-Communist era, has without doubt helped to shape the political discourse of contemporary Russia.

Jumping ahead of our chronology momentarily, it is worth noting that Vladimir Putin brought the duality of Russia's history into focus when he came to power, initially as acting president, on 31 December 1999. Russia's second post-Soviet leader succeeded President Yeltsin with – as he himself put it – the task of combining the universal principles of democracy, and a free market, with Russian reality. Putin, in his turn of the millennium statement, called Communism 'a blind alley, far away from civilisation'. However, he was not about to junk the entire Communist experience. Putin made clear early in his presidency, in an address to the Presidium of the State Council, that there was much to be proud of in Russia's past, and that the wholesale rejection of what had gone before was untenable:

Where shall we then put the achievements of Russian culture? Where shall we put Pushkin, Dostoyevsky, Tolstoy and Tchaikovsky? Where shall we put the achievements of Russian science – Mendeleyev, Lobachevsky and many, many others? Much of what all of us take pride in – what shall we do with all this? . . . And do we really have nothing, except the Stalin camps and repressions, to recall for the whole Soviet period of our country's existence? Where shall we then put Dunayevsky, Sholokhov, Shostakovich and Korolev and the achievements in outer space? What shall we do with Yuri Gagarin's flight, as well as the brilliant victories of Russian arms – from the times of Rumyantsev, Suvorov and Kutuzov? And the victory in the spring of 1945?

(For details of Putin's Russian Heroes see Box 1.2.)

Putin's argument provides a particularly pertinent context to understanding contemporary Russia. During his years as president, he sought to recreate a sense of national pride and identity of Russia as a 'great power'. The trickiest element in this narrative of renewal was the question of what to do with Communism itself, an ideology rejected by Presidents Yeltsin, Putin and Medvedev. For most of the twentieth century, the Soviet regime represented itself as being at the leading edge of global historical development. One does not have to be an apologist for the Communist system to note that this case was not a wholly ridiculous one. There was a logic to it, a mix of interpretation and fact which together created a powerful discourse and a powerful state.

To make the case for Russia leading the world in the twentieth century let us go back to our discussion of political thought, and the influence of European thought in particular. A distinction should be drawn between liberal thought and revolutionary thought: it is the latter that transformed twentieth-century Russia. Revolutionary thought had both European and Russian strands. The Populists in the nineteenth and early twentieth centuries saw the uniqueness of Russian civilization, with its overwhelming peasant majority and particular forms of local governance, as the basis for a future socialist society.

Those Russian socialists who took their lead from the writings of European counterparts had a more global perspective. Men such as the founder of the Soviet state, Lenin, drew on Western European political thought as developed by Karl Marx and Friedrich Engels. Marxism concentrated not on the peasantry, but on the industrial working class – the proletariat – and a rejection of capitalism. Revolution would come from the proletariat, revolution would eventually be global, and the final stage of history would be communism – an end to exploitation and oppression, the emancipation of humankind and the fulfilment of humanity's potential in a technologically advanced, rationally managed society. Russian and Soviet communism, as it developed in the twentieth century, placed itself unequivocally at the head of the Marxist camp, and the Populists were soon repressed following the Bolshevik revolution of October 1917.

Soviet Marxism placed an emphasis on being at the cutting edge of a developing global movement. Marxism provided a world view within the framework of which every aspect of life could be placed. Its adherents claimed it to be scientific and rational, with the

Box 1.2 Putin's Russian heroes

In a speech to the Russian State Council, President Putin singled out the following fourteen men as being indicative of the great achievers in Russian history. Putin's selection is a conservative group, in the sense that all these would have been acknowledged in the Soviet era as great men of Russian history.

Aleksandr Pushkin, 1799–1837. Known as the founder of Russian literature, and Russia's greatest-ever poet.

Fyodor Dostoevsky, 1821–81. One of the great novelists of the nineteenth century. His best known works are *Crime and Punishment* (1866) and *The Brothers Karamazov* (1879).

Isaak Dunayevsky, 1900–55. Composer, particularly popular during the Stalin years and best known for his film music which fostered an upbeat view of Stalin's Soviet Union.

Yuri Gagarin, 1934–68. In 1961 he became the first person in space.

Sergei Korolev, 1907–66. Instrumental in the development of the intercontinental ballistic missiles which underpinned the Soviet Union's status as a nuclear superpower.

Prince Mikhail Kutuzov, 1745–1813. Commander of the Russian forces that repelled Napoleon's invasion of Russia in 1812.

Nikolai Lobachevsky, 1792–1856. Mathematician and founder of non-Euclidean geometry.

Dmitrii Mendeleyev, 1834–1907. Developed the periodic table of chemical elements.

Marshal Pyotr Rumantsev, 1725–96. Hero of the Seven Years' War with Prussia in the mid-eighteenth century, and of later wars in Europe. Governor-General of Ukraine from 1764.

Mikhail Sholokhov, 1905–84. The only non-dissident Soviet writer to win the Nobel Prize for Literature (1965). His best known work is *Quiet Flows the Don*.

Dmitrii Shostakovich, 1906–75. One of the twentieth century's finest composers, and arguably its greatest symphonist.

General Aleksandr Suvorov, 1729–1800. Famed military commander of the latter half of the eighteenth century, Suvorov was known for his development of 'military science'.

Pyotr Tchaikovsky, 1840–93. Composer; best-known works are the *1812 Overture*, the opera *Yevgenii Onegin*, and the ballet *Swan Lake*.

Lev Tolstoy, 1828–1910. One of the great novelists of the nineteenth century, he wrote *War and Peace* (1865–9) and *Anna Karenina* (1873–7).

implication that it was therefore infallible. And the Marxist view was that a global workers' revolution was inevitable. This emphasis on scientific rationalism and the ongoing development of history to its end-point, communism, carried with it a contemporary edge in most areas of life. Communism was a creed for the newly emergent industrial working class, predominantly the younger generation:

- it embraced modern technology;
- it rejected superstition and religion in favour of the ability of human beings to construct a better world for themselves;
- it sought common ownership of goods and planned production to meet the needs of the people, as opposed to the vagaries of the market; and
- it was a teleological ('goal-orientated') ideology, with a momentum and a purpose.

That a successful workers' revolution leading to a socialist regime occurred first in Russia, rather than in the more industrialized states of Western Europe, took a little explaining in terms of the expectations of Marx. Lenin's explanation was that the chain of capitalism broke at its weakest link – Russia – and that global revolution would follow. Global revolution did not follow, at least not in terms of the European powers becoming Communist. However, much of the former Russian Empire became united under Communist rule as the Soviet Union by the early 1920s and thereafter – particularly in the Cold War era after the Second World War – numerous countries around the world became part of the Communist bloc. The Soviet Union established itself as the leader of this growing Communist camp, which stood in opposition to the US-led capitalist bloc. In its own terms, the Soviet Union was at the cutting-edge of history's inevitable progress to communism. In some sense the Russian nationalist concept of Moscow as 'the Third Rome', which would illuminate the world and never fall, can be said to have been taken up by the Communists.

In reality, the Soviet experiment soon soured. Whatever one's politics, for most people there can be little argument that the Stalin regime, which executed or imprisoned in labour camps around 20 million of its own citizens between 1929 and 1953, scarcely represented the fulfilment of Marxism's emancipatory mission. Historians and politicians have disputed whether the authoritarianism, repression and dictatorship of the Stalin years in particular represent a failure of Marxism or of its Soviet implementation. Some have sought the roots of Soviet totalitarianism in the political culture of Russia. Stalin implicitly encouraged parallels between himself, Ivan the Terrible and Peter the Great, and the suggestion that Russians are somehow predisposed to rule by a 'strong hand' is cited fairly often in the literature.

While the Stalin years represent the epitome of totalitarian dictatorship, from Lenin through to the late 1980s the Soviet Union was marked by:

- repression of opponents;
- the existence of a single party with no participation in politics by any other means;
- strict state censorship and ownership of all media;
- a preference for the rights of the state over the individual;
- a judicial system accustomed to political judgements; and
- the socialization of all citizens into the Soviet ideal.

Lenin ordered the arrest and execution of ideological opponents. Nikita Khrushchev's reformist reputation stems largely from his closure of many labour camps and his condemnation of Stalin in the Secret Speech of 1956, but none the less he himself instigated a brutal anti-religious campaign. In the years under Leonid Brezhnev (1964–82) dissidents were subjected to compulsory psychiatric treatment – after all, the argument went, if they oppose the Soviet regime, they must be mad.

Can we then still speak of the Soviet Union in any sense as leading the world? In short, yes, if only because of its development into one of two global superpowers by the middle of the twentieth century, and its consolidation of this position for over three decades. Even in the 1930s, as the Stalinist repressions swung into action and millions died in labour camps or as a result of state-induced famine, there was support for the Soviet regime on the European left. Stalin's repressions were largely hidden from the world. Only in 1956 did Khrushchev begin to acknowledge them. And only after the Soviet archives were opened in the late 1980s and early 1990s was their extent fully revealed.

To many observers at the time, the Soviet Union seemed to be demonstrating the superiority of the planned economy in comparison with the market. While the Great Depression devastated the economies of the United States and much of the capitalist world in the

1930s, the Soviet Union enjoyed rapid economic growth as it industrialized with unprecedented speed. As the Marxists had stated, capitalism appeared to be collapsing under the weight of its inherent
contradictions, while the new scientific rationalism of the Communist
regime apparently flourished. During the Second World War, the
contribution of the newly industrialized Soviet Union to the defeat of
Nazi Germany cannot be overstated.

From this perspective it is easier to gain that sense of unstoppable
momentum which is central to understanding communism's place in
the world in the middle decades of the twentieth century. Similarly,
an elaboration of the extent and speed of the global political map's
'reddening' in the immediate post-war decades, provides us with an
insight into the influence of Soviet Communism. By merely counting
the number of states that became Communist between 1945 and 1975
– albeit that many were coerced into the Communist camp – one
might have concluded that Marx's prediction of world revolution was
not completely far-fetched. With the benefit of hindsight and the
knowledge of Soviet Communism's eventual failure, it is too easy to
forget the enthusiasm and commitment of those in the Soviet Union
and elsewhere who genuinely believed that they were pushing
forward in history's vanguard.

We began this section by noting two problems with the catch-up
approach to Russian history. The Soviet experience is by and large a
demonstration of the first problem; namely, that Russia has not spent
its entire history in unsuccessful pursuit of a superior European ideal.
For much of this period the Soviet Union travelled a path not taken
by the Western nations – despite the provenance of Marxism being
European, even if the 'actually existing socialism' of the Communist
world had Russian snow on its boots.

The second problem is that the idea of a backward Russia is not one
held dear by most Russians. When considering the Soviet era, many
Russians hold a broadly positive view, particularly of the post-Stalin
years. In opinion polls in the 1990s, when Russian citizens were
asked to name the best Russian leader of the twentieth century,
Brezhnev repeatedly topped the list, with his time in office being
voted the best period in which to live (Bacon and Sandle, 2002).
Again, this perception cannot be dismissed as fanciful. Many
Russians look back on these years as a time when living standards
steadily increased, full employment and job security were the order
of the day, inflation was virtually non-existent, crime levels were low,
and national pride was high.

From communism to contemporary Russia

Using different but complementary approaches to Russian history, we have illuminated much of the context helpful to our understanding of contemporary Russia. It is worth emphasizing again – as will become apparent later – the resonance of history in contemporary Russian political debate. Politicians and population alike in Russia today are well-versed in their past and, given the nature of Russia's recent history, it is perhaps not surprising that it plays a significant role in shaping the contemporary agenda. In the final section of this chapter we shall consider the transition from communism to the present day. Much of what is covered here will be revisited in later chapters; again, our emphasis is on providing the context for studying contemporary Russia.

As noted above, during the 1990s in opinion polls of the best era in which to live from the last hundred years of Russian history, the Brezhnev years (1964–82) consistently came out on top. As well as the everyday factors that influence people's opinion of these years, the Brezhnev era was a time when the Soviet Union competed as an equal with the United States in both the space race and the arms race; a time when Soviet musicians, dancers and composers were renowned the world over; and a time when Soviet sportsmen and women regularly competed with and beat the world's best.

In 1980, the Olympic Games were held in Moscow, in what was the first – and until Beijing 2008, the only – Olympics held in a Communist state. The event was intended to crown the achievements of a great superpower, and was seen in the Soviet Union as an unqualified success despite a debilitating boycott by Western countries. Had it been suggested then that within little more than a decade the Soviet Union would have weakened to the point of collapse, few would have believed it. And yet, beneath the surface, there was much wrong with the Soviet regime by the 1980s.

Mikhail Gorbachev

Mikhail Gorbachev, when he came to power in 1985, began to refer to the Brezhnev years as an 'era of stagnation'. He characterized it as a time when an ageing leadership clung to power and gave little thought to the future development of the country. After Brezhnev died in 1982 his two successors, first Yurii Andropov and then Konstantin Chernenko, both took power as sick men and died after a very short time in office. The economy stopped growing, and Gorbachev inherited what he called 'a pre-crisis situation'. The later joke was that in 1985 the Soviet Union stood on the edge of the abyss, and under Mikhail Gorbachev it took a great step forward.

Gorbachev's characterization of the Brezhnev years provided the context in which he began his reform programme. It could also be argued that the military weakness of the Soviet superpower was exemplified by the inability of Soviet forces to secure victory in the Afghan War (1979–88). For a state that owed its superpower status almost entirely to its military strength, this failure in a low-tech conventional war was compounded by the Soviet Union's inability to compete with the United States in the high-tech stakes. As the arms race between the superpowers moved increasingly towards the development of smart conventional weaponry and missile defence shields (the so-called 'star wars' programme announced by US President Ronald Reagan in the early 1980s), Gorbachev, along with many of the generals and most of the party leadership, saw that reform was needed in order to catch up with the West.

The Soviet economy was shrinking, and Gorbachev's solution was a radical reform of socio-political relations, gradually reducing the reach of the authoritarian state and giving the people a genuine democratic vote for many key positions – though never for his own. Unfortunately for Gorbachev, a simultaneous reduction in authoritarian control and an invitation to elect political leaders led many in the national republics that made up the Soviet Union to vote for leaders who sought independence from the Soviet state. The biggest of these national republics was Russia itself, and once Russia, under its newly elected president, Boris Yeltsin, declared independence from the Soviet Union in 1991, no Soviet state remained. If Gorbachev inherited a pre-crisis situation, then by the end of his period in office it had turned into a terminal crisis for the Soviet Union.

In December 1991, the leaders of Russia, Ukraine and Belarus met and declared that their republics were forming a Commonwealth of Independent States. By the end of the month the majority of Soviet republics had joined this Commonwealth, and those that had not insisted resolutely on complete independence. The Soviet Union no longer existed.

Boris Yeltsin

When Yeltsin rose to power in Russia in the late 1980s and early 1990s he did it with the support of the emergent broad democratic movement, Democratic Russia. Like many post-Soviet politicians, Yeltsin had been a member of the Communist Party of the Soviet Union for much of his adult life, and was brought into the Party's highest body – the Politburo – by Gorbachev in 1986, having been put in charge of the Party in Moscow in December 1985. Yeltsin soon came to national and international attention as something of a maverick with a populist touch. He advocated faster and more far-reaching reform than that proposed by Gorbachev, and in 1987 Yeltsin resigned from the Politburo. Gorbachev removed him from his senior position as head of the Moscow Communist Party, but, to the surprise of many, then gave him a ministerial post in the Soviet government. In the past, this might have been the end of Yeltsin's influence, but as Gorbachev's reforms opened up the Soviet electoral system Yeltsin was able to gain election first to the new Soviet parliament – the Congress of People's Deputies – in 1989, and then, in 1990, to the parliament of the Russian republic.

In the Russian parliament, Yeltsin, with the support of the reformist deputies, was elected Speaker – at that time the highest position in the Russian, as opposed to the Soviet, political hierarchy. In March 1991, Gorbachev organized a referendum across the Soviet Union on the preservation of the Soviet state. Yeltsin again saw his opportunity and, with the support of the Russian parliament, placed a second question on the referendum ballot, asking the people of the Russian republic to support the creation of a Russian presidency. Approval was duly gained, and in June 1991 Yeltsin became the first-ever directly elected leader of Russia, albeit that he remained constitutionally – if not democratically – in an inferior position to Soviet President Gorbachev. It was from this position of strength that President Yeltsin moved to take Russia out of the Soviet Union.

In August 1991, Gorbachev's conservative opponents in the higher echelons of the Soviet government and party structures staged a coup attempt. Gorbachev himself was put under house arrest, a state of emergency was declared by the coup plotters, and troops were brought in to take control of Moscow. The Russian parliament and president became the focus of opposition to this coup. Thousands of supporters gathered there to hear Yeltsin – having climbed up on one of the tanks sent to enforce the coup – declare the state of emergency illegal and call for the immediate return of Gorbachev to Moscow and to his position as head of the Soviet Union. Though there was a real danger of an assault on Yeltsin and his parliament by special forces under the command of the coup plotters – and indeed three civilians were killed in skirmishes outside the parliament building – within a couple of days the coup had collapsed and Gorbachev came back to Moscow. However, he returned to a very different political landscape. Yeltsin's moral authority and popularity had been boosted by his opposition to the coup. Furthermore, he could point to the fact that he had been elected to his position by the Russian people, whereas Gorbachev, in contrast, had never stood in a democratic election. It was from this strengthened position that Yeltsin moved rapidly through the Soviet endgame, and to the creation of the Commonwealth of Independent States noted above.

After Communism – from Yeltsin to Putin

The collapse of the Soviet Union at the end of 1991 marked the culmination of an astonishingly short period during which the Soviet bloc, which had shaped world affairs since the end of the Second World War, disappeared. In 1989, the Soviet 'satellite states' of central and eastern Europe embarked on a democratizing path, establishing constitutions, political institutions, independent judiciaries and multi-party systems. In the economic sphere, they moved away from state planning and towards a market. When an independent Russia emerged out of the failed Soviet Union in 1991, it also intended to take this path.

It is a commonplace of political life that to be in opposition is easier than to govern. In the last years of the Soviet Union many disparate forces had been able to unite around a common cause, that of democratic opposition to the Communist regime. But once the common goal had been achieved, these disparate forces began to fracture around the question of 'What next?' In broad terms, the democratic opposition, Yeltsin included, wanted to establish democracy and a market economy. When it came to the specific implementation of policy, however, many differences and questions emerged:

- What about the sequencing and pace of reform? Should economic reform precede political, or vice versa? Should everything be done at once, taking the often cited 'shock therapy' approach, or would a more gradualist approach be beneficial?
- What about relations with the other former Soviet republics? A good number of those in the broad Yeltsin camp had fought for a democratic Soviet Union, but had not envisaged its total disappearance.

- And when it came to democratic transition, what form of democracy should be adopted? Parliamentary or presidential? An electoral system based on proportional representation or a majoritarian system? A single chamber or a bicameral parliament?
- And what about relations between Russia's regions and the centre?

There was clearly much to decide. Unfortunately the decision-making process was not clear. Yeltsin had risen to power in Russia with the support of the parliament, or Supreme Soviet, which, thanks to Gorbachev's democratizing moves, had at last been able to lay hold of the authority to which it had been nominally entitled throughout the Soviet period. Once elected president, though, Yeltsin had a mandate direct from the people, rather than having to rely on the maintenance of a parliamentary majority. However, many of his powers as president were granted to him by the parliament, under the terms of the much amended Russian Constitution. This Constitution had been in force since 1978; it was a Soviet Constitution in desperate need of replacement. Yeltsin wanted to replace it with a constitution setting out a presidential democracy; the parliament wanted to change it for a constitution establishing a parliamentary democracy.

There was deadlock, and for the best part of two years (1992–3), when the newly independent Russian state was in desperate need of fresh legislation and clear governance, President Yeltsin and his parliament had reached a stalemate. One solution would have been the holding of simultaneous presidential and parliamentary elections; Yeltsin was confident of re-election, but many parliamentary deputies were less confident, and so the parliament rejected this option. Yeltsin was unable to dissolve parliament himself, as this lay outside his constitutional powers.

Finally, after move and countermove, and an inconclusive national referendum, Yeltsin unilaterally – and in constitutional terms, illegally – dissolved the parliament in late September 1993 and announced new elections for the following December. Parliament refused to accept its dissolution, and, with the Constitutional Court ruling in its favour, it remained in session. After a stand-off of several days, fighting broke out in Moscow, as troops loyal to the parliament attacked the building of a national television station. Yeltsin responded by ordering a full-scale assault on the parliamentary building, where only two years before he had led the parliament in its opposition against the Soviet coup plotters. The parliament building was shelled, over a hundred of its defenders were killed, and Yeltsin stood as the undisputed ruler of Russia. On 12 December, a national referendum passed a new and heavily presidential Constitution on the same day as the people voted for the new parliament that this Constitution created.

It is this Constitution of 1993 that remains in force in Russia today. Its provisions include the right of the president to issue decrees with the force of law, and the clear separation of the executive (presidency and government) and legislature (parliament). No member of parliament may serve in the government at the same time as being a parliamentary deputy, and the only oversight that parliament has over the government is the ratification of the president's choice of prime minister. Should parliament reject the president's nominee, then the president can dissolve parliament. These provisions are discussed in more detail in Chapter 4.

Since the elections of December 1993 there have been parliamentary elections in 1995, 1999, 2003 and 2007. Yeltsin stood for the presidency again in June 1996 and was re-elected in a second-round run-off against his Communist opponent, Gennadii Zyuganov. This victory owed much to the support of a coterie of rich businessmen and media owners, who collectively became known as the oligarchs, because of their subsequent influence on the president.

For much of his second term in office, Yeltsin was in visible decline both physically and mentally. He underwent a major heart operation after his re-election in 1996, and throughout his period in office was prone to bouts of heavy drinking. Ironically, having sent troops against his parliament in his pursuit of a heavily presidential constitution, Yeltsin increasingly seemed unable to govern Russia as the twentieth century came to an end. A presidential constitution demands a strong president – Boris Yeltsin was physically weak, owed a political debt to the increasingly powerful oligarchs, relied heavily on a small group of advisers known as 'the family', and had to make a series of bilateral agreements with regional leaders in which he negotiated the division of power between the centre and the components of the Russian Federation.

It became ever more apparent that the Russian state was weak, and this impression was emphasized by the fact that between 1998 and 2000 Russia had five prime ministers. With hindsight, it was as if Yeltsin were casting around for a successor, and the fact that three out of the four prime ministerial appointments he made in this period were of men with security service backgrounds indicates the sort of figure for which he was searching. Yeltsin wanted a technocrat rather than a politician to succeed him, someone able to strengthen the state, and someone who would both protect his legacy and guarantee him a safe and comfortable retirement.

By the end of 1999 Yeltsin believed he had found that man. Vladimir Putin had risen from relative obscurity to the post of prime minister in August of that year, and on 31 December Yeltsin resigned the presidency and – in accordance with the constitution – appointed Putin as acting president pending an election in March 2000. Putin duly won this election. Boris Yeltsin enjoyed a comfortable retirement until his death at the age of 76 in April 2007.

From Putin to Medvedev

Vladimir Putin became president of Russia in May 2000, at the age of 47, and remained in that position until May 2008, having served the constitutional limit of two successive four-year terms. On leaving the post of president, he was immediately appointed prime minister by his successor as president, Dmitrii Medvedev.

Putin's period in office as president saw a process of stabilization by a leader viewed as strong and resolute in comparison to the more emotional, elderly and erratic Yeltsin. Much of what happened in Russia under President Putin forms the basis of the remaining chapters in this book. None the less, it is worth presenting here a brief overview of his years as president, particularly in relation to the framework of Russia's history established in this chapter.

Putin devoted considerable effort throughout his presidency to placing twenty-first-century Russia within a historical narrative, drawing on precedents from the nation's past and engaging in the debate on Russia's relationship with the West. As noted earlier (see Box 1.2), Putin attempted at an early stage to create a sense of Russian continuity within, and to some extent despite of, the Soviet era. He consistently sought to play down communism whilst at the same time holding on to the notion of Russia as a great nation. A good example of this approach can be seen in his move, within months of becoming president, to replace the Russian national anthem of the 1990s with an anthem composed of new words set to the music of the old Soviet era national anthem. Putin sought to build bridges with émigré communities descended from those forced out of Russia by the Bolsheviks. He also abolished 7 November, formerly Revolution Day, as a national holiday.

These symbolic moves are just that – symbols. None the less, a good deal of effort was put into the creation of a narrative that emphasized pride in Russia and in great Russians, even from the Soviet years, while remaining critical of communism and its leaders (this narrative is explored in some detail in Chapter 7). Such a balancing act could not always be carried off successfully, particularly in relation to the seminal event of the twentieth century – the Second World War. To laud the achievement and sacrifice of the Russian people without appearing to celebrate the leader of the state in that period, Stalin, has proved difficult.

The importance to Putin of creating an appropriate national narrative was apparent too in the way in which the Yeltsin years were presented. Increasingly during his period as president, Putin and his team talked of the 1990s as a period of chaos and weakness, comparable to the 'Time of Troubles' at the turn of the seventeenth century. This fitted well with the idea that a strong 'tsar' and a strong state were required after Yeltsin.

The process of strengthening the power of the Russian state became a key feature of Putin's presidency, particularly in the first term. The oligarchs, who had exercised significant political influence under Yeltsin, were reined in by Putin. The message was clear – they should stay out of politics and stay loyal. Some of the most prominent oligarchs refused to do so and now live in exile – for example, Boris Berezovsky and Vladimir Gusinsky – or languish in prison, as is the case with Mikhail Khodorkovsky. Similarly, Russia's regions were brought more firmly under the control of the federal authorities.

The process of 'strengthening the state' was tackled by a variety of means, including greater state oversight of political parties, an end to elections for regional leaders, political interference in the judicial process, and increased state control over the media – partly via companies in which the state owns a majority share. At the end of the 1990s, almost all commentators agreed that the Russian state needed strengthening. By the end of Putin's second term, the consensus was that democracy and pluralism had declined in Russia during the previous eight years. Within this consensus, however, there is room for analysis and debate. In the rest of this book, questions over the legitimacy, wisdom and outcome of Putin's methods and goals are considered.

Political developments in Russia during the Putin presidency took place in a climate of rapid economic growth. Increasing standards of living, accompanied by the state's ability to pay off debts and to spend more, came on the back of high energy prices, thus providing a boost to the largest sector of the Russian economy, the oil and gas industries. Economic success is one of the reasons why Putin's popularity remained remarkably high throughout his presidency.

Against the background of this brief account of the Putin era, 2000–8, we conclude our overview of Russian history up to the present day by returning again to the recurrent theme of Russia's place in the world. There is no doubt that, as Russia and its state became stronger under Putin, so relations with many countries in the West, notably the United States and the United Kingdom, declined. Critical observers in the West see a Russia that has returned to its default position as an undemocratic and expansionist state. As we have seen, though, if Russia has a default position it is not static. The key questions of modernization and relations with the West remain at the heart of contemporary Russia.

In 2008, Vladimir Putin came to the end of his second term as president. He had the political support and legislative means to change the constitution and remain as president, following the examples set by the presidents of Kazakhstan and Uzbekistan. None the less, he stood down. He threw his and the state's weight behind the candidature of his younger and long-standing colleague, Dmitrii Medvedev, thereby ensuring Medvedev's election as president of Russia. On taking power, Medvedev spoke forthrightly and clearly about Russia's role as a European nation, modernizing by integration with the global economy. He spoke too of a commitment to values such as freedom and the impartiality of law. The rest of this book assesses the nature of the Russian Federation and its people, considering their geography, economy, society, polity, culture and place in the world. Only through such a multi-faceted approach can we gain a full understanding of the country over which Medvedev presides: contemporary Russia.

2

Land and People

Russia covers roughly 17 million square kilometres, significantly larger than its nearest rivals in terms of being the world's largest country – namely Canada, the United States and China – each of which covers between 9 and 10 million square kilometres. Before it collapsed in 1991, the Soviet Union was a third bigger again. Yet Russia easily retains its lead position, even with the post-Soviet loss of the vast territories of Central Asia (Kazakhstan, Kyrgyzstan, Tajikistan, Turkmenistan and Uzbekistan), the Transcaucasian countries (Armenia, Georgia, Azerbaijan), the Eastern European lands (Belarus, Moldova, Ukraine), and the Baltic States (Estonia, Latvia and Lithuania).

In terms of population, Russia ranks ninth in the world with a population in 2007 of 142.2 million. The Soviet Union before its collapse had ranked third in terms of global population, and at the beginning of the twenty-first century, Russia ranked seventh. Russia's population is declining; its death rate is remarkably high, particularly for men, and serious health problems exist. All of this is reflected in demographic predictions for the coming decades which set out a number of scenarios, all of them negative. Russia's official demographic predictions remain relatively optimistic, with the Ministry for Economic Development predicting a population of 143 million in 2030. The Organisation for Economic Co-operation and Development (OECD), on the other hand, estimates that Russia's population will have fallen to 124 million by then.

Russia's capital city, Moscow, ranks sixth in terms of the world's most populous cities, keeping to a strict definition of city boundaries. If estimates are made for urban areas, Moscow slips to nineteenth in the global rankings. Moscow and St Petersburg are the two cities in Russia that have the status of federal regions. Moscow is Europe's biggest city,

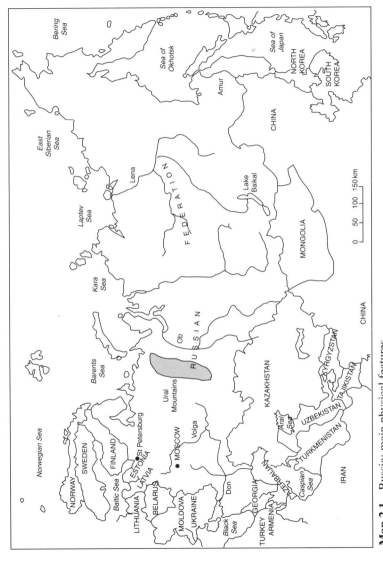

Map 2.1 Russia: main physical features

with a population of 8.3 million in 2007, though if the greater Moscow area is included that figure rises to 10.8 million. Making allowances for the high number of unregistered inhabitants in Russia's capital would push this number higher still, with some estimates claiming 13 million inhabitants of Moscow and its environs. St Petersburg is Europe's third biggest city, with a population of 4.7 million. London is in second place, between these two Russian giants, with over 7 million.

Moscow is a European city and the centre of the country's political, economic and cultural life. It is too easy to forget the vast Asiatic expanse of Russia when so much in terms of contact with the West is mediated through crowded, commercial, cosmopolitan Moscow. Almost a fifth of Russia's population live in the *millioniki* – those cities that proudly boast a population of more than a million (see Box 2.1) – and 60 per cent of the population live in the Central, Volga and Southern federal districts of Russia. Or, to put it the other way round, those areas officially classified as 'the North' (the Far East, Siberia

---

Box 2.1 The '*millioniki*' – Russian cities with over a million inhabitants (largest to smallest)

1 Moscow, population 10.8 million (see Box 2.2).
2 St Petersburg, population 4.7 million (see Box 2.3).
3 Novosibirsk, population 1.4 million. Russia's third-largest city, the largest in Siberia, and the furthest million-plus city from Moscow.
4 Yekaterinburg, population 1.3 million, a key gateway for the Urals region, and the third-largest city economy in Russia.
5 Nizhnyi Novgorod, population 1.3 million, the nearest million-plus city to Moscow.
6 Omsk, population 1.1 million, on the main route between Yekaterinburg and Novosibirsk.
7 Samara, population 1.1 million, an administrative and industrial centre on the Volga river in southern European Russia.
8 Kazan, population 1.1 million, capital of the majority non-Russian region of Tatarstan.
9 Chelyabinsk, population 1.1 million, situated in the southern Urals region.
10 Rostov on Don, population 1.0 million, centre of the Southern Federal District.
11 Ufa, population 1.0 million, capital of Bashkortostan.
12 Volgograd, population 1 million, formerly Stalingrad, situated on the Volga at its nearest point to the Don.
13 Perm, population 1 million, in the Urals region, known as Europe's most easterly city.

Box 2.2   Moscow

Moscow was founded in 1147 by Prince Yury Dolgoruky. With Constantinople falling to the Turks in 1453, Moscow came to be seen by the Russian Orthodox Church as the home of true Christianity – the 'Third Rome'. From Muscovy, Ivan the Great (1462–1505) united the Russian principalities.

In the sixteenth century, Moscow grew to become one of Europe's largest cities, and by that time the Kremlin, Red Square and St Basil's Cathedral had all been established. Moscow remained the seat of Russian power until Peter the Great moved the court to St Petersburg. Moscow was re-established as the capital in 1924. May Day parades of troops, tanks and missiles on Red Square – watched by a line of Communist leaders from the mausoleum containing the preserved body of their predecessor Lenin – symbolized for many the power of the Soviet state. In 2008, this military element was restored to an annual Red Square parade, but this time for Victory Day on 9 May, commemorating the end of the Second World War, rather than for May Day.

A visitor to Moscow in the mid-1980s would have found a sterile city compared with the one seen today. Communist Party slogans stood in place of advertising, there were relatively few cars, shops were dull and poorly stocked, and conformity and cleanliness were abiding features. By the mid-1990s all this had changed, as Moscow had become a vibrant city, full of traffic, advertising, shopping malls, restaurants, political demonstrations, noise, crime, beggars and a chaotically hedonistic nightlife. From 1998 onwards, Moscow also became the scene of terrorist acts such as the blowing up of random apartment blocks in 1999, and the suicide bomb on a metro train in 2004.

In recent years Moscow has seen vast capital projects, such as the rebuilding of the Cathedral of Christ the Saviour, the construction of the Manezh shopping centre next to Red Square, and the ongoing development of the Moscow International Business Centre – complete with contemporary skyscrapers and, by 2011 if all goes to plan, the location of Europe's two largest towers – the Federation Tower at 506 metres, and the Russia Tower at 612 metres. The flipside of these vast construction projects is the destruction of many Moscow buildings, including the hotels Moskva, Rossiya and Intourist. Heritage campaigners have fought, largely in vain, for the preservation of landmark buildings across the city in recent years.

Contemporary Moscow is also marked by the curse of many of the world's super cities – traffic congestion. Growing prosperity has brought increasing numbers of cars on to the streets, despite the fact that Moscow's super-efficient metro train system carries a staggering 9.5 million passengers every day, more than the underground systems in London and New York combined.

Moscow's most famous landmark, situated next to the Kremlin on Red Square.

Illustration 2.1   St Basil's Cathedral

and northern European Russia) make up 70 per cent of the territory of the Russian Federation, but contain only 8 per cent of the population. According to the 2002 census, over a quarter of Russia's population can still be classified as rural dwellers.

The final point to make by way of creating a true picture of Russia which moves beyond the Moscow-centric European perception is that it is a multi-ethnic federation. Over 160 different national groups were identified in Russia by the 2002 census. While 80 per cent of the population are ethnically Russian, the diversity of the country is represented in its federal structure, in its religious make-up (with around 10 per cent of the population being Muslims), and – most acutely – in its vicious conflict with the ethno-religious rebels in and around the republic of Chechnya, which formally ended in 2009. All

---

Box 2.3   St Petersburg

S. Petersburg was founded in 1703 as Russia's 'Window on the West', built on the orders of Peter the Great, the Westernizing Tsar who saw Russia's future firmly in Europe. The city became his capital, and remained the capital of Russia until the Soviet era.

In 1914, with the outbreak of the First World War, St Petersburg changed its name to Petrograd, which sounded less Germanic. Petrograd was the scene of the Russian Revolution in 1917, and in 1924 was renamed again: Leningrad, after the revolutionary leader and founder of the Soviet Union, Vladimir Ilyich Lenin.

For around 900 days during the Second World War, from September 1941 until January 1944, Leningrad remained under siege by the German armed forces. Over half a million inhabitants died during this period. In 1991, with the Soviet Union on the brink of collapse, a city-wide referendum restored the name of St Petersburg.

Still spoken of as one of Russia's two capitals, St Petersburg enjoys a rivalry with Moscow, sharpened by the fact that Russia's current and previous presidents (Vladimir Putin and Dmitrii Medvedev) come from there, as do many of their senior colleagues.

---

these issues are dealt with in this chapter, which outlines the physical, demographic and social bases of the Russian state.

The physical setting

Covering as it does a seventh of the earth's land surface, Russia stretches more than 10,000 kilometres across Europe and Asia, from the port of Kaliningrad on the Baltic Sea (an enclave cut off from the rest of Russia) to Cape Dezhneva in the far north-east (the easternmost point in the Eurasian land mass, named after the Cossack explorer who was the first European to sail round it). Russia extends over eleven time zones, and journeying overland on the Trans-Siberian railway from one end of the country to the other will take the traveller over a week. The distances involved have been a problem for successive governments seeking to make their mark across such a vast land area.

There are a number of other points about the geographic conditions in Russia that help us to understand its development and present situation. First, most of Russia is of course located very far north. Half of its land mass is above the latitude of 60° north – that is, north of a line running through Oslo, the Shetland Islands, the southernmost tip of Greenland, the middle of Canada, and southern Alaska. Sub-Arctic conditions prevail along its north coast, and through all of Siberia apart from the far south-east, since the high mountain ranges on Russia's southern and eastern borders prevent warm tropical air masses from further south in Asia reaching the north. Average winter temperatures, a mild −1° in the south-west, fall as low as −45° in the diamond-mining centre of Yakutsk, where temperatures only rise above freezing point for four or five months a year.

Second, Russia has relatively low levels of rainfall. It is a long way from the Atlantic Ocean and mountains block airstreams from the Pacific. The Arctic Ocean is too cold, and the Black and Caspian Seas too small to provide much water vapour. Unfortunately, peak rainfall in the better agricultural areas occurs in late summer and autumn, rather than earlier in the growing season. This growing season, particularly in the more northerly parts, lasts for a relatively short period, when intensive agricultural efforts have to be made, which has tended to foster collective rather than individual forms of agricultural organization.

Just 13 per cent of the land area, virtually all of it located south of a line from St Petersburg in the west to Novokuznetsk in south-western Siberia, is used for agricultural purposes. Of the rest, 45 per cent is forested, and the remainder largely tundra, mountain and swamp, which are too cold for cultivation. Even the most fertile areas in the so-called black earth (*chernozemnyi*) region along Russia's border with Ukraine often suffer from the lack of rainfall.

Russia, then, is not well placed for productive agriculture. It is, however, blessed with an abundance of natural resources, with substantial coal, oil, natural gas and iron ore reserves as well as non-ferrous metals, gold and diamonds. There are very few naturally occurring minerals in which Russia is not self-sufficient. Indeed, so much of its territory is undeveloped that there may well be many resource deposits yet to be discovered. Many of the easily accessible resources in European Russia and the Urals regions are being depleted, however, and most of the important deposits are now found in more remote and inhospitable parts of the country.

Attempts to exploit these less accessible resources were heightened during the industrialization drive under Stalin from the 1930s onwards, largely on the back of forced labourers who had no choice about where they worked. Consequently, millions of people lived, and died, in remote regions where they might never have settled under a market economy. As the Gulag system of forced labour

Box 2.4 Closed cities

The phenomenon of Russia's 'closed cities' provides a particularly interesting example of the range of difficulties to be had in moving from the Soviet system towards more democratic arrangements. Closed cities were set up in the Soviet era as urban centres closed off from the world around them. Not only were foreign visitors barred from them, but so too were citizens of the Soviet Union if they did not have the correct documentation. These cities were declared 'off bounds' for security reasons, as they contained key military facilities or were centres for research into defence technology, usually nuclear.

When the Soviet Union collapsed, many of the larger closed areas (such as Kaliningrad, Vladivostok, Nizhny Novgorod and Murmansk) were opened. None the less, a number of smaller closed cities remain. There are ten cities closed under the instructions of the State Corporation for Atomic Energy, and a further unknown number – probably more than thirty – cordoned off by the Defence Ministry.

The world of the closed city is fascinating. In the Soviet years, isolation was compensated for by prestige and privilege – the inhabitants were engaged in work that would see the Soviet superpower lead the world in military power, and as a reward they lived well in comparison with workers elsewhere. In the 1990s, subsidies to these cities were hit by the economic downturn. None the less, the cities remain, and offer a tantalizing research subject from a sociological point of view. Generations of families have lived in these cities in relative isolation, marrying and bringing up their children within the closed community. They have had limited access to the mass media, and censorship on information coming in and going out of the cities has been constant. Human rights activists are concerned that the laws on closed cities allow restrictions on basic rights, such as the right to freedom of movement. Entrepreneurial activity is also tightly constrained in these cities, particularly when it comes to foreign engagement.

At the end of the 1990s, two former closed cities in the Urals petitioned the authorities for the return of their closed status. Most of their inhabitants – like many Russians in the 1990s – preferred the safety and predictability of their previous existence to the influx of new ideas and new people.

camps declined from the mid-1950s onwards, compulsion largely gave way to material incentives and continued ideological exhortation as a means of attracting workers to the industrial cities of Siberia and the far north, such as Norilsk. None the less, it was the economic system of central planning and subsidy that sustained many of them. Since the collapse of the Soviet Union and the introduction of a market-based economic system, the plight of these remote settlements and their inhabitants has worsened, as many are simply unable to survive economically. Russia's economic life, as exemplified by its major transport routes, is overwhelmingly centred on European Russia and on the east–west route of the Trans-Siberian railway, which runs across the south of the Federation.

The environment

The particular difficulties of Russia's physical setting outlined above have in many cases been exacerbated by problems of pollution and environmental degradation. While the process of industrialization produces environmental difficulties the world over, a number of factors exist which mean that contemporary Russia carries an especially negative environmental legacy from the Soviet era. In addition to this, the process of global climate change presents Russia with an uncertain path into the future. The locations of Russia's major cities, transport infrastructure and economic resources all stem to a large extent from climatic factors. Furthermore, Russia's size means that the impact of changes in the climate will differ across the country.

The relative lateness of the Soviet Union's industrialization – in comparison to the rest of Europe – coupled with the desire to catch up rapidly (as noted in Chapter 1) and to prove the superiority of the Communist system, meant that the middle decades of the twentieth century saw rapid and large-scale industrialization. This prioritization of rapid industrialization left little room for the serious consideration of environmental effects, and many of the environmental problems being faced in contemporary Russia stem from decisions made in the Soviet years.

The Communists' ideological stance with regard to the relationship between humankind and nature seriously exacerbated the environmental problems that generally accompany industrialization. The Communist view was constructivist and scientific, believing that enlightened human beings could build, on the basis of ever-increasing knowledge, a better world. While this approach is most often thought of in terms of its application to building a new society and economy, it applied also to the natural world. Natural resources existed for people to use, exploit and improve, with little attention being paid to the potential consequences. So, for example, the 'virgin lands scheme' initiated by Khrushchev (Soviet leader 1953–64) saw

30 million hectares of previously uncultivated land in Kazakhstan and southern Russia put to the plough, sown with grain, and doused with chemical fertilizers and pesticides, in a grand scheme to increase grain supplies massively. Ecological issues were scarcely considered and, after the scheme's initial success, soil erosion and environmental degradation set in.

There are numerous other examples of the environmental devastation wreaked during the Soviet era, most notably the Chernobyl nuclear power station disaster of 1986. Details of one other case in particular illustrate the sorts of ecological problems caused. Even though the Aral Sea, which straddles the border between Uzbekistan and Kazakhstan, is no longer (since the collapse of the Soviet Union) ruled from Moscow, the fate of this particular body of water illustrates the lack of environmental concern displayed by the Soviet authorities. The relative shortage of water in the Soviet Union led to numerous schemes being touted for the diversion of rivers. Happily, many of these got no further than the planning stage. However, the irrigation of cotton and rice fields by the diversion of water from rivers feeding into the Aral Sea in Central Asia from the 1960s onwards resulted in what had been the world's fourth-largest inland sea shrinking in size by three-quarters. Former fishing ports now find themselves some distance from the shoreline, increasing levels of salinity have killed virtually all the fish and many crops, and dust from the dried-out seabed, contaminated by salt, pesticides and fertilizers, has increased rates of cancer, respiratory diseases and miscarriages. Life expectancy in communities close to the Aral Sea fell from 64 years in the late 1980s to 51 years by 2005 (Lean, 2006).

As if all this were not enough, from the 1930s to the 1990s the Soviet armed forces used Vozrozhdeniye Island in the Aral Sea to test biological weapons, including anthrax and strains of diseases made resistant to antibiotics. With the shrinking of the sea, Vozrozhdeniye is less and less the isolated testing ground it once was. The shore is now only six miles away. The island's name means, with a sad irony, 'Regeneration' – though what is left on it is the most likely cause of the sudden deaths, in separate incidents, of a large shoal of fish in the Aral Sea in 1976, and thousands of antelopes on the nearby steppe in 1988.

In the 1990s, the authorities in Kazakhstan, where the 'small', or northern, Aral Sea is situated, began to investigate ways of reversing the environmental catastrophe that was occurring. In 2005, a dam was completed that doubled the water flow from the Syr Darya river into the North Aral Sea, and sea levels have risen rapidly since then. The effects are yet to be felt in the South Aral Sea, where the Uzbek authorities are less engaged in the process of environmental protection.

The Aral Sea is not in Russia, but serves as a clear example of the lack of environmental concern that is the Soviet Union's legacy to its successor states. There is a story that, when the heavily polluting Baikalsk paper and pulp mill was built in the 1960s, a Soviet minister, challenged about a development that would see toxic waste pumped into the world's largest freshwater lake, declared that 'even Lake Baikal must work for the advancement of the Soviet regime'. It was only in November 2008 that the Baikalsk mill, now controlled by billionaire Oleg Deripaska, was closed down.

Perhaps the worst ongoing environmental disaster on Russian territory is in Norilsk, a city in remote northern Siberia that regained its closed status in 2001. Norilsk has been named, in a study in 2007 by the US-based Blacksmith Institute, as one of two Russian cities in the top ten most polluted sites in the world. The other Russian city named in this report is Dzerzhinsk, a chemical industry city 250 miles east of Moscow.

The Norilsk region contains over a third of the world's nickel reserves and two-fifths of its platinum-group metals, as well as important cobalt and copper resources. Norilsk was first developed by forced labour in the 1930s. These days it is claimed that the Norilsk Mining Company produces a seventh of all industrial pollution in Russia, and the maximum allowable concentration of toxic air pollution is exceeded most days of the year. Given such conditions, it is scarcely surprising that average life expectancy for factory workers in Norilsk is ten years below the national average. That national average at the end of the twentieth century was 59 years for men.

Norilsk and Dzerzhinsk are at the extreme end of environmental problems in today's Russia. None the less, the legacy of the Soviet era continues to be felt more widely. Russia has just under a quarter of the world's supply of fresh water, but the ecosystems of 200 of its rivers are being undermined by the effects of the dams built as part of the hydroelectric programme of the 1960s and 1970s. In the late 1980s and into the 1990s, when increased political freedom meant that environmental concerns became more openly expressed, such concerns were of low political priority when set against a growing economic crisis. A lack of public investment over recent decades has resulted in a situation today where, according to official statements, around two-thirds of Russia's public water supply is not fit to drink. Only recently have Russia's politicians begun to give serious thought to the passing of clearer environmental laws. President Medvedev has talked of enshrining high environmental standards in new laws and introducing sanctions for polluting businesses.

Medvedev's stated environmental aims deal not only with long-standing issues of pollution, but also with wider environmental issues around the question of climate change. He has spoken with regret about how far Russia is behind in the development of renewable energy technology, and in waste disposal and recycling. Predictions of climate change suggest that by 2030 there could be an average temperature increase across Russia of 1.5°C, though this would vary between regions. In addition, rainfall levels and occurrences of extreme weather, particularly flooding, may increase.

Russia's development over the centuries has been shaped by the fact that much of its vast area is not easily habitable, and certainly not amenable to farming. Global warming might therefore bring some benefits, in particular by decreasing the area covered by permafrost and increasing both arable land and the growing season. Any such impacts from climate change are not, however, adapted to easily – farming habits and expectations need to be adjusted, land cultivated for the first time, and infrastructure built. At the same time, the changes brought about by warming will have negative effects in terms of shortening the lifespan of buildings, increasing the area of marshland, and, in Russia's south, creating more droughts and water shortages.

Geostrategic location

Russia has long been a player in the international affairs of a number of regions, straddling as it does two continents and having land borders with no fewer than fourteen sovereign states. In security terms this geostrategic position has often translated into wide-ranging threat assessments and the fear of encirclement by hostile powers. An important point to appreciate is that, situated largely on the great Eurasian plain, Russia has few natural borders such as mountain ranges or oceans. Russia's international borders have shifted frequently, indeed a clear answer to the question 'Where is Russia?' remains elusive.

Russia, including the Russian enclave of Kaliningrad, has land borders with:

- Azerbaijan
- Belarus
- China
- Estonia
- Finland
- Georgia

- Kazakhstan
- The Korean People's Democratic Republic
- Latvia

- Lithuania
- Mongolia
- Norway
- Poland
- Ukraine

Since the military conflict with Georgia in August 2008, Russia has also recognized Abkhazia and South Ossetia – with which it also shares land borders – as independent states. However, neither Abkhazia nor South Ossetia are recognized internationally as anything other than Georgian territory.

In addition, Russia has sea borders with Japan and with the United States. The state of Alaska, sold by Russia to the United States for $7.2 million in 1867, lies just 56 miles across the Bering Strait.

In the aftermath of the collapse of the Soviet Union at the end of 1991, many Russians felt that parts of several former Soviet republics – in particular, Northern Kazakhstan, Eastern Ukraine, Belarus, the Narva region of Estonia, and Abkhazia and South Ossetia in Georgia – should be incorporated in the new Russian state. Border disputes have complicated bilateral relations with a number of Russia's neighbours, such as the continuing controversy with Japan over ownership of the Kurile Islands, seized by Russia at the end of the Second World War. The popular post-Soviet mood was reflected in the speeches of more nationalistic politicians, with, for example the mayor of Moscow, Yuri Luzhkov, calling on a number of occasions for the transfer of the port of Sevastopol, in Ukraine, to Russia. The Communist Party of the Russian Federation did not recognize the collapse of the Soviet Union, and the head of the Liberal Democratic Party of Russia (LDPR), extreme nationalist Vladimir Zhirinovsky, even called for the re-establishment of Russia within her 1860 borders, including Finland, Poland and Alaska. Such a call might have been treated with wry amusement by observers, had the LDPR not garnered almost a quarter of the votes in the 1993 general election and only a little less than 10 per cent of the national vote in the following four Duma elections up to 2007.

Russian politicians of all political hues continue to distinguish between the 'near abroad' of former Soviet republics, and the rest of

---

Box 2.5   The rise and fall of the Russian Empire

9th century	First Slavic settlements, in present-day Ukraine and Western Russia. Known as the Kievan Rus period
1237–40	Mongol (Tatar) Invasion, led by Ghengis Khan's grandson, Batu Khan; Russia under Tatar control
1480	End of Tatar rule in Rus
1552	Battle of Kazan signals beginning of empire building
16th–17th centuries	Expansion through Siberia to Pacific coast
18th century	Conquers present-day Western Ukraine, Belarus, Lithuania, Latvia and Estonia; Russians settle Alaska and parts of Northern California
1809	Finland acquired from Sweden
19th century	Conquers Central Asia, the Trans-Caucasus and Bessarabia
1867	Sells Alaska to the United States for $7,200,000 (2¢ an acre)
1875	Exchanges Kurile Islands with Japan for possession of the whole of Sakhalin
1917–23	Constituent parts of the Empire reconquered by Bolsheviks; Finland, Baltic States, Poland, Western Ukraine and Bessarabia lost
1922	Country renamed Union of Soviet Socialist Republics
1941–5	Stalin reincorporates parts of the Soviet Union lost after 1917; Yalta Conference (1945) gives USSR control over most of Eastern Europe
1989	Collapse of Communist rule throughout Eastern Europe
1991	Belovezha Agreement between leaders of Russia, Ukraine and Belarus dissolves the Soviet Union into fifteen independent states

Further reading: Hosking (1998)

---

the international community. Just as three-quarters of Russians had voted for the preservation of the USSR in the referendum held by Gorbachev in 1991, so, as of early 2007, a poll by the Public Opinion Foundation found that two-thirds of the Russian population regretted the fall of the Soviet Union and only a quarter had not felt sorrow at its passing.

None the less, despite these regular expressions of popular opinion, there is a realism among the population and politicians alike. The Yeltsin, Putin or Medvedev administrations have not sought to change the borders of Russia as constituted at the collapse of the Soviet Union in 1991, though some would claim that military conflict with Georgia in August 2008, and the subsequent recognition of Abkhazian and South Ossetian independence, comes perilously close to a *de facto* border change.

The nearest that the restoration of the Soviet Union has come on any formal level is in the shaky relationship between Russia and Belarus. These two states signed the Treaty on the Formation of a Union State in December 1999. This was more a statement of intent than substance, however: Russia would prefer Belarus to become a component of the Russian Federation, while Belarus wants a more equal relationship. Relations between the two countries have subsequently fluctuated, but a formal mutual commitment remains.

The peoples of Russia

Russia has always been a multi-ethnic country. The first Russian state, Kievan Rus, from its foundations around the ninth century, consisted of Slavs, Varangians (Vikings) and Finnic peoples. As Russian colonists moved southwards and eastwards across the Eurasian continent over the centuries, they found themselves coexisting with a wide variety of ethnic groups, including Caucasian, Finno-Ugric, Hunnic, Turkic and Mongol peoples, as well as a wide variety of indigenous inhabitants across the expanses of Siberia.

Russia today remains a multi-national country. Results of the most recent census, carried out in 2002, counted over 160 separate ethnic groups. Of the total population of 145 million, 80 per cent are Russian. According to the 2002 census, six other ethnic groups had populations of more than 1 million: Tatars number over 5 million, with Ukrainians not far behind. The Bashkirs and Chuvash number just under 2 million each, and the Chechens and Armenians just over the million mark. A further eleven ethnic groups number more than 500,000 each.

When the Soviet Union ceased to exist at the end of 1991, more than 25 million ethnic Russians suddenly found themselves living abroad, in one of the fourteen non-Russian Soviet republics. The reality of this situation took some time to sink in, for people and politicians alike. Many of the newly independent states had not only been part of the Soviet Union for decades, but had been part of the Russian Empire before that. One of the great projects of the Communist state had been the creation of the 'new Soviet man' (or woman), to whom nationality would be far less important than solidarity with workers across the globe. On a less ideological level, there was substantial geographical mobility within the Soviet Union; young people went to universities or served in the armed forces far away from their homes, skilled workers moved to different parts of the country as the planning system established industries in particular areas. Naturally, there was a significant amount of 'intermarriage', though it was not often thought of in those terms, particularly among related ethnic groups. The cities in particular reflected such mobility. Across the non-Russian republics of the Soviet Union, Russians made up 16 per cent of the population as a whole, 24 per cent of the urban population, and 30 per cent of the population in capital cities.

Put yourself in the shoes of a Russian from Moscow who, say in the late 1970s, married a Ukrainian from Kiev and then lived, with their children, in Minsk (the capital of the then Soviet Republic of Belorussia). Such a family may have had little perception of themselves as anything other than a normal Soviet family unit settled in an area of their country, in a city not too far removed either geographically and culturally from their own home cities. Suddenly, as 1991 turned to 1992, they woke up one morning to find themselves living in a new country – Belarus, separate from both Russia and Ukraine. Should they stay there, in a relatively small country with an uncertain future? After all, their children were presumably Belarusians. Or should they return to their home country? And, if so, to which country, since Ukraine and Russia were now two separate states?

With 25 million ethnic Russians suddenly finding themselves living abroad in the early 1990s, similar dilemmas were widespread, and the solutions settled on were as varied as the number of complex combinations of circumstances. Many Russians returned to Russia in the 1990s, in a reversal of the trend of 500 years of expansion outwards from the Russian heartland. Between 1989 – the date of the last Soviet census – and 2001, there was a total immigration to Russia from the other former Soviet republics of more than 5.5 million people, and a net immigration of just under 4 million. This flow rose to a peak in 1994 and seems, by the beginning of the twenty-first century, to have more or less come to its natural end so far as Russians returning to Russia is concerned.

As in many other countries, the immigration issue in Russia is controversial politically. The Russian situation is particularly complex, since the distinction between immigrant and returnee has not always been clear. In some ways there were good reasons for allowing the relatively lax immigration policies of the 1990s. First, for ethnic Russians entering Russia there were few difficulties with cultural and linguistic assimilation – though economic integration was not so straightforward given the state of the Russian economy in the 1990s. Of course, it must also be remembered that those returning to Russia were in many ways coming back to a different country from the one they left – to Russia, not the Soviet Union. Second, net immigration of 4 million went some way towards off-setting the decline in population caused by emigration, low birth rates and high death rates.

Despite these factors that would seem to undermine the arguments of the anti-immigration lobby, from the end of the 1990s onwards the Russian authorities began to tighten up the rules on immigration, bringing them more into line with those in most European states. Responsibility for overseeing migration issues was transferred in 2002 to the Ministry of the Interior, which oversees the Russian police force. This move was accompanied by much discussion among politicians, including government spokesmen, of the alleged higher propensity of immigrants towards criminal activity. By the early years of the twenty-first century, the immigration of the ethnic Russians who suddenly found themselves living abroad at the Soviet collapse had all but run itself out, and immigration debates took on more of a racial character.

Opinion polls show that the existence of xenophobic or racist attitudes is more widespread in Russia than in most developed countries, and racially motivated attacks are fairly common in Russian cities with ethnic communities. In Moscow, the situation became so bad that a delegation of ambassadors from around the world complained in 2003 to the authorities about the lack of protection against such attacks given to their citizens. Into this mix must be added the regularly reported propensity of the Moscow police to stop 'blacks' (the Russian term for anyone of a slightly dark complexion) for questioning – a propensity heightened, and justified in the minds of the authorities, by terrorist attacks carried out by Chechen terrorists at the end of the 1990s and into the 2000s.

Labour migration, particularly from the former Soviet republics in Central Asia, continues to be a source of both valuable labour and xenophobic tension in Russia today. A 2007 report by the International Fund for Agricultural Development said that the economies of two Central Asian states in particular – Tajikistan and Kyrgyzstan – were dependent on remittances sent back from labour emigrants working abroad, and that figures for Uzbekistan were also high. Many of these migrants found work in Russia, particularly during the boom years up to 2008. Lawyers working on behalf of migrant workers in Russia report thousands of complaints each year about poor labour conditions, low wages and xenophobic mistreatment. Such complaints will be likely to increase during an economic downturn.

The Chechen conflict

Chechnya is a republic within the Russian Federation, on its southern border with Georgia. This simple statement would, of course, be hotly disputed by those Chechens who believe that their republic should enjoy full independence from the Russian Federation. It is this age-old desire for independence that is at the root of the Chechen conflict.

Chechnya's geographical position makes it a far more likely candidate for secession than another occasionally independence-minded republic, Tatarstan. The latter is firmly within Russian territory and surrounded by other regions of Russia. Chechnya, on the other hand, is on the periphery of Russia.

The history of the Chechen people is one of repeated conflict with Russian invaders. Even when firmly part of the Soviet Union, Stalin felt at the end of the Second World War that the Chechens were not to be trusted, and so organized the brutal forced resettlement of the entire Chechen people to Central Asia. It was not until the 1950s that the Chechens returned to their homeland.

In November 1991, as one by one the Union Republics of the Soviet Union declared their independence, the Chechen leadership – under former Soviet air force general Dzokhar Dudaev – declared their republic independent. The difficulty was, however, that Chechnya was not one of the fifteen Union Republics, but was a republic within the Russian Soviet Federative Socialist Republic (RSFSR), as Russia was officially known in the Soviet era. The newly elected Russian president, Boris Yeltsin, while actively encouraging the Union Republics – including his own – to secede from the Soviet Union, was determined that Russia itself would not break up. He declared a state of emergency in Chechnya and insisted that it remain within Russia.

An uneasy stand-off between Chechnya and Moscow held until December 1994, when Yeltsin sent in troops to try to subdue the rebel republic. The Russian army was used as a blunt instrument, engaging in indiscriminate bombing and shelling of the capital, Grozny, where many of the remaining inhabitants were ethnic Russians unable to flee to family in the Chechen mountains. The Chechen rebels, on the other hand, were skilled at guerrilla and terrorist tactics. By the summer of 1996 the stalemate was broken by a deal that gave some autonomy to the Chechens, but no real hope of independence.

In late summer 1999, Chechen rebels encroached into the neighbouring Russian republic of Dagestan. This was followed in September of that year by a series of devastating bomb attacks on apartment blocks in Moscow and elsewhere, which were blamed on the Chechens. Yeltsin, backed by his new prime minister, Vladimir Putin, sent troops into Chechnya again. The result was similar to that of the first Chechen War, with the exception that reported brutality on both sides was if anything fiercer. Putin, soon after becoming president in 2000, talked in terms of the Russian troops in Chechnya being the first line of defence for Europe against militant Islam. After the terrorist attacks on New York and Washington of 11 September 2001, he repeatedly placed the Chechen conflict within the framework of the global war on terrorism.

At the same time, the Chechen rebels increasingly adopted the symbols of radical Islam and tactics of Islamist terrorists, as well as developing links with other Islamist terror networks. They took terrorism to the heart of Moscow on several occasions, using suicide bombers on the Moscow metro, outside a city-centre hotel, and at a summer rock festival. In October 2002, a group of Chechens took several hundred people in a theatre audience hostage. The siege was ended by Russian special troops, who stormed the building, killing all the terrorists. Tragically, over a hundred of the hostages were also killed, not by terrorists but by the gas that the Russian troops pumped into the theatre to debilitate those inside. Within a week in August and September 2004 Chechen terrorists planted bombs that destroyed two separate passenger airliners, detonated a device outside a metro station in Moscow, and – in horrific scenes that captured global attention – killed hundreds of school children after taking them hostage in Beslan, southern Russia.

The horror of the Beslan school siege turned out to be the final event in this period of terrorist attacks. President Putin's policy for dealing with terrorism in the North Caucasus was to cede regional power to local leaders, on condition that they remained loyal to the Kremlin and kept order within their own republics. To the extent that Russia is no longer engaged in a quasi state-to-state conflict with Chechnya, and terrorism no longer spills over into the Russian heartland, this policy has been a success. The price to pay for it has been supporting, both politically and economically, the undemocratic regime of the Chechen president, Ramzan Kadyrov, in power. While to a great extent Chechnya has been pacified, sporadic violence occurs as rival groups clash and separatists continue their struggle against troops loyal to Kadyrov. None the less, Moscow announced a formal end to the anti-terrorist operations in the republic in March 2009.

Religion in Russia

As well as being multi-ethnic, Russia today is also religiously diverse. Religious activity has increased since the collapse of communism. Survey evidence from 2008 suggests that just under 70 per cent of the adult population describe themselves as religious believers. One in three Russians attends religious services more than once a year, though only one in fifty attend weekly. Practising believers are more likely to be older, and to be women rather than men.

The dominant religion in the country is Russian Orthodoxy. There are also many other Christian confessions, a substantial Islamic minority, and established Jewish and Buddhist communities, as well as a few adherents of pre-Christian pagan religions. Of Russia's eighty-three regions, five are Islamic republics and one, Kalmykia, is a Buddhist republic. Table 2.1 provides data on the number of registered religious communities at the beginning of 2006.

Table 2.1 does not provide a complete picture, because a number of religious groups either do not wish, are unable, or cannot afford to register. Estimates from religious groups themselves suggest that up to 9,000 Muslim groups and over 1,000 Christian groups remain unregistered.

The religious revival in Russia dates from 1988, the millennium of the conversion of Russia to Christianity, which, thanks to official support from previously anti-religious state authorities, became a

Table 2.1   Registered religious organizations in Russia, January 2006

Russian Orthodox Church		12,350
of which, Moscow Patriarchy	12,214	
Muslim		3,668
Pentecostal		1,486
Baptist		965
Evangelical Christian		812
Jehovah's Witnesses		408
Lutheran		288
Old Believers		285
Jewish		284
Roman Catholic		251
Buddhist		197
Presbyterian		187
Methodist		115
Other		1,217
Total		**22,513**

nationwide celebration. It has a number of elements. The Orthodox Church has been resurrected as a national symbol, as indeed it was before the 1917 revolution, although it now maintains a formal independence from the state. The Orthodox Patriarch – up to his death in December 2008, Aleksii II, and since February 2009, Kirill I – blesses the president on his inauguration, and in times of political crisis has played a mediating role. Other politicians from across the political spectrum have been keen to associate themselves with Orthodoxy. The post-Communist period has seen the building or restoration of many churches, cathedrals, monasteries, seminaries and theological academies. Charitable and educational work by churches has become increasingly common after decades of complete prohibition. The Orthodox authorities continue to argue for the restitution of land and property lost in the Soviet period. While the current (1993) Russian Constitution and the 1997 Law on Freedom of Conscience and Religious Associations guarantee religious freedom, there have been concerns about an overly close relationship between the Orthodox Church and the Russian state, and about harassment of some religious minorities, a topic we examine in detail in Chapter 6.

Dating from the early sixteenth century this cathedral is the oldest building in the Orthodox convent of Novodevichy in Moscow.

Illustration 2.2   The Cathedral of Our Lady of Smolensk

Islam is the second-largest religion in Russia, and – along with Christianity, Judaism and Buddhism – is recognized in the preamble to the 1997 Law on Freedom of Conscience and Religious Associations as one of Russia's traditional religions. As a proportion of the population of the Soviet Union, Muslims made up a greater percentage than is now the case in Russia, since the break-up of the USSR brought independence to Kazakhstan, Uzbekistan, Kyrgyrztan, Tajikistan, Turkmenistan and Azerbaijan. None the less, there are more than 14 million Muslims in the Russian Federation, some 10 per cent of the population. Virtually all of them are Sunni Muslims, though in a few areas – significantly Chechnya – there is a tradition of Sufism. In the current demographic downturn afflicting Russia, the Islamic population is notable for its growth rate compared with the rest of the population.

The size of the Jewish community is far smaller, with the 2002 census reporting that there are now only around 300,000 Jews left in Russia, down from over half a million in 1989. The emigration of Jews from Russia, mainly to Israel, has been particularly marked since the end of the 1980s, when restrictions were eased. From a peak of over 180,000 emigrés in 1990 the figure fell to an average of around 60,000 in the first half of the 1990s and has fallen still further since then. Reasons behind this emigration are varied, and there is no doubt that economic factors played a major role, as they did with emigrants of all faiths or none from Russia in the immediate post-

---

Box 2.6   What is Russian Orthodoxy?

Contemporary Orthodoxy, like all religions, encompasses many different elements and interpretations. While we can hardly do justice to the richness of the tradition, the following distinctive features are noteworthy:

- *The role of tradition*: the split with Catholicism in 1054 was a rejection of changes that the Western Church wished to introduce. Since then, Orthodoxy has seen itself as being the closest of all the branches of Christianity to the traditions of the early Church. Doctrinally and in practice there have been few changes since the eighth century. Participation in an Orthodox service indeed involves an experience of changelessness and timelessness. Doctrine does not change, because faith is seen as a matter of practice, not doctrine, an attitude that often causes confusion among foreign observers.
- *Greater emphasis on mysticism and spirituality*: Western religion, like Western thought, has since the Enlightenment been dominated by a tradition of rationalism; that is, the belief that the human mind is capable of explaining everything, eventually. This attitude applies to theology as much as to philosophy: theological statements must be susceptible to proof and human reason. Orthodoxy does not reject truths that arise out of reason, but takes much more seriously extra-rational sources of truth: the symbolic, inspiration and spiritual transcendence. The religious icon, the form of the service, Russian religious music, the emphasis on artistic aspects of worship, all arise out of an emphasis on experience and adoration rather than analysis.
- *Less hierarchical*: at least in the experience of worship. There are, for example, no pews in a Russian Orthodox church, and the congregation is able to come and go as it pleases, giving rise to a much more flexible an informal atmosphere than is familiar in many Western denominations. There is no equivalent in Orthodoxy of the Pope, no individual with universal jurisdiction. What holds the Church together is that its members understand it as a communion of the faithful.

Soviet years. To some extent, though, Russia's tradition of anti-semitism was also a factor, particularly with the rise of fascist and far right movements during this decade, marked by the significant vote for the Liberal Democratic Party of Russia in 1993 (see Chapter 4).

The place of Buddhism as a legally acknowledged traditional religion in Russia owes more to its longevity and its identity with specific groups of people than to any large Buddhist community. Estimates of the number of Buddhists in Russia are not easy to find, but the country's only Buddhist republic, Kalmykia, has only around 150,000 Kalmyks, and a figure of about twice that for the number of Buddhists in Russia would not be far wide of the mark.

Who are the Russians? Culture and traditions

The culture of a group is not a fixed or given set of attitudes and ways of behaving. However, members of a society do tend to share beliefs about themselves as a collective, and about right ways of acting, and these beliefs have an important impact. They are embodied not just in social discourse, but also in religious practices, art and literature, folk traditions, notions of social justice, and national symbols. Generalizing about these matters is a risky business: values are not shared by everyone, and social beliefs and practices change over time. However, at the risk of stereotyping, there are cultural beliefs which, while not necessarily being shared by all sections of society, are none the less central to understanding current reality.

The importance of the 'Russian Idea'

The term 'Russian Idea' indicates a set of interpretations by Russian thinkers of various political and philosophical persuasions, of what is distinctive about Russia. These formulations are not identical, but they do tend to share common features. The most important of these is that Russia is different from the West. Western societies are often lumped together and stereotyped as being overly individualistic, excessively materialistic, immoral, and generally unpleasant places to live. Russia is defined, crudely, as not the West. Russians allegedly share a uniquely spiritual, communal existence, a life that concentrates not on the squalid pursuit of individual material goals, but on what is most important in existence. Values such as spirituality and communality are, of course, not easy to measure. However, figures for attendance at religious services or membership of those organizations that make up civil society are far lower in Russia than in the United States – casting great doubt on claims that Russians are in some way more spiritual and communal than are Americans. None the less, even if hard statistics do not back up the common perception, the widespread existence of that perception has influence in itself. It contributes to the construction of a national identity, and from there into the formulation of voting preferences and policies. (For more details on civil society, see Chapter 6.)

Proponents of the Russian Idea, the 'Slavophiles' of the nineteenth century and their modern-day successors, idealize the role of the Orthodox Church in 'Holy Russia', the co-operative values of the peasant commune and, often, the desirability of political autocracy. The way in which these are conceived is, it scarcely needs to be said, an idealized version of reality. There is no point in history when Russians did live in this way. Furthermore, basing a system of thought on how different the society is from Western societies is not a feature unique to Russian culture. Thinkers in many other countries – for example, in the Islamic world or East Asia – like to argue that their societies are less materialistic, or more co-operative, though the precise emphasis obviously varies from culture to culture, and it must be said that the level of egalitarianism found in many versions of the Russian Idea is high by comparison with most other parts of the world.

The 'Russian Idea' tends to have a distinctive view of the role of the state and the nature of political leadership. One way to understand this is to compare Russian political ideas with those of the founding fathers of the American Constitution. James Madison, in *Federalist No. 51* (Hamilton *et al.*, 2008), wrote that the political arrangements proposed were necessary because this was a government of human beings:

> If men were angels, no government would be necessary. If angels were to govern men, neither external nor internal controls over government would be necessary. In framing a government which is to be administered by men over men, the great difficulty lies in this: you must first enable the government to control the governed; and in the next place oblige it to control itself.

The American political system is therefore one that manifests a suspicion of power. There has been a tendency in Russia, on the other hand, to invest new governments with inflated expectations, as if they were indeed governments of angels not of men; in Tim McDaniel's (1996) phrase, a 'government of Truth'. Governments of this kind do not need to be politically restrained, hence the lack of countervailing political institutions compared to some other parts of the world. Governments of truth also like to believe that they have unique access to the way in which the country should develop, which is a feature of administrations from Peter the Great through Stalin to Putin and Medvedev. If you know the answer, you are building the New Jerusalem, so political opposition serves little purpose, and hence the concept and the practice remain underdeveloped in Russia.

This concept of the place of the state and its powers became increasingly evident during the Putin presidency (2000–8). Although formally holding to democratic procedures, the notion that there should be opposition forces offering genuine alternative views had little purchase with the Putin administration. The space in which opposition forces might operate was squeezed by bureaucratic control over party formation, state oversight of the media, and the need for successful businesses and their owners to stay in line with the Putin project. In terms of the Russian Idea, the Putin administration put a good deal of effort into creating a national narrative in line with Russian traditions. A new public holiday, National Unity Day, symbolized this well in its fusion of Orthodoxy, a distinct – that is, non-Western – national identity, and the need for unity among the diverse groups that make up Russia.

One important consequence of this conception of politics is that it tends ultimately to undermine government when rulers turn out after all not to be perfect. When their actions begin to favour some groups over others, which is inevitable, and fail to realize their utopian promises, disillusionment sets in. This disillusionment has periodically in Russian history, including the end of the periods of rule of Gorbachev and, to a lesser extent, his successor Yeltsin, led to legitimacy crises and a real breakdown of state power. At the time of writing it is too soon to say, but the economic crisis of 2008–9 may once again begin to eat away at public confidence in the Putin–Medvedev regime.

The belief system has some important consequences. The glorification of the notion of equality between people can lead to a tendency to be suspicious of individual success. The vision of a society in which fundamental values are basically shared leaves little space for difference of any kind, whether physical, racial or just a difference in lifestyles. The prioritization of supposed common-sense values of the community over abstract laws from outside makes it very difficult to operate, for example, a contract-based free market economy, or even to preserve a reasonable degree of law and order, matters without which it is difficult to imagine a modern society operating effectively. Russia's first three post-Soviet presidents, Yeltsin, Putin and Medvedev, as well as the last Soviet leader, Gorbachev, have all proclaimed their belief in the rule of abstract law. None the less, Russia remains a country where connections, influence and political expedience regularly appear to undermine the equitable application of the law. Not for nothing was the team around Yeltsin at the end of the 1990s known as 'the Family'. In anointing Putin his successor, Yeltsin made sure that the first act of the new president would be to grant him immunity from prosecution.

The Slavophiles versus Westernizers controversy

One consequence of the controversy surrounding the Russian Idea has been that intellectual life in Russia, both throughout the nineteenth century and again in the present day, has seen a marked tension between those who want a society and political system unique to Russia, and those who are less convinced about Russian 'specialness' and want to adapt practices used elsewhere to Russian circumstances. The tensions between these two positions have been an important driving force in Russian politics. In opinion polls, clear majorities regularly state a preference for a uniquely Russian path of development, rather than a Western one.

Social mood

The national mood in Russia has changed with some volatility over recent decades. In the 1950s and 1960s there was, among the elite at least, and probably more widely in Soviet society, a sense of national pride and optimism. Soviet successes in the space race saw the launch of the first artificial satellite (Sputnik) in 1957, and then four years later Yuri Gagarin became the first man in space. The sense that the Soviet Union was at last beginning to fulfil its promises was memorably captured in the boast contained in the 1961 Programme of the Communist Party that the country would catch up with and overtake the United States in economic terms by 1970, and that by 1980 Soviet citizens would be living under true communism.

Of course, by the end of the 1980s the Soviet Union was on its last legs, and finally collapsed in 1991. In the rest of the 1990s, against a background of economic decline, mass poverty, lawlessness and environmental devastation, such promises, and the optimistic era from which they came, were just a distant memory. Commentators who are more critical of the Communist experience stress the negative influences on morality of the 'double life' Russian citizens were compelled to lead under Communist rule, paying lip service to an ideology of public service and striving to build a Communist utopia, while in practice not being able to discuss social problems which everyone knew to exist and being party to a culture of irresponsibility both at work and in public life. Those who dislike the economic policies of the 1990s and beyond, stress how these have led directly to a rise in undesirable behaviour such as greed, nepotism, corruption and organized criminality. Whatever the case, the first post-Soviet decade created a mood in Russian society of deep pessimism, powerlessness and hopelessness about future possibilities, moral decay, cynicism and general despair.

Under Putin's leadership, the national mood undoubtedly changed. Putin himself retained exceptionally high levels of personal popularity throughout his presidency, scarcely falling below 70 per cent approval ratings in the opinion polls. Such figures were retained throughout 2008 as he became prime minister, and his successor as president, Medvedev, enjoyed only slightly lower levels of popular support in the same period. Such popularity can be attributed partly to the impressive economic growth that accompanied the Putin presidency, chiefly facilitated by high oil prices. Beyond economic good news, however, Putin was initially popular because he was not Yeltsin. For much of his time in office, Yeltsin was an erratic and impulsive leader, prone to public and private drunkenness and suffering from a variety of illnesses. He oversaw a period of national decline in terms of living standards, the strength of the state, and international prestige. Though his time in office may well go down – with sufficient passage of time – as the most democratic years in Russia's long history, Yeltsin regularly comes last in polls seeking the best leader of Russia's recent history. Under Putin, and then Medvedev, in contrast, Russia again had energetic, intelligent leaders. Putin was widely seen to have restored the authority of his office and the state, both at home and abroad. Such a restoration of authority and national pride, though, increasingly came to be seen abroad as bullying and bluster. Chapter 8 charts the international implications of a Russia growing again in self-confidence in the first decade of the twenty-first century.

3

Social Structure and Social Policy

In many former Communist countries, the period of transition from communism to whatever followed it – democracy in some cases, authoritarianism in others, and various points in between for the rest – has proved to be a time of great social and demographic upheaval. According to estimates put forward by UNICEF, the transition process was responsible for over 3 million early deaths. The UN Development Programme posits a population deficit of over 10 million 'missing men'; that is, premature deaths plus the number otherwise expected to be born, as a consequence of the transition process. A report published in the UK's leading medical journal, *The Lancet*, in 2009 showed that, of the countries that emerged out of the Soviet collapse, Russia was an extreme case in terms of demographic impact. Life expectancy declined by almost five years between 1991 and 1994. The research showed that the chief explanations as to why Russia fared even worse than other post-Communist countries in this respect were the rate of privatization and the lack of engagement with social organizations on the part of the Russian population.

Later chapters deal with the process of privatization in Russia (Chapter 5) and the relative absence of engagement with those social organizations that make up civil society (Chapter 6). In this chapter, though, we are concerned with the related questions of social structure, demography and social policy in contemporary Russia. From a consideration of the fall, rise and possible fall again of living standards in the Yeltsin, Putin and Medvedev eras, respectively, we move on to an assessment of health policy and indicators. Living standards and health status both have a clear impact on the demographic crisis that is perhaps the greatest threat facing Russia in the first half of the twenty-first century. The chapter also looks at developments in, and policy proposals for, other key areas of social policy in Russia today – specifically, criminal justice, housing and education.

Russia after the collapse of communism was faced immediately with social and demographic problems on a huge scale. As noted in Chapter 1, such large-scale human hardship has been far from uncommon in Russia's twentieth-century history. The historian Christopher Read (2001) has written of 1990s Russia having witnessed 'economic mass murder', with excess deaths comparable to Stalin's purges. In fact, best estimates suggest that excess pre-war deaths in Stalin's Russia were over 10 million, while the highest serious estimate for the Yeltsin years is 3.5 million. There is also a clear difference in intent between the famine, forced labour and executions of the Stalin years, and the severe economic hardship of the 1990s. While to some extent economic transformation lay at the root of policy in both eras, direct causes of early death are less easy to establish in the Russia of the 1990s than in the Soviet Union of the 1930s. Such factors as poverty, increasing income differentials, declining standards of medical care, and psycho-social stress are all cited as causes of excess deaths during the post-Soviet transition in Russia, alongside more immediate causes such as drinking, smoking and accidents.

The Soviet Union was known for its 'cradle to grave' model of free social welfare provision. While the reality of this provision was often wholly inadequate for people's needs, the post-Soviet period saw a deterioration in many respects. The disruption of even this basic level of provision caused severe difficulties for the population as a whole. Similarly, the years after 1991 saw a huge transformation in social structure. During the Soviet era, Russia went from being a rural country to being predominantly urban, in terms of both its demographic structure and its political priorities. The population became much more highly educated, and the number employed in administrative and professional capacities grew substantially. However, Soviet social structure acquired a very different shape from that found in industrial democracies. The basis of social divisions was access to administrative power, rather than wealth. In terms of monetary income differentials, the Soviet Union was notably egalitarian. However, the Party-state elite exerted monopolistic and unaccountable control over resources and people. Unsurprisingly, this led to the development of an elaborate system of special privileges. Officials had access to goods that were unavailable to the wider population, networks of special schools for their children, exclusive hospitals with superior facilities, luxurious dachas (country retreats), and their own holiday resorts.

Such privileged access was, partly by its nature and partly by deliberate policy, concealed from the view of most citizens. This apparently egalitarian state of affairs suited Soviet propaganda well, especially when contrasted with income differentials in the capitalist countries. However, the impact of monetary income on the life of a Soviet citizen was in fact minimal, with the problem for most being access to goods, rather than the ability to pay for them. However, all of this changed in the 1990s. Suddenly money became, as across most of the world, the key factor in obtaining goods and services. What is more, while the Soviet Union had been a shortage economy with next to no access to Western consumer goods, post-Soviet Russia witnessed an influx of Western shops, brands and technology. In the Yeltsin years, while most Russians were suffering both materially and physically from the transition process, a few were becoming very rich, with their lifestyle visible to all. Following an era when goods were few, privileges relatively hidden, and egalitarianism the state creed, the ostentatious wealth of these few super-rich 'new Russians' was particularly galling for the majority, who appeared to be disadvantaged. The notion that wealth would 'trickle down' and spread through the economy seemed to be an empty excuse for most of the 1990s, and it was only really in the boom years of high oil prices when wealth did indeed begin to spread more widely. Even then, though, at the end of the Putin presidency in 2008, around half of all Russians were seeing their wages rise more slowly than prices.

Standards of living

The immediate post-Soviet period saw a sharp decline in overall living standards in Russia, and then a gradual improvement from around the turn of the millennium. The United Nations Development Programme (UNDP) estimated that, in purchasing power parity terms (that is, adjusting national incomes for relative prices), as of the year 2000, Russia's per capita gross domestic product (GDP) was US\$8377. This was just under a quarter of the US\$34,142 figure for the United States, over a third of the US\$23,509 for the United Kingdom, and put Russia, according to these data, on a par with countries such as Libya and Mexico. By 2008, the CIA's estimate of

Russia's GDP at purchasing parity power per capita was US$15,800. This was slightly under a third of the United States' US$48,000, and over 40 per cent of the United Kingdom's US$37,400. According to these data, Russia is now ranked at just above 50th among almost 200 countries in the world, on a par with countries such as Malaysia and Chile.

The decline in living standards in the first decade after the Soviet collapse had a number of identifiable causes:

- the dramatic reduction in state subsidies for basic services such as rents, public transport and energy;
- the hyperinflation of 1992 which led to rises of some 2,500 per cent in price levels and the wiping out of personal savings;
- the economic slump and rise in unemployment;
- the non-payment of wages and an inadequate welfare system; and
- the collapse of the rouble in 1998, which again wiped out the savings of many Russians.

As noted above, income inequality also increased sharply after the end of the Soviet Union. By 2007, the official ratio between the incomes of the richest and the poorest 10 per cent, known as the decile coefficient, was around 17:1 in Russia, having risen from 13:1 in 1997. Independent estimates put the ratio significantly higher. These figures are a useful corrective to aggregate data showing economic growth. Similarly, regional variations facilitate a more nuanced perspective on the living standards of Russians. That 'Moscow is not Russia' is a helpful maxim to bear in mind if one wants to understand fully contemporary Russia. According to the UN, in 2006, Russia's GDP per capita – in US dollars, not adjusted for purchasing power parity – was US$8800. In Moscow it was US$16,700. Only one other Russian region, oil- and gas-rich Tyumen oblast, has a higher GDP per capita (US$31,742 in 2006). None the less, Moscow also has a decile coefficient of 41:1, which demonstrates a vast gap between its richest and poorest inhabitants.

Just as Russian politics polarized in the early 1990s, with the concept of the 'middle ground' giving way to an almost elemental struggle between reform and reaction, so standards of living also moved in opposing directions. The 'new poor' and the 'new rich' appeared. Among the 'new poor' were many professional people – teachers, academics, scientists – whose wages scarcely pretended to keep up with the rising costs of everyday life, even when they were being paid, which often they were not. A common sight in the centre of Moscow in 1992 and 1993 were groups of people, from all walks of life, standing outside metro stations selling their possessions in order to buy the necessities of survival. The practice ended on this large scale in the mid-1990s not because the problem went away, but because the city authorities put a stop to it.

Popular resentment of the 'new rich', more commonly known as the 'new Russians' – that is, the section of the population that prospered materially in the post-Communist period – was fuelled by conspicuous consumption. Their expensive foreign cars, lavish lifestyles and luxurious new dachas were evident to all. For some of the 'new Russians', the word 'rich' seems inadequate. A very small, but highly visible, proportion of the population made serious money in the privatizations of the mid-1990s, when vast state-owned resources were sold at prices that turned out to be gross underestimates of their true market value.

For the men in control of these resources, foreign cars and lavish lifestyles were only the beginning. In 2003, one such businessman, 36-year-old Roman Abramovich, bought one of London's top football clubs, Chelsea, and proceeded to astonish the world of European football by using his wealth to pay huge transfer fees and wages for almost any player the club desired. With an estimated personal fortune of around US$7 billion, made chiefly in the oil industry, he could afford to transform the landscape in the home of the world's most popular sport.

Abramovich remained close to President Putin. A number of other high profile 'oligarchs', however, fell into disfavour with the Russian government. Men such as Vladimir Gusinsky and Boris Berezovsky both left Russia for 'voluntary' exile in western Europe during Putin's first term in office (2000–4), under threat of prosecution should they ever return to Russia. In the summer of 2003, another young and seriously rich oil tycoon, Mikhail Khodorkovsky, was imprisoned in Russia, pending prosecution for financial irregularities (see Box 3.3). Putin's stated desire, in a deliberate echo of a Stalinist phrase used to describe the campaign against the Soviet Union's 'rich peasants' in the 1930s, was to 'destroy the oligarchs as a class'. Many observers have noted, however, that only those oligarchs who display politically oppositionist tendencies seem to attract the negative attentions of the Russian state.

Berezovsky, Gusinsky, Abramovich and Khodorkovsky belonged to the super-rich among the new Russians. By 2008 there were 101 dollar billionaires in Russia, second only to the United States' figure of 415, though this number fell rapidly to 49 in early 2009 as a result of the global financial crisis. As well as these billionaires, many others made a great deal of money in the chaotic marketization of the post-Soviet period. It is folly to use generalizations in judging any particular individual, nevertheless there are features of the 'new Russians' as a whole that apply sufficiently well to be worth identifying:

- There was an element of elite continuity from the post-Soviet era, as those who had access to, or *de facto* control of, resources – such as factories or local networks of influence – were in a favourable position when it came to gaining ownership on privatization. Research by David Lane and Cameron Ross (1999) showed elite continuity in the older areas of economic activity, but less continuity in new areas such as retail and commerce.
- There is some truth in the assertion that no one who made money in Russia following the collapse of the Soviet Union did so without paying bribes, protection money and so on. The common view, in Russia as much as outside, is that corruption has been so rife that material success is itself a sufficient indicator of guilt. Some mitigation might be offered, on two grounds. First, a market economy needs to be regulated by a complex framework of laws, none of which existed under the Soviet command system. Factors such as political upheaval and lack of expertise meant that the development of a privatized, proto-market environment outpaced the construction of a renewed legal framework. Inevitably, old and inadequate laws were broken. Second, there were those who saw the arrival of an 'incipient acquisition class' as a necessary precursor to the creation of a regulated market economy. Once wealth had been acquired, so the argument went, then it would be in the interests of those who held it to support a protective legal framework. Two decades later, there are cautious signs that a legal environment of this nature is emerging, though these are vitiated by an apparent willingness on the part of the judiciary to take the side of the state when required. (For discussion of legal affairs, see later in this chapter.)
- There was a shadowy crossover between corruption and organized crime in Russia. Turf wars between groups seeking control of profitable areas of activity – for example, banking or trade – resulted in hundreds of contract killings of business people.

- Success in the marketizing economy often came more easily to the younger generation, who did not need to adjust from the old way of doing things and were far more likely to have gained business expertise abroad or with Western companies. Of course, by no means all Russian companies in the first decade of the twenty-first century are tainted by corruption and links with organized crime. As the market economy has become established, so have respectable companies – for example, in manufacturing and the service industries – with high-quality products, staff, and standards of customer service.

Below the level of the seriously rich, Russia has a growing middle class emerging out of Moscow, St Petersburg and other urban centres. According to official government data, the percentage of the Russian population falling into the middle-class income bracket had reached 21 per cent by early 2008. In the light of this figure, the government optimistically forecast that by 2020 around half of Russia's population would be middle class. However, this was before the economic difficulties that were felt around the world from late 2008. By the end of that year, 20 per cent of Russia's population, according to survey data, had experienced job losses and wage cuts, with many more expecting to do so in the near future.

As noted in Chapter 2, Russia's major cities have changed almost beyond recognition since the late 1990s, with the most immediately evident innovation being the arrival of large shopping malls and out-of-town stores. Anyone arriving at Moscow's Sheremetevo Airport these days will notice a vast IKEA furniture store on the outskirts of the city, along with restaurants and leisure complexes; in the centre of Moscow, more and more shopping malls, replete with fashionably expensive goods, are evident; and a short metro ride from the centre to the Gorbushka market will reveal a bustling indoor complex, crowded with Muscovites buying the latest electronic goods. The amount of retail space in Moscow grew rapidly from the early years of the twenty-first century, and such activity can only be supported by a large number of people with ready disposable income. The emergence of a middle class has been seen by theorists of democratic transition as a key driver in establishing a liberal democratic system in Russia. However, while an identifiable middle class is apparent, there is still some way to go before it becomes the bedrock of support for deeper democracy, as it has not yet established itself as a stable element of society confident of its position. Members of the middle class do not yet represent the 'average citizen' in Russia in the same way as they are often deemed to do by politicians in most Western countries.

There is a disparity between statistical indicators of 'middle-class-ness' based on income, and what might be deemed 'middle-class atti-tudes'. The parliamentary elections of 2003 represented a virtual wipe-out for the liberal parties who would like to see themselves as representing the middle classes, and this was repeated in 2007. There are, of course, many explanations for this, but one of them is that many educated, professional people – academics, teachers, doctors – are not middle-class in terms of income, and many of those who now fit into the middle class from an income point of view are as likely – according to some studies, *more* likely – to be nationalistic and authoritarian in attitude, as to be supporters of liberal ideals.

The proportion of the population living in poverty before the collapse of the Soviet Union was usually estimated at around 1 in 10. Official estimates were putting the figure at around 1in 5 of the popu-lation by 1994, and around 1 in 3 by the start of the twenty-first century, with incomes below the official subsistence minimum. Official figures released at the beginning of 2004 showed that during President Putin's first term in office, the proportion of people living below the poverty line of US$70 per month had fallen from 1 in 3 to 1 in 5. By the end of Putin's second term, in 2008, official data placed approximately one in eight of all Russians below the official poverty line. However, there are three caveats that might undermine an other-wise impressive reduction in poverty:

- Independent experts assert that official figures do not give a true picture. In particular, the subsistence minimum is set at a lower level for retired people, artificially excluding many from the offi-cial data. Even the normally loyalist Chairman of the Federation Council (the upper house of Russia's parliament) has stated that official statistics understate the situation, and that, in reality, 30 per cent of the population live in poverty.
- The reduction in poverty happened during a time of economic growth, and it is far from clear that mechanisms are in place to support the poor during an economic downturn.
- Individuals' own assessments of their family's economic situation do not always reflect this apparent improvement, especially in times of potential economic hardship. In any case, having at least 20 million people living in poverty remains a major problem for Russia to tackle.

A survey undertaken in December 2008 across Russia (see Figure 3.1) showed the beginnings of a decline in optimism about individual living standards, and a growing awareness of economic trouble ahead.

When Russians are asked, 'What is preventing you from living better?', the top five reasons cited are related to poverty – low wages, unemployment, inflation, pensions and inadequate state benefits. The situation has improved since the 1990s, but none the less the picture presented for the poorest remains a bleak one, and some sections of the population are in particular need. These groups include pensioners (both old-age pensioners and the disabled), one-parent families (increasingly common, given rising divorce rates, rising numbers of extra-marital births, and the high mortality rates among middle-aged men), the unemployed and migrants. Also included are workers in public services such as teachers, health professionals, military personnel and employees in the state sector, who during the 1990s suffered from persistent non-payment of wages.

Though pensions have risen steadily since the start of the twenty-first century, their rise has not kept pace with wage increases or the official subsistence minimum. The average monthly pension in Russia in 2006 was only 80 per cent of the subsistence minimum, and just

Figure 3.1   Top three problems facing Russian society, December 2008

What problems facing our society alarm you most and you think are the most serious? (Choice made from list of 24 options covering politics, economic, international relations, social problems and human rights.)

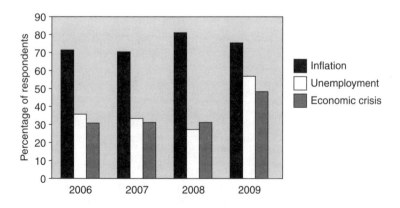

Source: Levada Center website: www.levada.ru/eng/, accessed February 2009.

over a quarter of the average monthly wage. In early 2005, tens of thousands of pensioners took to the streets across Russia in an unprecedented series of demonstrations against the monetization of benefits such as access to transport and prescription medicines, which they argued would see most of them in an even worse financial position.

Box 3.1   Ranking Russia

In an age seemingly obsessed by lists, it is a fascinating exercise to see where Russia appears in various 'league tables'. While there are always arguments, particularly where the placing is based on estimates, the following examples give us a picture of Russian society in the early years of the twenty-first century.

1st	in the incidence of abortions, with 53.7 per 1,000 women between the ages of 15 and 44. The next highest are Vietnam with 35.2 and Kazakhstan with 35.0 The second highest abortion rate in Europe is in Estonia, with 33.3 abortions per 1,000 women in the 15–44 age group (*UNData*, 2009)
2nd	in the number of people in prison per capita (Kings College, London, International Centre for Prison Studies, *World Prison Brief*, 2009)
2nd	lowest sex ratio, with 0.86 males to each female. Estonia has a ratio of 0.84, and Russia, Ukraine and Latvia are joint second (CIA, *World Factbook*, 2008)
3rd	in the list of countries with the most dollar billionaires, behind the United States and Germany (*Forbes Magazine*, 2009)
3rd	in the global suicide rate per capita, behind neighbouring Lithuania and Belarus (World Health Organization figures for 2005)
3rd	in the medals table at the 2008 Olympics
3rd	in global divorce rate per capita, behind the United States and Puerto Rico (www.nationmaster.com/graph/peodiv rat-people-divorce-rate)
5th	in the global murder rates per capita, behind Colombia, South Africa, Jamaica and Venezuela (www.nationmaster.com/graph/cri mur percap-crime-murders-per-capita)
5th	in the global male smoking rates, with 60.4 per cent of men being smokers (World Health Organization, 2008)
130th	out of 191 countries in the World Health Organization's ranking of health systems (World Health Organization, 2000)

The most vulnerable groups include the homeless, estimated at between one and two million – mainly children who have run away from home, or newly released prisoners, and inmates of prisons, mental institutions and children's homes. By 2003, unofficial Russian estimates placed 45 per cent of families with children below the poverty line, or – to translate the Russian phrase more precisely – below the living wage.

Demographics and health policy

The existence of widespread poverty is storing up problems for Russia for many years to come. Children brought up in such a situation have poor diets, are ill more often, and have lowered life expectancy. Throughout the post-Soviet period, life expectancy in Russia has been remarkably low, particularly for Russian men. By 2008, life expectancy was 73.1 for women and 59.1 for men. This represents the lowest life expectancy for males in any developed country, and the biggest gap between male and female life expectancy in the world. Why are so many Russian men dying early? Some suggested reasons are listed below:

- Rising alcoholism, accompanied by the Russian pattern of drinking, has been identified in studies as a major contributory factor to the decline in male life-expectancy. An anti-alcohol campaign spearheaded by Mikhail Gorbachev in the second half of the 1980s led to a slight improvement in male mortality rates, but by 1994 twice as many Russian men between the ages of 15 and 64 died than had been the case in 1986. A slight drop in mortality rates in 2006 and 2007 was linked by analysts to a temporary problem in alcohol supplies to the shops, which created a shortage for a few weeks.
- A particularly high rate of death through external causes (accidents or violence) afflicted Russian men in the 1990s, with such causes resulting in 80 per cent of deaths in the 15–24 age group in some years in that decade. Within this category, the highest identifiable cause was suicide, followed by vehicle accidents and homicides. The male suicide rate in Russia is more than six times that for females. Alcohol poisoning *per se* came at the bottom of the list of 'external causes', but clearly alcohol abuse could have played a part under a number of the other headings. For the sake of compar-

ison, though, it is worth noting that in 2006 in Russia, over 31,000 people died from accidental alcohol poisoning. In the United States – without adjusting for the fact that the US population is getting on for double the size of Russia's – around 300 people a year are recorded as dying from the same cause. One further comparison emphasizes the scale of the problem: a baby boy born in Russia in 1995 would have almost a 1 in 4 chance of his eventual death being through an external cause; in the UK, the corresponding risk would be 1 in 30. Since the early 2000s, death rates resulting from suicide and homicide have begun to decline a little, but still remain high in terms of international comparison.

- Cardiovascular diseases account for almost double the number of deaths among Russian men than do external causes. Again, alcohol consumption is a contributing factor, as 'binge drinking' is associated with an increased risk of cardiovascular disease. In addition, in Russia, the ratio of smokers to non-smokers is twice as high as in Western Europe, with nearly 70 million smokers out of a population of 144 million. Each year, around a million Russians die from these causes – 400,000 from smoking-related illnesses and 600,000 from alcohol-related causes.

In 2002, Russia carried out its first national census since the Soviet collapse (the previous Soviet census had taken place in 1989). The results of the 2002 census reveal what can accurately be described as a demographic time-bomb. A number of commentaries noted positives such as the fact that the overall population of Russia was more than two million higher – at 145 million – than many had estimated. None the less, projections for Russia's future into the middle of the twenty-first century and beyond provide serious cause for concern in relation to the decline of, and the shifting age structure within, the population.

In many developed countries, the birth rate is below the replacement rate necessary to maintain the population level. Russia's birth rate, however, has been well below that in most developed countries for many years, though it has experienced a slight upturn in the past few years: 2007 saw the highest number of births in Russia since the Soviet collapse. Optimism about this rise in the number of births, however, may be misplaced:

- For a complex of reasons – largely to do with economic hardship, poor medical care and lack of confidence in the future – the number of children being born in Russia has been insufficient to prevent population decline. A return to more straitened economic times could see birth rates declining again.

- President Medvedev has spoken of the birth rate (11.3 per thousand in 2007) exceeding the death rate (14.7 per thousand in 2007) by the year 2014. Reports in 2008 suggest, however, that infant mortality rates are increasing in more than half of Russia's regions. Clearly, population growth is dependent on both births and deaths, and improvements in medical care, alongside massive reductions in smoking and drinking, are essential to decrease death rates. Demographic trends are not subject to short-term fixes, as a decline in one age cohort is reflected later when that generation reaches child-bearing age.

Lower levels of population in turn affect overall well-being in a number of ways, particularly as they are combined with a changing age-structure. In 2007, 60 per cent of the population were of working age, 23 per cent were younger and 17 per cent older. In the coming decades, however, the percentage of pensioners will continue to increase, with some estimates putting them at about 40 per cent of the Russian population by the middle of the century. This matters for a number of reasons – most obviously because it means that an ever-smaller proportion of the population will have to provide for an ever-growing pensioner sector. This is not a problem unique to Russia, but the existence of widespread poverty within the country at the present time makes persuading working people to contribute to private pension funds extremely difficult, especially when combined with a distrust of financial institutions. Aside from issues of pension provision, the combination of population decline and changing age structure means fewer people able to contribute to economic growth and – seen as particularly important in Russia, which is still apparently wedded to military conscription and a trained reserve – fewer people to staff the armed forces. Projections for the decline in the working-age population of Russia over the next decade suggest a percentage decline of more than double the 7 per cent predicted for most of Europe. It is against this background that any plans for economic growth must be judged.

The demographic problems outlined above are similar to, though worse than, those experienced in a number of developed countries. However, these difficulties are compounded in Russia because of its specific features of size, ethnic mix and political culture. Where allowing an increase in immigration might be seen as an obvious solution to population decline in the abstract, in reality socio-political attitudes – including relatively widespread xenophobia and exaggerated security concerns – make such an option difficult politically. Furthermore, although a number of the demographic features outlined above may be similar in type to those experienced in many developed countries, they are greater in scale and differ in certain key details.

Fears of the depopulation of Russia on the basis of the birth rate deepen when turning to the health of children. According to the Russian Ministry of Health, 70 per cent of Russian teenagers suffer from chronic diseases, and the mortality rate in 2000 for 10–17 year olds was an extremely high 213 per 100,000. High levels of drug addiction and alcohol abuse are reported for teenagers in the 15–17 age bracket, along with an increase in gynaecological ailments for girls of the same age as the phenomenon of teenage maternity becomes more prevalent. These health problems at a young age have an immediate effect in terms of the proportion of the biannual call-up to the armed forces who do in fact get to serve. All Russian men aged 18–27 are required to serve one year in the armed forces, reduced from the previous two-year requirement in 2007, but up to 90 per cent avoid the draft – more than half by means of the legal right to draft deferment for students, but many of the remainder on health grounds. The reduction of the period of service to one year was intended partly to increase the number of conscripts actually serving. Such immediate effects as the poor health of young men are also compounded by long-term effects. If the staggeringly low life-expectancy levels of Russian men in particular are to be improved, then it is important that children's health is not neglected, since illness as a child makes the adult more vulnerable.

One further major health problem in Russia that has not yet been mentioned is the especially acute threat from tuberculosis and AIDS. Tuberculosis is a disease that was relatively well controlled in the Soviet era, but weaknesses in the public health system and increasing poverty have meant a resurgence. However, in recent years a new strain known as multi-drug-resistant tuberculosis (MDR-TB) has emerged, and most cases of MDR-TB reported in the world occur in Russia. At the same time, the far more publicized spread of AIDS has constituted a growing global health threat – and, of course, the combination of these two threats is mutually destructive to health, as TB is one of the main infections to which AIDS sufferers become vulnerable. As can be seen from Figure 3.2, the incidence of TB has increased dramatically in the post-Soviet period, up to levels which exceed those of half a century ago.

In 2007 there were around 150,000 cases of TB in Russia, compared with, for example, just over 13,000 in the United States, which has almost twice the population. Russia also has one of the fastest-growing rates of AIDS cases in the world, with the World Health Organization (WHO) noting that two-thirds of new AIDS cases in eastern Europe occur in Russia. For many years, the Soviet and then the Russian governments appeared to live in a state of denial about HIV/AIDS. In 2003 and 2004, signs appeared of an increasingly active awareness of the issue among policy-makers. President Putin even noted the dangers in his State of the Federation address in 2004, and in 2006 he convened a session of the State Council devoted to combating HIV/AIDS. In the same year, a government commission on HIV/AIDS was formed. None the less, commissions and political support for action do not in themselves solve the problem. Responsibility for the provision of treatment lies with regional rather than national authorities, and not all of them are willing or able to respond adequately. There are fears among some experts that the combination of a growing HIV problem, high rates of TB infection, and an inadequate medical infrastructure could create a 'perfect storm' in Russia.

Figure 3.2   Incidence of tuberculosis in Russia, 1955–2010, per 100,000 population

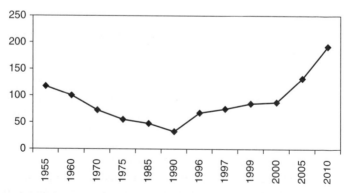

Source: Olga Govor, Vladivostok State University, cited in Johnson's *Russia List Research and Analytical Supplement*, January 2004.

Table 3.1   Russian health indicators, 2008

Life expectancy	
• Total population	65.9
• Male	59.1
• Female	73.1
Infant mortality, under one year old, per thousand	
• Male	12.3
• Female	9.2
Infant mortality, under five years old, per thousand	20.9
Total health expenditure, percentage of GDP	5.2

Source: CIA, *World Factbook*, 2008.

In 2000, the World Health Organization ranked the health systems of 191 countries. Russia was ranked at 130, between Peru and Honduras. During the Soviet era, the state created a system of health care that entitled every citizen to access to medical services, free at the point of use. Official health statistics for decades showed improvement across a range of indicators – albeit from a low base. Health care was, of course, far from perfect; stories abound of poor treatment in unhygienic hospitals, and there were inevitable regional discrepancies across the vast territory of the Soviet Union. In general, the Soviet health system used techniques, equipment and treatments that were far below the level of developed nations. The health system suffered too from the vagaries of the centrally planned economy, with its emphasis on quantity over quality, and its sometimes counterproductive use of targets. For example, targets for the number of 'bed days' led hospitals to keep patients in hospitals longer than necessary, and to prioritize the number of beds rather than the quality of other resources. Furthermore, health spending in the Soviet Union was low as a percentage of GDP – typically around 3 per cent, compared with 10–12 per cent in the West. According to figures from the Russian Ministry of the Economy, around 6 per cent of all hospitals were financed and run by places of work, such as an industrial enterprise or collective farm. This figure related to the country as a whole, and in some regions the percentage could have been significantly higher.

Health care was not a government priority in the same way as defence spending or spending on heavy industry, and so in a shortage economy the budget and the flow of resources diminished when other demands came to the fore. Doctors' wages were relatively low – only about three-quarters of the amount received by high priority indus-trial workers – and it was common for patients to give money or goods in kind to medical staff to ensure a certain level of service. Over time, such payments took on the character of expectations rather than gratuities. As with so much in the Soviet Union, the best-quality service came in those facilities reserved for the party elite.

As the Soviet system collapsed in the late 1980s and early 1990s, so the health system worsened severely as its funding declined dramatically in real terms. Such a situation clearly had some impact on the serious downturn in health statistics noted above. Policy responses to this took a number of forms, chief among these being the introduction of health insurance funds, and the decentralization of the funding and delivery of services. Health reform legislation was passed in Russia in 1991, and again in an amended form in 1993. This legislation put responsibility for all but forty of the country's hospi-tals in the hands of regional government, and introduced a system of mandatory medical insurance to be paid via a uniform payroll tax. The health insurance fund would operate alongside central state funding.

In reality, such reforms, though perhaps necessary, fell far short of what was needed to provide adequate, let alone high-quality, health care coverage for the population. Despite government promises regarding improvements in the quality of and access to health care services, by the end of Putin's first term as president in 2004, the increase in national wealth resulting from booming oil prices was still not reflected in public funding of the health system:

- An official report for President Putin in 2003 found that Russia's health insurance funds received only a fifth of the amount neces-sary to sustain the health system adequately. Health insurance paid for by a payroll tax leaves those not in employment out of the equa-tion, and it is often such people who are likely to need medical services. A separate insurance fund exists for non-working people, payments into which were supposed to be made from the federal and regional budgets. Payments were officially estimated to have fallen 75 per cent short of requirements in 2001.

- Statistics from the WHO suggested that a quarter of all health care in Russia was funded from the patients' own pockets in 2000, despite the Russian Constitution's guarantee of universal access to health care. By 2005, this figure had grown to over 30 per cent of health care being funded in this way. What this means in practice is that an episode of illness can have devastating economic consequences for poorer households.

- A lack of resources to pay for immediate needs was contributing to a low level of investment in infrastructure and equipment, leading to worsening conditions and out-of-date treatment.

Health policy and the national projects

In keeping with his long-standing emphasis on issues relating to standards of living, President Putin sought to address health care provision as a priority within the framework of the 'national projects' that were introduced at the beginning of his second term in office. In September 2005, following policy debates about how the Russian state could best use the significant increase in income that had come its way as a result of high oil and gas prices, Putin launched the 'national projects' as the key domestic policy of his second term (see Box 3.2). Their aim was to focus government attention, and expenditure, on areas of social provision deemed to be most significant.

National projects in the areas of health, education, housing and rural life were announced in September 2005. In relation to health care, the staffing situation was to be improved by higher pay for doctors and nurses, and the training of more staff. There is an emphasis too on technological solutions, with new, high-tech medical centres to be built, more ambulances bought, and higher levels of technological provision in hospitals. The projects outlined had very specific targets, such as 12,120 new ambulances and the retraining of 13,848 doctors in two years.

The projects were initially put under the charge of then first deputy prime minister, Dmitrii Medvedev, who succeeded Putin as president in 2008. At the end of 2008, a government 'Healthcare Development Concept to 2020' was published, designed to work with the national project on health. In terms of aspirations, this health care concept targets areas of clear need, and sets specific targets; for example, reducing strokes and heart attacks by 20 per cent, and increasing average life expectancy from 66 to 75 years by 2020. The concept also sets out plans for a complete move to a centralized mandatory health care insurance scheme.

Box 3.2   The national projects

'National projects' in the areas of health, education, housing, and rural life were announced in September 2005.

Health The focus is on higher pay for doctors and nurses, the training of more staff, and increasing the technological levels in hospitals. New high-tech medical centres are to be built, and provided with ambulances. There is an emphasis on preventive medicine, particularly immunization, and increasing the population through improved ante- and post-natal care.

Education The education project has a strong competitive element, with universities and schools competing for substantial grants to develop innovative programmes, and annual competitions with cash rewards for talented youngsters and leading teachers. Funding will go towards giving more schools internet access, providing school transport for rural pupils, and creating new universities and business schools.

Housing The provision of 'affordable and comfortable' accommodation is to be achieved by increasing the amount of new housing being built by a third within two years, and subsidizing mortgages to enable certain groups – in particular, service personnel, refugees and young families – to buy housing. Targets include the provision of state support for 181,700 young families in relation to mortgages by 2010. In 2008, President Medvedev proposed the creation of a Federal State Fund for the Promotion of Housing Construction, to bring unused land owned by the state into a programme of mass construction of individual housing – specifically, new towns and cities.

Development of the agro-industrial complex To be achieved by encouraging smallholdings, increasing the availability of housing for 'young specialists' in rural areas, and subsidizing modernization and the leasing of equipment. A set of production targets include specific figures for the increase in meat and milk production.

In addition to these four projects, there is a fifth 'quasi-national project', namely, the 'gasification of the regions' – providing gas to many more households across Russia, particularly in rural areas.

Judicial policy

All of Russia's recent leaders, including the last Soviet leader, Mikhail Gorbachev, have committed themselves in principle to the rule of law. As president, Putin repeatedly emphasized that the law should not be applied differentially on political grounds – though his choice of phrase left something to be desired when, in an echo of the

Communist Party's commitment to a 'dictatorship of the proletariat', he called for a 'dictatorship of the law'. Despite this formal commitment to the rule of law, however, cases such as the Yukos affair (see Box 3.3) suggest that political control over the courts still prevailed where it was deemed necessary.

President Medvedev, a lawyer by profession, has similarly made a public commitment to the rule of law. In one of his first speeches as president, in May 2008, he declared that 'our main objective is to achieve independence for the judicial system', implicitly accepting that such a situation had not been arrived at during the presidency of his predecessor.

If there was one area of social policy where the Soviet Union's international reputation plumbed the depths, it was judicial policy. In the Stalin years (1928–53) around 18 million people suffered in the Gulag forced labour camps – some of them criminals, but most simply designated as criminals by a system with political and economic values that trumped natural justice at every turn. During the Brezhnev era (1964–82), political prisoners were 'sentenced' to terms in psychiatric hospitals, where they underwent forcible treatment with drugs, electric shocks and physical restraint. The working assumption seemed to be that anyone foolish enough to doubt the wisdom of the state must be genuinely mad. Throughout the Soviet period, the concept of an independent judiciary remained completely alien. The law was what the Party declared it to be, and judges took their orders from the political authorities – where necessary, regardless of the niceties of evidence. Under Soviet law, the presumption of 'innocent until proven guilty' was turned on its head.

When the Soviet Union collapsed, Russia inherited not only the attitudes and procedures of the Soviet era, but also many of the personnel. There was no tradition of or training in liberal democratic norms of justice. Consequently, despite reforms since the late 1990s, many of the old practices continue:

- The presumption of guilt until proven otherwise is to some extent apparent in the fact that, on average, 99 per cent of cases heard by judges in Russian courts result in the conviction of the accused (though in jury trials that average falls to 85 per cent). Anyone attending a Russian court case will be struck immediately by the fact that defendants – whether dangerous or not – give their evidence from inside a cage in the courtroom, as if to emphasize the fact that they are almost certain to be found guilty.

- Courts often depend on the good offices of the local executive for funding, and so to cross the authorities can result in difficulties for the judiciary.
- In the late 1990s, the New-York-based Human Rights Watch reported that torture 'now appears endemic to the Russian criminal justice system' (Bivens, 2003).
- In 2003, an International Helsinki Federation for Human Rights report claimed that pre-trial detention, occasionally for long periods of time, is used in order to break the will of prisoners 'with the intention of eliciting confessions and information' (International Helsinki Federation, 2003). In 2007, the President of the European Court of Human Rights again called for the period of pre-trial detention to be reduced, down to a maximum two years, which the court recommends.

Box 3.3   The Yukos Affair, Khodorkovsky and Basmanny justice

Any claim on the part of the Russian authorities to support an independent judiciary and fair legal system must be considered against the Yukos Affair. This represented a watershed in several key elements of Russia's recent development, from both political and economic perspectives. For the purposes of this chapter, however, the main focus is its judicial aspect.

Yukos was Russia's largest private oil company, the CEO of which, Mikhail Khodorkovsky, was arrested in October 2003 and charged with tax evasion and fraud. There are several explanations as to why Khodorkovsky was singled out for arrest and prosecution, especially given that Yukos was renowned for being the first Russian company to comply with international accounting standards in terms of releasing financial data, and paid a higher proportion of its earnings in tax than other leading oil companies. Khodorkovsky had supported opposition parties financially and was said to be 'buying' Duma deputies in order to influence legislation. Political engagement went against the spirit of the alleged agreement between Putin and Russia's leading businessmen in 2000, that, if they kept out of politics, the state would not revisit the legality of the privatizations of the 1990s, in which lay the root source of their wealth. Khodorkovsky was also a strong critic of corruption in the Russian government.

Aside from the politics, some argue that Yukos's intention to create the country's largest oil company, by merging with Sibneft, cut across the ambitions of other companies with state influence. Or that Yukos showed a willingness to disrupt the state's oversight of pipeline policy, viewed by the administration as a critical economic and foreign policy tool.

Whatever the precise weight of the different elements, the Parliamentary Assembly of the Council of Europe summed up the

||||➡

This list of apparent failures in the Russian judicial system should not be taken to imply that nothing at all has changed since the Soviet era. At the fundamental level, Russia's Constitution, adopted by national referendum on 12 December 1993, forms the basic law of the Russian Federation and is a recognizably liberal democratic document. There is a fundamental commitment within it to the separation of powers and equality of citizens before the law (for more details of the Constitution, see Chapter 4).

Under Boris Yeltsin, Russia ceased to apply the death penalty, in line with the conditions for membership of the Council of Europe. Russian citizens are also able to take their cases to the European Court of Human Rights and, as of January 2007, approximately 20,000 of the 90,000 cases pending before the Court originated in

---

impression of many, particularly in the West, by passing a resolution calling the arrest of Khodorkovsky arbitrary and arguing that it was carried out in order to 'weaken an outspoken political opponent, intimidate other wealthy individuals and regain control of economic assets'.

Khodorkovsky's trial has given rise to the phrase 'Basmanny justice', after the Basmanny district court in Moscow where it took place, as a description of a Russian judicial system where the state can rely on, or lean on if necessary, the judiciary to deliver the desired verdict. Besides the bigger question of why Yukos was singled out, Khodorkovsky's lawyers allege a whole series of procedural and due process violations during the case. Mikhail Khodorkovsky was found guilty and sentenced to nine years' imprisonment. In 2007, further charges were brought against him, and the case in relation to these was ongoing as of early 2009.

Even as Khodorkovsky's trial was continuing, the Russian state began to break up and sell Yukos to recover some of the alleged tax debts. In December 2004, the little-known Baikalfinansgrup bought Yuganskneftegaz, Yukos's prime asset, for an amount reported to be significantly below market value, and swiftly sold it on to the state-owned company, Rosneft.

As CEO of Yukos, Khodorkovsky himself has attracted the most attention. However, several other Yukos employees have been arrested, along with Platon Lebedev, Director of Yukos's holding company. The court proceedings and detention conditions of those arrested in the Yukos Affair have caused serious concern, particularly the case of Vasilii Aleksyan, who was held in prison between 2006 and 2008 while seriously ill with HIV/AIDS and cancer. The European Court of Human Rights issued several injunctions to transfer Aleksyan to a civilian facility where he could receive appropriate treatment. Eventually, he was released in December 2008 after posting bail of US$1.8 million.

Russia. The fact that more citizens of Russia than of any other country petition the European Court of Human Rights is an indication of the failure of the Russian court system to uphold these rights. President Medvedev has spoken of the need to reform Russia's judiciary in order to stem the flow of cases to Strasbourg.

In 2002, a much-trumpeted judicial reform package was introduced by President Putin. Among its provisions was enabling legislation to introduce the constitutional provision of trial by jury on a nationwide basis, as previously it had only been available in limited locations. The reforms also sought to enhance the status and independence of the judiciary by improving judges' pay by 40 per cent, increasing the number of judges, and ending their lifetime tenure and immunity from prosecution. Measures were introduced to enhance the rights of suspects and create a level playing field for defence lawyers in relation to the previously overwhelmingly influential prosecutors. Trials in absentia were banned; searches, arrests and detention beyond 48 hours must now be sanctioned by courts, rather than by prosecutors; plea bargaining was introduced for offences with a prison term of less than five years; and the practice of sending criminal cases back for 'additional investigation' – that is, enabling the prosecution to patch up a poor case – was ended.

As a package of reforms, the measures introduced in 2002 and 2003 were impressive. At the very least they indicated an awareness of continuing problems and of international norms. None the less, the problems with the Russian judicial system are deep-rooted in terms of culture. It is one thing to produce a list of reform measures, and quite another to change judicial culture. In early 2005, Dmitry Kozak, one of the presidential officials behind the judicial reforms, admitted that the public remains convinced that 'the system is corrupt through and through'. Similarly, in 2007, research by the Russian Academy of State Service found that 38 per cent of respondents distrusted the judiciary, compared to 26 per cent who trust it. The key point, according to those who conducted this survey, was that trust in the judiciary was increasing, not that it was at so low a level and easily dwarfed by those expressing distrust.

The success, or otherwise, of judicial reform is one of the key factors to watch out for in Russia over the coming years. Corruption in all walks of public life was noted by President Medvedev as a key problem that he aimed to tackle during his presidency, and in his speeches he has returned regularly to the rhetoric of legal transparency and an unbiased court system. In December 2008, Medvedev again spoke of the need to turn courts' *de jure* independence into *de facto* reality, but at the same time specific reforms to the system under his watch have included restricting jury trials in terrorism cases, and legislative amendments making it easier for judges to return cases for additional investigation. If the Russian judicial system itself leaves a good deal to be desired, then this applies doubly so to the prison network. A report from the Public Centre for Judicial Reform in late 2003 illustrates a situation that is not uncommon across Russia. Prisoners smuggled a mobile phone into their cell in order to call the Centre and publicize the conditions in which they were being held – 76 inmates in a cell designed for 36, icy temperatures, prisoners taking it in turns to sleep on the few cots under threadbare blankets, meals of rice for breakfast and dinner and a watered-down meat-and-potato soup for lunch. This account matches well a similar description from five years earlier, by an American who spent nearly two years in a Russian prison for possession of a small quantity of marijuana. He too describes over-crowding (100 prisoners in a cell built for 30, 'shoulder-to-shoulder, like riding in a bus at rush hour'), sleeping in shifts, lice-ridden mattresses, two meals of rice and one of watered-down soup. His conclusion was that 'it's hell on earth . . . I'd never seen so many rats, and the cell walls were carpeted in cockroaches.'

Given conditions like those described above, it is not surprising that the Russian prison system is a breeding ground for disease, particularly for TB. Out of around 800,000 prisoners in Russia, roughly 10 per cent have active TB, and of these a third have the multi-drug-resistant strain. The high turnover of prisoners means that each year several hundred thousand prisoners leave the system and go back into the general population, taking the disease with them, but with inadequate access to treatment. The general sickness rate of people in prison is about five times that of those outside.

In addition to health concerns, there have also been regular reports from human rights groups, including Russia's official Human Rights Ombudsman, about violence against prisoners by prison authorities. Prison riots, in protest against conditions, are on the increase, and in May 2008 President Medvedev publicly committed the Russian state to improving conditions in prisons. A law on public oversight for safeguarding human rights in prisons was passed by parliament with presidential support, making Russia's Public Chamber responsible for monitoring prison conditions. Medvedev has also stated that alternatives to pre-trial detention will be used, including technology such as electronic bracelets.

Education

As with the judicial and the health care systems, the story of contemporary Russia's educational provision is one of contending on two fronts: first, with the legacy of the Soviet era; and second, with the economic difficulties of the post-Soviet years.

In terms of the Soviet legacy, perhaps the most interesting feature of the education system from a political point of view was its propagandistic content. The state taught what it wanted its citizens to know, including compulsory lessons in Marxism–Leninism. The history curriculum was replete with uncritical praise for all that the Party had done, and studiously avoided topics such as the Stalinist terror or the ideas of 'the renegade Trotsky'. English-language textbooks included accounts of poverty-stricken Londoners oppressed by the bourgeoisie. Economics and law followed narrow ideological courses, and sociology barely existed until Gorbachev embraced some of its findings to bolster his reform programme in the mid-1980s. Political reliability was not only central to curriculum content; it could also have an influence on admission to the best universities. In the Soviet period, the drive to recruit working-class children to higher education gave them priority, but such priority could always be trumped by members of the new ruling class, the Communist Party leadership, and their families.

A far more positive spin on the Soviet education system would emphasize its achievements in providing universal education, and creating a literate and highly educated population with specialists capable of rivalling the world's best. Political bias aside, there was nothing second-rate about the Soviet education system. In the post-Soviet era, however, the difficulties facing the public sector at large swept away much of the good from the old system. While debates about curriculum reform occupied many specialists, schools were undermined by salary arrears, equipment shortages and a lack of teachers. The teaching profession in Russia became so unattractive in the 1990s that by the end of the decade only about half of those graduating from teacher training institutions went on to teach in schools. The difficulties in attracting teachers were felt in particular in remote regions, as the Soviet practice of requiring teachers to work in designated schools on qualification was discontinued. At the tertiary level, Russian higher education became increasingly expensive and open to corruption.

Education appears to have come low down the list of priorities of the Russian government in the 1990s, faced as it was by the massive problems of economic and political reform. The major 'achievement' of the 1992 law on education, backed up later by Article 43 of the Russian Constitution, was to break the commitment to universal secondary education, of which the Soviet Union had been justly proud. The law guaranteed state-funded education up to Year 9, rather than Year 11 as had previously been the case, thus opening the way for schools to charge fees for pupils beyond the age of 15.

It may have been that other priorities came before education and prevented a serious reform of the system in the 1990s. Just as likely, though, is that barriers to reform came from the relative chaos of Russia's weak state in that decade. Attempts at reform were obstructed by an exodus from the classroom by teachers, as real incomes declined or salaries were simply not paid; regions with large ethnic minorities, or even majorities, sought to establish their own systems of education; and funding shortages were exacerbated by problems with budgetary transfers between the regional and federal levels. At the same time it was reported by the education minister in 2001 that up to two million children of school age in Russia do not in fact attend school.

When President Putin came to power in 2000, reform of the education system fitted with his declared focus on domestic issues. In August 2001, the State Council – a body set up by Putin, with a membership made up of the heads of regions, but with only advisory status – considered the issue of education reform. In a speech to the State Council, Putin called free education 'the cornerstone' of the state system, but also talked positively of the contribution to be made by an ordered private system. The major reform announcement was that educational spending would become a national priority. The most obvious immediate beneficiaries of this change in policy were teachers, who saw their salaries doubled – but this was to a figure equivalent to a meagre US$80 to US$100 per month. A further 50 per cent pay rise followed in 2005. In a reversal of decades of Soviet practice, in 2004 the Ministry of Education proudly announced that state spending on education outstripped that on the defence industries, a significant shift away from the priorities of the Soviet era.

The reforms of 2001 included a move to a 12-year schooling system, which would allow pupils to specialize before going on to higher education. In addition, plans were announced for a standard school leaving exam, on which entry to university would be based. This latter reform was introduced to make entry into higher education more egalitarian, and less prone to the corruption that beset it in the immediate post-Soviet era. Further reforms to the school system included a change in teachers' terms and conditions, so that pay was related more closely to hours taught and thus 'moonlighting' diminished. Changes too are also gradually being introduced in the way that pupils are taught, with the old Soviet emphasis on rote learning of facts and figures supposedly giving way to the teaching of independent and creative thinking.

These initial education reforms of the Putin years were followed by the introduction of the national project for education (see Box 3.2), specifically aimed at creating an education system capable of supporting the development of civil society and of an economy suited to technological innovation. The aims of the project are framed on the one hand in terms of support for innovative approaches, support for the best teachers and most talented young people, and the development of regional centres of excellence. On the other, there is a more universal commitment to the provision of internet connection and computers, adequate school transport, improvements in school meals, and repairs to buildings. As with the national projects as a whole, there is a clear sense of trying to integrate the more remote towns and cities of Russia into the development process.

President Medvedev has also sought to focus attention on reform of the higher education system, even making it the subject of one of his regular video blogs on the presidential website. In recent years, initiatives have been developed to reduce the level of corruption involved in gaining university places – in particular, the standardized national test at the end of secondary schooling, discussed above, has been introduced and is being used increasingly. A poll in 2007 found that 66 per cent of Russians consider their higher education system to be corrupt, with some families spending over a third of their income on what is supposed to be free education. There are regular stories of university staff accepting bribes for good marks – thirty to forty cases coming to light each year in Moscow alone – and of university authorities selling building permission for private profit, or using state funds for purposes other than those intended. Medvedev, with an eye to such activities, was careful to emphasize, while announcing new financial measures to support students in February 2009, that 'universities exist for students, and not for earning money'.

Other initiatives in the sphere of higher education follow the same priorities as for the national project for education as a whole; namely, support for innovation and moves to widen the geographical base of the system. Since 2006, extra state funding has been provided for those higher education institutions chosen, on a competitive basis, as being innovative. Also in 2006, new universities were established in the Siberian and Southern Federal Districts. The ambitious aim is for Russia to have five or six institutions in the world's top hundred universities by 2020. At present, only Moscow State University features in the Shanghai Jiao Tong ranking of global universities – in 70th place in 2008.

4

Politics and Government

In May 2008, 42-year-old Dmitrii Medvedev became the third president of the Russian Federation. Medvedev's background is in many ways similar to that of other modern world leaders in developed countries: he is an urbane and educated figure with a middle-class upbringing, the son of two university professors. Like his American counterpart, President Barack Obama, Medvedev gained a postgraduate law degree and has taught law at university. He worked his way up through the political system, having key jobs in the presidential administration and the government before being elected president. So far, so 'normal'. But in fact, beyond some surface similarities in background and style, Medvedev's claims to political normality do not measure up well against either Russian or Western models.

From the Russian perspective, Medvedev is a departure from what has gone before. His two immediate predecessors were Vladimir Putin (2000–8), a working-class child who went on to serve in the foreign intelligence arm of the Soviet security service – the KGB – before working in the administration of St Petersburg mayor, Anatolii Sobchak; and Boris Yeltsin (1991–9), a hard-drinking, impulsive and physical man who had for many years been a senior figure in the Communist Party of the Soviet Union. Medvedev, in contrast, became head of state at a relatively young age, a sober and softly-spoken figure given to expressing broadly liberal opinions and with a reputation as a considerate and polite boss. He also came to office in line with constitutional principles, as Putin had served the maximum two consecutive terms and so could not stand again in the 2008 election. In these ways, Medvedev is breaking the Russian mould.

From the Western perspective, Medvedev's succession to the presidency does not fit the 'normal' democratic template. His candidacy in the 2008 presidential election was the first time he had ever stood for election in his life. He had been nominated by Putin as his preferred successor and, even though there were other candidates on the ballot paper, there was never any serious question as to whether Medvedev would win. While no doubt genuinely popular, Medvedev's victory was seriously tarnished from the democratic perspective by the regime's use of media control, election law and administrative resources to curtail dramatically the opportunities for the opposition to campaign effectively against him. Even when in office, the extent to which Medvedev is fully in power has been far from clear, since his mentor and predecessor, Putin, occupies the position of prime minister and leads the party with a huge majority in Russia's parliament – United Russia.

It is this question of where the Russian political system fits in relation to Western democracy that shapes this chapter, and has been at the heart of discussions about Russian politics ever since the collapse of the Soviet Union in 1991. The immediate post-Soviet paradigm, adopted by President Yeltsin's regime and by Western observers and interlocutors, was that of democratic transition. For much of the 1990s, given the broad acceptance that Russia was in transit from Soviet totalitarianism to democracy, the key questions were technical ones about how to build a democratic system: questions such as whether power should ultimately lie with president or parliament, or how relations between the regions and the centre should be structured. Towards the end of the Yeltsin era, however, the centre ground shifted and talk turned more to whether Russia was still progressing towards a Western-style liberal democracy at all, or was instead floundering in a mire of corruption, oligarchic in-fighting, and regional conflict that might result in a failed state.

During the Putin years, the notion of rapidly completing a transition to Western liberal democracy began to lose all currency, and the dominant discourse turned to state strengthening and the possibility of a Russian variant of democracy. By the time Medvedev entered office in May 2008, the Putin/Medvedev regime had consolidated executive and legislative power. Across various areas of policy, today's government in Russia sets targets to be achieved by 2020, apparently assured of continuing in power until then at the earliest. In the same vein, the major political reform of Medvedev's first year as president was to extend the presidential term from four to six years, and the parliamentary term from four to five years, both effective from the next series of elections.

This chapter surveys post-Communist Russian politics on a number of levels. It begins with the institutional, the formal ordering of power, the 'rules of the game'. However, institutions are clearly not the only source of power. Informal aspects of politics are of particular relevance, given Russia's historical tradition. Power does not often interact with institutions in quite the way that the formal structure suggests. During the Soviet period, four Constitutions set out the institutional structure of the state over their respective periods. However, these Constitutions masked the true picture, which was that supreme power lay with the Communist Party of the Soviet Union and was exercised by means, such as the power of appointment, that, though not unconstitutional, simply by-passed the constitution. The culture of political behaviour that exalts networks and connections above the formally constituted powers of institutions carried over into the post-Soviet era. This chapter therefore will not only lay out the formal rules of power relations in contemporary Russia, but it will also deal with the relative incoherence of power relations within and beyond the formal constitutional framework.

The collapse of the Communist political system in Russia in the period 1989–91 was the end of what had become widely known as the command administrative system. This was politics by central *diktat*. Power was concentrated at the centre among the senior ranks of the Communist Party, and the function of other elements of the system – parliaments, central government, republican, regional and local authorities – was to put central instructions into practice. Nor was the exercise of power restrained by legality, since laws were applied only arbitrarily, and elements of the legal code, such as the notion of 'anti-Soviet activities', were interpreted so broadly that they were frequently taken to mean any activities of which the authorities disapproved.

Command administrative politics were largely non-political politics. That is, what was missing in this political system were information flows, and the free interchange of ideas and alternatives for society. The atmosphere was one of instinctive secrecy and obsessive official control over information presented in the media or through the arts and literature. Soviet Russia was largely cut off from foreign influences, both benign and malign. The use of a particular language of political discourse, the language of Marxism–Leninism, ruled out certain alternative directions of development, including calls for the introduction of market mechanisms into the economy. It also deified other practices, such as the leading role of the Communist Party, which at its worst became the belief that the Communist Party collectively was never wrong. There was no role for political opposition, let alone any possibility of the opposition one day becoming the government, which is the essence of democratic politics. The lack of opposition and the lack of an independent system of policing and the courts meant that a chronic problem for the system was accountability. In the Stalin period, officials were held accountable for their actions via an all-pervasive mass terror, but after the abandonment of widespread terror during the General Secretaryship of Nikita Khrushchev, the system demonstrated inherent tendencies towards corruption and nepotism on a large scale.

This was broadly how Soviet politics operated in the period before Mikhail Gorbachev's abortive attempts to reform and purify the system during 1985–91. It was an environment that encouraged habits of command and elitism, and of seeing politics not as the comparison of alternatives and a search for compromise but as a means for the political destruction of opponents. Clearly, it would be difficult for those acculturated by such 'non-political politics' to adapt and operate in a new democratic system with new virtues of openness and honesty about the country's problems, compromise, and respect for the electoral choices of ordinary people.

Many observers looking at Russia under President Putin, and then under the apparent co-leadership of President Medvedev and Prime Minister Putin, see a country where, after the upheavals of the 1990s, 'non-political politics' has reasserted itself:

- Russia is something of a political desert, with few alternative voices or policy proposals being heard;
- it has a constitutionally democratic presidential system, but after nearly two decades of Russian democracy there has still not been a genuinely competitive transfer of power;
- the ruling regime has taken steps to control key media outlets and limit the opportunities available to the political opposition;
- Russia's parliament, from the elections of December 2003 onwards, has been firmly in the hands of the United Russia party, which is led by Putin and is unfailingly loyal to the regime; and
- public opinion in Russia has long been sympathetic to 'strong leadership', and now widely associates the term 'democracy' with the political chaos and economic decline of the Yeltsin period.

Despite all this, however, it would be wrong and too simplistic to state baldly that Russia has returned to a Soviet-type system of government. There are features of contemporary Russia's government that are recognizable from the Soviet era – notably the lack of political space for an effective opposition to operate; the tendency of parliament to act more as a rubber-stamping body than a debating chamber; and the creation of a party that dominates legislatures at both the regional and national level. However, for all the echoes of the former regime that can be identified, a more nuanced and accurate understanding of today's Russia requires an awareness of differences as well as similarities. Specifically, the lack of opposition, parliament's rubber-stamping role, and the creation of a dominant national party are all of a qualitatively weaker degree than in the Soviet era; there is no overarching political ideology to dictate or guide policy; and in institutional terms, Russia's formal structures are radically different from those existing under communism.

The 1993 Constitution

Our starting point for understanding the distribution of power in contemporary Russia are those formal institutional structures, as set out in the Russian Constitution, that were passed by national referendum on 12 December 1993. The need for a new Constitution for Russia after the collapse of the Soviet Union was clear on three counts – institutional, ideological and legal:

- At the institutional level, the operative constitution in Russia in 1992–3 was the 1978 constitution of the RSFSR (Russian Soviet Federative Socialist Republic) – the old name for Russia in its Communist-era existence as one of fifteen republics in the Soviet Union. This 1978 Constitution was therefore predicated on the existence of an institutional framework that had disappeared in 1991 along with the Soviet state. It assumed implicitly the existence of a one-party state. The Communist Party of the Soviet Union was the institution that had held the Soviet state together. Once this had gone then decision-making processes reverted to the formal procedures of a Constitution that had been written for another political age, and even then had never borne much relation to the way the state was really governed. In particular, the means by which the centre controlled the regions – a relationship known in Russia as the 'power vertical' – virtually disappeared along with the Party.

- At the ideological level, the old constitution adhered to communist ideology in its Marxist–Leninist form, whereas the Russian Federation after 1991 saw itself more as a Western-type liberal state. This makes a fundamental difference to the underlying concept of any constitution. In a liberal state, the rights of the individual are supreme. Under Marxist–Leninist ideology, individuals and their rights come second to the rights of and obligations to the workers as a collective, and to the state.
- At the legal level, the need for a new Constitution was evident if one considers what constitutions are for: a constitution is supposed to be the fundamental law of a state, containing concepts that, if not unchangeable, are certainly meant to have a depth of durability. The constitution of the United States, for example, has only been amended around twenty-seven times since its adoption over two centuries ago, in 1787. By 1992, the old Constitution of the RSFSR had been amended more than 300 times in fourteen years. It could scarcely be seen as a fundamental law.

Virtually all politicians in Russia accepted the need for a new Constitution after the collapse of the Soviet Union. Despite this, it took two years from the end of the USSR for the new Constitution to come into existence. The primary cause of this delay was the power struggle between President Yeltsin and the parliament in 1992–3. Having abandoned Marxism–Leninism and chosen a democratic path, the Russian Federation and its political elite had to decide on their preferred form of democracy. The two key issues to be resolved were the relationship between president and parliament, and the relationship between the centre and the regions. These issues, of course, are central elements of the 'rules of the game' and therefore of the Constitution.

President versus parliament, 1992–3

The failure to decide between presidentialism and parliamentarism held up agreement over a new constitution. Participants in this dispute between president and parliament couched their arguments largely in terms of which system better suited the nascent democracy of Russia in the immediate post-Soviet era. However, the dispute had as much to do with the past and present as with democratic guarantees for the future. It was a power struggle between parliament and the president fought in terms of not only the relative democratic legitimacy of these two institutions, but also ultimately the extent to which they could command the use of force.

The Russian word 'soviet' literally means 'council' or, at the highest levels, 'parliament'. As its name suggests, the Soviet Union throughout its existence had claimed to be run by a series of workers' councils, which culminated with a central Supreme Soviet where, in theory, state power lay. As we have seen, in practice, power lay with the Communist Party, which dominated the soviets and reduced them to virtual rubber-stamping bodies through most of the twentieth century. Only after Gorbachev's reforms in the late 1980s did some real power begin to return to the soviets, and particularly to the Russian soviet, or parliament. Therefore, at the collapse of the Soviet Union, the Russian parliament enjoyed more power than it had known before. Many members were understandably reluctant to see this long-denied power being swiftly removed again and given to the president, particularly since the parliament had been reasonably democratically elected in 1990.

The president, on the other hand, could lay claim to a more recent, and arguably more democratic, mandate. Boris Yeltsin had been elected as Russia's first democratically chosen leader in June 1991. Not only had he won the election, but he had won it overwhelmingly. Yeltsin had received a majority over all the other candidates combined, thereby removing the need for the second round of votes provided for in electoral rules. He believed, with some further justification from opinion polls, that the people favoured a presidential system.

As if to demonstrate its inadequacy as a fundamental law, the old Constitution offered no clear way out of the dispute between president and parliament. The obvious solution would have been a general election or binding referendum. However, only parliament had the constitutional right to implement such a course of action, and was unwilling to exercise this right and dissolve itself mid-term. President Yeltsin wanted to dissolve parliament but was constitutionally barred from doing so. The impasse held up policy-making and the enactment of a new Constitution until September 1993, when Yeltsin unilaterally – and, strictly speaking, illegally – dissolved parliament. Some parliamentary deputies refused to accept this dissolution and remained under armed siege in the parliament building until, provoked by attempts by armed parliamentary supporters to seize the central television building in Moscow, President Yeltsin ordered a military attack on the parliament building in early October, which left over a hundred defenders of the parliament dead.

The 1993 Russian Constitution was therefore drawn up against the background of the power struggle between president and parliament, and near civil war on the streets of Moscow. More importantly, it was drawn up by the winning side in this dispute – the presidency. The resulting constitution consequently provides for a strong presidency and a comparatively weak parliament. As Box 4.1 sets out, under this Constitution, Russia has an executive (president, presidential administration and government) almost wholly independent of parliament. The legislature (parliament) consists of upper and lower chambers, the Federation Council and the State Duma, respectively, known collectively as the Federal Assembly. The document also establishes a constitutionally independent judiciary, a Constitutional Court and a Supreme Court. Other sections of the constitution define the Russian Federation as a democratic, law-based state where a range of human rights are observed.

This presidential Constitution was put before the Russian people in a referendum on 12 December 1993, alongside a general election of deputies to the Federal Assembly. The 1993 general election therefore chose members of a parliament whose very existence would depend on the result of the constitutional referendum. To critics, even the process by which Russia adopted its new democratic constitution was not entirely democratic. Referendum and election happened simultaneously, making it difficult for anyone running for election to parliament to urge a vote against the Constitution that would create the very parliament in which they were seeking a seat.

In addition to a democratic deficit in terms of procedure, the actual voting on the Constitution did not indicate the wholehearted support of the Russian people for their new system of government. To be binding, the referendum on the Constitution had to attract a turnout of over 50 per cent of the electorate. In the event, the Constitution was adopted by 58 per cent of the vote, with a 55 per cent turnout. That is, it was adopted on the basis of the votes of under one in three of the Russian electorate, amid accusations from many quarters about falsification in the conduct of the referendum.

These difficulties surrounding the adoption of the Constitution mean that the method by which constitutional amendments are introduced has considerable political significance. The procedure is quite elaborate. Two-thirds of each chamber of parliament and two-thirds of regional legislatures must approve changes. It is this procedure

---

Box 4.1   The powers of the president of the Russian Federation

The president:

- is head of state;
- is supreme commander-in-chief of the armed forces;
- issues decrees, the implementation of which is mandatory through-out Russia;
- directs foreign policy;
- nominates the prime minister;
- appoints, dismisses and has the right to chair the government;
- forms the presidential administration and the Security Council;
- schedules elections to the State Duma; and
- dissolves the State Duma (according to constitutional procedures).

---

that was used in 2008 to introduce amendments extending the presidential and parliamentary terms to six years and five years, respectively, and requiring the government to present an annual report to parliament. In the case of changes to chapters 1, 2 and 9, which are the sections containing the basic principles of the constitution (democracy, rule of law and the structure of the federation, as well as bans on official ideology and a state religion), individual rights and the procedure for constitutional amendment, there is an additional need for the convening of a Constitutional Assembly and, if this assembly so decides, a national referendum in which at least half the electorate must participate.

Executive

The formal powers of the presidency in the Russian Federation enable him, or her, to rule with relatively little reference to the parliament. The president ultimately appoints the government and decides on the size and personnel of the influential presidential administration. It is the presidential administration which usually prepares the decrees – binding throughout the Russian Federation – issued by the president, though, as we note later, the number of such decrees has decreased as the number of laws passed by parliament has increased. From 2012, the president will serve for a six-year term, as opposed to the current term of four years.

There is a fluidity within the presidential administration as the president can set up and close down different executive bodies freely, for example, between 1996 and 1998 a Defence Council existed, created by President Yeltsin to rival the Security Council. In 2004, President Putin declared that the size of the presidential administration should be reduced, and so once again the structure changed; the current structure is set out in Box 4.2. Alongside this presidential administration, and under the president within the executive branch of power, there exist five other institutions or types of institution, namely: the government, the Security Council, the State Council, Presidential Commissions, and Presidential Councils. In addition, the Public Chamber, although not part of the executive, is made up initially of presidential nominees and so is dealt with in this section.

The government

Russia's government is headed by the prime minister, who is appointed by the president with the approval of the lower chamber of parliament, the State Duma. The president has the right to preside over meetings of the government and to dismiss the prime minister

---

Box 4.2   The presidential administration, 2009

Leadership of the administration
Head of administration, 1 first deputy head, 2 deputy heads,
7 presidential aides.

Other key officials
Including presidential press secretary, head of presidential protocol,
9 presidential advisers, 7 presidential representatives in the regions,
presidential representatives in the upper and lower houses of
parliament and the Constitutional Court.

Branches of the administration
Including the State-Legal Directorate and the Directorate for the
Civil Service.

Source: www.president.kremlin.ru.

Box 4.3   The Russian government, 2009

Prime Minister

2 First Deputy Prime Ministers, 6 Deputy Prime Ministers

18 Ministers
(for Agriculture, Communications, Culture, Defence, Economic
Development, Education, Emergency Situations, Energy,
Environment, Finance, Foreign Affairs, Health, Industry and
Trade, Internal Affairs, Justice, Regional Development, Sport
and Tourism, Transport)

Source: www.government.ru

and government. For most of the post-Soviet era, Russia's government has focused on domestic policy, chiefly economic affairs, under a technocratic prime minister. However, during Putin's second spell as prime minister, from May 2008, the responsibilities of the government in relation to the president increased somewhat in practice, though there was no formal change in the institutional balance. The structure of the government is set out in Box 4.3.

The Security Council

After the government, potentially the most important body in the executive branch is the Security Council, which is identified specifically in the Constitution. Formally, this council has sweeping powers to oversee social, political and economic threats to security, and it serves as an inter-agency body, bringing together key political actors and the 'power ministries' of defence, foreign affairs, the emergency ministry, the security service and the foreign intelligence service. The Security Council exercises its power under the president, and so at times has been influential and at other times peripheral, according to the president's wishes. In recent years it has been quietly significant, providing a forum where the key players in the Russian state meet regularly to discuss key issues. Its membership under President

Medvedev includes the prime minister, defence minister, foreign minister, the speakers of both chambers of parliament, and the heads of the presidential administration, the government administration, the Federal Security Service, and the Foreign Intelligence Service.

The State Council

The State Council of the Russian Federation is an advisory body, chaired by the president as head of state and made up of the heads of all of Russia's federal regions. Unlike the Security Council, there is no constitutional mandate for its existence. The State Council was established by President Putin in 2000, partly as a sop to regional leaders after their right to sit in the upper chamber of parliament, the Federation Council, was removed. The use of the title State Council is a deliberate reference to the imperial State Councils, which advised the Tsars in pre-revolutionary Russia. In the twenty-first century, the State Council meets at least four times a year, and sometimes in joint session with the Security Council. Its business is typically a major theme of national importance, usually put forward by the president.

In establishing the State Council in 2000, President Putin created a major state body that was not mentioned in the Constitution. President Yeltsin had done this at a lower level, by creating a Defence Council within the presidential administration, but the State Council represented – in terms of symbolism and informal power at least – a more significant innovation, in that it brought together the executive heads of all the regions that make up the Russian Federation, under the chairmanship of their head of state, the president of Russia.

Presidential Commissions and Presidential Councils

The final bodies that go to make up the executive *per se* are the Presidential Commissions and Presidential Councils, which are essentially part of the presidential administration. The difference between the two is that commissions are orientated to specific tasks – for example, the Commission on Questions of Reforming and Developing the Civil Service – and councils are concerned more generally with particular areas of activity – for example, the Council for Relations with Religious Organizations. In 2009, there were five Presidential Commissions and thirteen Presidential Councils.

The Public Chamber

The extra-constitutional, rather than explicitly anti-constitutional, creation of state institutions by the president, which was seen in the case of the State Council in 2000, was repeated in 2005 with the establishment of the Public Chamber. The Public Chamber's remit is to ensure co-operation between citizens and the organs of state power at both federal and regional level, including analysing draft legislation and monitoring the performance of federal and regional bodies. In essence, it brings together representatives of civil society into a formal structure. Its formation can be interpreted partly as stemming from three policy strands apparent in Russian politics from the late 1990s onwards:

- A process of securitizing domestic politics in Russia (see Bacon and Renz, 2006) meant that a number of areas of activity began to be interpreted increasingly in terms of their threat to Russia's security. The activities of NGOs represented one such area. There were concerns within the regime, and particularly within the security services, that NGOs were being funded too easily from abroad, and so becoming means of undermining Russia's security, either through their open activities or by serving as a front for espionage.
- Since the Yeltsin years, Russia's government had been putting the bodies that make up civil society on a more formal footing, reflecting on the part of the authorities at local and national level a distrust of independent organizations acting in areas that had in the Soviet era been tightly controlled by the state. As a result, laws requiring the registration of religious organizations, political parties and NGOs had been passed (see Chapter 6). The law on NGOs, finally passed in 2006, caused some disquiet among supporters of civil liberties both at home and abroad.
- During the Putin presidency (2000–8), the notion of adopting a Russian model of democracy, rather than being dictated to by the West, came increasingly to the fore. Within this discourse there was support for establishing a strong indigenous Russian civil society, rather than allowing free rein to foreign NGOs. This approach differs from Western attitudes to civil society, in that it smacks of the state creating civil society, and is therefore seen as something of a contradiction in terms.

The creation of the Public Chamber seemed to tick all the boxes in relation to these policy strands. It brought civil society into a state-led structure, while emphasizing support for Russian NGOs and encouraging them to exert appropriate pressure on the state. The rules by which the Public Chamber is formed reflect this tension between being state-led and yet independent of the state. The Chamber has 126 members. The first forty-two of these are nominated by the president – and would normally not include politicians or businessmen. The next forty-two are nominated by NGOs. These eighty-four together then select the final forty-two members of the Public Chamber. There are also regional-level public chambers.

From the point of view of the institutional structure of Russia's political life, both the State Council and the Public Chamber can be seen as shadowing institutions that have already been established constitutionally. The State Council can be seen as a shadow executive, and the Public Chamber as a shadow legislature. Neither has anything but advisory power, but none the less they have a presence on the political scene, the regime asks for their opinion on key issues, and the decisions and resolutions of both are reported as having some weight in policy discourse. In short, when the state creates institutions such as these, they find a role, and that role arguably diminishes to some extent the constitutionally established bodies of the executive and the legislature.

Legislature

Russia's parliament, or Federal Assembly, is made up of two chambers. The lower chamber, the State Duma, consists of 450 members elected by means of proportional representation under the party list system. A party must get at least 7 per cent of the national vote in order to gain seats in the parliament.

Electoral procedures for the State Duma were changed during Putin's second term in office. Before the 2007 election, the Duma was formed by an unusual combination of proportional representation and 'first-past-the-post' systems, whereby half of the deputies gained their seats under a party list system and the remaining deputies were selected on a constituency basis, and may or may not have had a party affiliation. The abolition of the constituency element of the Duma in favour of an entirely party-based proportional representation system was part of a process designed to strengthen the role of political parties and to encourage smaller parties to amalgamate. The threshold to be passed in order to gain seats was raised from 5 per cent to 7 per cent from the 2007 election onwards, and the Law on Political Parties dating from 2001 had already introduced requirements in terms of size of membership and geographical spread before parties could run in elections. From 2011, the Duma will be elected for a five-year term, instead of the current four years.

The upper house, the Federation Council, represents Russia's eighty-three regions, and each one has two seats, regardless of the size of the region. These seats are filled by a representative of the regional legislature and a representative of the regional executive. The upper house has employed three different methods for selecting its members since its foundation in 1993. Its first convocation consisted of members elected on a regional basis at the 1993 general election, two for each region. From 1995 to 2000, deputies gained their seats in the upper chamber on an *ex officio* basis; these seats were taken by the heads of, respectively, a region's legislature and executive. In the latter case, this would be the governor or president of a region, or, in the case of the 'city regions' of Moscow and St Petersburg, the mayor. Regional heads were, until 2005, elected on a regular basis. Now, however, they are appointed by the president, and ratified by the regional assembly.

When Putin came to power in 2000, he put forward proposals, accepted by the Federation Council, that ended the filling of the upper house on this *ex officio* basis. Instead, as the terms of office of each region's head came to an end these individuals were replaced in the upper house by representatives of the regional legislature and executive, rather than by the heads of the legislatures and executives themselves. By way of compensation, the heads of Russia's then eighty-nine regions were given membership of the advisory State Council.

Power relations between president, prime minister and parliament

In terms of international comparison, the parliament's powers in relation to the president are weak and, should differences between the two institutions prove irreconcilable, the last word almost always rests with the president. For example, the Constitution allows parliamentary involvement in government formation on one issue only – that of the appointment of the prime minister. The president nominates a candidate whose appointment must be confirmed by parliament. However, should parliament not confirm the candidate, then the president, after three rejections of his nominee, dissolves parliament.

There are three other levers of influence with which a legislature might exert its influence over the executive branch of power:

- First, through its legislative power; that is, by means of passing laws or blocking bills. Under the terms of the Constitution, a law passed by parliament outranks a presidential decree, even though the latter has the force of law pending any legislative act that supersedes it. In the early period of the post-Communist transition in Russia there was a legislative gap, which was filled to some extent by presidential decrees, drawn up and signed in their thousands. If the parliament passes a law it is submitted to the president, who either signs it or sends it back to the parliament. If the parliament then passes the law a second time, unaltered, the president is constitutionally obliged to sign it.
- Second, the parliament might pass a vote of no confidence in the government. To force the president to take action, such a vote has to be carried by a majority of the 450 members of the State Duma twice in three months. Even then the president may decide either to dismiss the government or to dissolve the Duma.
- Third, the final sanction the legislature might apply against the executive is the impeachment of the president. Under the Russian Constitution, this procedure is not easy. The only grounds allowed are those of treason or 'some other grave crime', and the process can only be completed with the agreement of the Supreme Court, the Constitutional Court and a two-thirds majority of both legislative chambers. Although half-hearted impeachment procedures were begun by the Communist Party of the Russian Federation against Boris Yeltsin over his decision to go to war against Chechnya, there was never any serious prospect that the stringent conditions for impeachment might be met.

In addition to these potential levers of influence over the executive in the hands of the parliament, a constitutional amendment of 2008 now requires the government to submit an annual report of its activities to parliament, including the answers to questions put by the State Duma.

Listing these ways in which the parliament might in theory hold the executive to account is not by any means to suggest that it is likely to do so in the near future. By a combination of factors – including legislation on elections and political parties, the use of administrative

Box 4.4   Russia's prime ministers since 1992

Viktor Chernomyrdin	December 1992–March 1998
Sergei Kirienko	March 1998–August 1998
(Chernomyrdin nominated unsuccessfully August–September 1998)	
Yevgeny Primakov	September 1998–May 1999
Sergei Stepashin	May 1999–August 1999
Vladimir Putin	August 1999–March 2000
(Putin was acting president from 31 December 1999)	
Mikhail Kasyanov	May 2000–February 2004
Mikhail Fradkov	March 2004–September 2007
Viktor Zubkov	September 2007–May 2008
Vladimir Putin	May 2008–

resources to electoral benefit, media bias in favour of the ruling regime, corruption among parliamentary deputies, and the fact that Putin and Medvedev have enjoyed genuine popularity among the Russian population – Russia's parliament is now for the most part unquestioningly supportive of the executive branch of power. It would take a serious crisis or a split in the executive branch to upset this equilibrium.

In short, then, the Russian Constitution is strongly presidential in comparison with other constitutions within the democratic pale. However, after the accession of Medvedev to the presidency in May 2008, it became clear that he was sharing far more power with his prime minister, Putin, the former president, than had any of his predecessors with their usually technocratic heads of government (see Box 4.4 for a list of Russia's prime ministers in the post-Soviet era). There are two broad reasons for this relative dilution of the power wielded by the president, and understanding them is useful in demonstrating both the importance of institutions and the influence of informal factors in Russian politics.

First, in terms of the formal constitutional arrangement of power with regard to the president and prime minister, nothing has changed. President Medvedev has the power to dismiss his prime minister and government at will. However, Prime Minister Putin also leads the United Russia party, which has a clear majority of seats in the State Duma and, through its domination of around 90 per cent of regional legislatures, in the Federation Council. This combination of power in the executive, the legislature and the regions is not one envisaged in the Constitution, and it demonstrates that while Russia's constitution is heavily weighted in favour of presidential power, such power is not boundless. In particular, as political parties – or at least the dominant party – become stronger and more disciplined, there are more barriers placed in the way of arbitrary presidential action as national and regional parliaments are more able to use what power they have.

Second, the creation of what swiftly became known as a 'tandem' of power, shared by President Medvedev and Prime Minister Putin after May 2008, is, of course, also explained by factors beyond the formal constitutional arrangement. In particular, the personal relationship between the two men was always one where Medvedev was the junior figure and Putin his boss and mentor. Medvedev only became president because of Putin's endorsement. Furthermore, Putin, as a highly respected and popular ex-president, has immense experience and influence, which have naturally played a part in enhancing the power of his office as prime minister. Medvedev in turn has been happy to benefit from both the support and the skills of Putin.

At the time of writing – just nine months into Medvedev's presidency – it would be unwise to predict whether the Medvedev–Putin relationship will remain harmonious, whether their intention is to continue sharing power, or for Medvedev to gradually take on more fully the mantle of president, and whether Medvedev will serve two terms or step down after one in order to allow Putin to return to the presidency, having observed the constitutional provision that forbids more than two *consecutive* terms as president. What is clear, however, is that institutions matter. Even though there is much wrong with Russia's version of democracy, formal observation of the constitutional rules does matter to both Putin and Medvedev. Furthermore, should any political crisis arise, such rules come into their own as the only guidelines available for the resolution of disputes.

Contemporary Russia and democracy

Almost two decades since the Soviet Union collapsed and the Russian Federation declared itself a liberal democracy, there has still been no democratic change of regime in Russia. In the rest of this chapter, we investigate the reasons for this lack of democratic

United Russia, led by Vladimir Putin, is the dominant party in Russian politics.

Illustration 4.1   A United Russia rally next to the Kremlin

consolidation. It is not just that there has been no regime change – after all, there have been elections, and it is feasible, and within the bounds of the democratic process, for the people to want the existing president or his preferred successor to hold power – but that the potential for opposition forces taking power scarcely exists at all in contemporary Russia. As has been emphasized already in this chapter, to understand Russia's politics requires the understanding of both its formal and informal elements. The formal institutional means for a transfer of power in a genuinely contested election are present, but the institutions' nature and the context in which they exist militate against such an event happening.

The institutional relationship between executive and legislature has implications for the sort of politics that has existed in contemporary Russia. This institutional structure partly explains the failure of democracy to consolidate. In particular, the presidential nature of the constitutional settlement arrived at in 1993 has brought into play several of the 'perils of presidentialism' – to use Juan Linz's phrase (Linz, 1990) – which militate against the development of a genuine multi-party system with open competition.

First, the 'winner takes all' nature of a presidential system means that if a presidential candidate gains, say, 54 per cent of the vote, as Boris Yeltsin did in 1996, he gets 100 per cent of the power. Whereas in a parliamentary system where the government relies on the support of a proportionally representative parliament, a party with 54 per cent of the vote would have to form a government that took more account of its narrow margin of victory. As a result, a culture of compromise between winners and losers, and motivation for creating strong and disciplined parties, would be encouraged.

Second, the president of Russia is also the head of state, which promotes the idea that the president is above factional politics and instead in some way embodies the nation. Yeltsin certainly presented himself in this way. Putin and Medvedev have similarly refused to join political parties, although Putin's decision to decline actual membership in United Russia while still leading it requires a semantic technicality of some precision.

The relative lack of power held by the Russian parliament, in comparison with the president, means that much of the 'politicking' that has gone on within and around the institution of the parliament in the post-Soviet years has had little impact on actual policy formation. To illustrate this, let us consider the general elections of December 1993, December 1995 and December 1999 (see Tables 4.1 and 4.2). The most popular single parties in these elections were, in 1993, the extreme-right Liberal Democratic Party of Russia, and in 1995 and 1999, the nationalist anti-reform Communist Party of the Russian Federation. These parties headed the party list ballot with around a quarter of the national vote. None the less, despite the vast effort put into electioneering and the inevitable wide coverage by domestic and foreign media, these elections had no direct means with which to change the regime. The prime minister remained the same; the president, of course, remained in office; and the 'victors' could not even demand successfully so much as a single minor ministerial position. This divorcing of much 'public politics' from the substance

Table 4.1   Percentage of votes on the party list ballot for the Russian Duma, 1993 and 1995

Party	1993	1995
Agrarian Party	8.0	3.8
Communists	12.4	22.3
Liberal Democratic Party of Russia	22.9	11.2
Our Home Is Russia	–	10.1
Russia's Democratic Choice	15.5	3.9
Russian Unity and Accord	6.8	0.4
Yabloko (Russian Democratic Party)	7.9	6.9

of politics (that is, power) can serve to alienate people from the political process. Furthermore, the parliament becomes marginalized, encouraging gesture politics and inhibiting the direct representation of the electorate. The real levers of power are in the hands of the president who, despite being popularly elected, has little subsequent check on his powers by the people or a party organization.

The context in which the institutional structure exists similarly serves to restrict the opportunity for opposition forces to become a serious threat to the power of the incumbent regime. Elections in Russia in the 1990s provided genuine uncertainty in relation to the results – for example, the surprisingly high vote for the Liberal Democratic Party of Russia in 1993, or the close-run presidential election of 1996, when Boris Yeltsin required a second round to beat the Communist leader, Gennadii Zyuganov (see Table 4.3, p. 117). Such uncertainty has diminished greatly in the twenty-first century, partly as a result of the changes in electoral law noted above. The introduction of the law on political parties has resulted in a reduction in the number of parties eligible to stand. The removal of the constituency element of the Duma election has made for a more predictable and straightforward party-list vote without the independent candidates of previous elections. Similarly, when it comes to presidential elections, potentially dangerous candidates – such as former prime minister Mikhail Kasyanov in 2008 – have been prevented from standing, on the grounds that they have breached election rules. In Kasyanov's case, the election commission ruled that too high a proportion of the signatures on the nominating petitions required were forged. In such a situation it is impossible to judge from outside whether the signatures were forged or not. However, the fact that election commission chief, Vladimir Churov, told a newspaper that his first rule was 'Mr Putin is always right' made some observers sceptical of his impartiality in this and other cases, to say the least.

In addition, the abolition of elections for regional leaders in 2005 means that they are now appointed – or dismissed – by the president. This reliance on the Kremlin for their position brings echoes of the Soviet command-administrative system, and politics by central *diktat*. It has led many to claim that regional leaders who fail to deliver an appropriate vote in their region when federal elections come round might be removed from their positions. The means by which such a vote might be achieved include the use of what is known as 'administrative resource'. In other words, regional leaders may use their position to influence the election by, for example, leaning on businessmen to fund favoured candidates, mobilizing state-funded employees to vote the 'right' way, hindering the campaign of opposition candidates by such means as instigating tax inspections or safety audits, or – in extremis – falsifying voting returns.

As well as this, most national broadcast media are owned by the state or are state-friendly companies, and the same applies to regional broadcast companies. Reports by the Organization for Security and Cooperation in Europe (OSCE) on the Russian parliamentary elections in 2007 found that United Russia received as much airtime on state-funded television as all the other parties put together. In addition, the OSCE found evidence of the selective application of election rules, such as the ban on negative campaigning or the requirement to show TV debates in prime time, to the benefit of United Russia. Similar contextual factors go some way to explaining the near certainty, from the day Putin announced his support, that Medvedev would be elected president of Russia in March 2008. To point to these factors is not to deny the popularity of United Russia or of Medvedev and Putin. However, it does perhaps partly explain this popularity, in that people's perceptions of political actors are shaped by what they know of them. It also demonstrates that the ruling regime in Russia, though happy to allow some opposition voices to be heard, dissenting newspapers to be published, and even critical broadcasts to be made, has created a context where it can be sure of victory, and is able and willing to act should there be any danger of a different result occurring.

As noted above, despite the number of elections that have taken place in Russia since June 1991 (five parliamentary and five presidential), Russia has not yet experienced a democratic change of regime. Parliamentary elections do not change the regime. In terms of the presidential elections, neither of the two successions witnessed in Russia since it formally chose the democratic path in 1991 have been truly competitive and democratic, and both have witnessed regime continuity, with the outgoing president's preferred successor gaining an assured victory:

- Boris Yeltsin won presidential elections twice (1991 and 1996) before resigning early, thereby creating an electoral advantage for his chosen successor, Putin. The advantage created was twofold. First, Putin could campaign from the position of incumbent, since, as prime minister, he became acting president on Yeltsin's resignation. Second, the election had been due in June 2000; by resigning early, Yeltsin forced an election in March, as the Constitution stipulates that a presidential election must take place within three months of a vacancy. Yeltsin knew what he was going to do, and could make preparations accordingly. Opposition figures, however, had to go to the polls earlier than they had expected.
- Putin won presidential elections twice (2000 and 2004) before backing Medvedev as his successor. There had been speculation for several years over whether Putin would indeed step down in 2008, as required by the Constitution. That he did so was perhaps the most democratic element of the process. Speculation had also raged over whom he would support to succeed him, since the more destabilizing but more democratic options of supporting either no one or more than one candidate were not seriously considered. The moment Putin backed Medvedev, it was clear that his candidate would be the next president. Such was the regime's control over political life and the electoral process by then – backed, it must be said, by popular support on the back of a growing economy and a sense that Russia was regaining its pride and strength internationally – that the only question was by how many votes Medvedev would win.

After President Putin came to power in 2000, the relationship between the executive and the legislature shifted from that of the Yeltsin years. Under Yeltsin, as we have noted above, the influence of parliament on policy-making was minimal. Yeltsin preferred to issue presidential decrees, as he could not be certain of a parliamentary majority. Presidents Putin and Medvedev have both shown a clear preference for passing laws through parliament rather than issuing such presidential decrees. This is largely because the political make-up of the parliaments elected since December 1999, and particularly since 2003, have made it increasingly easy for the president to be sure of support in parliament.

The current make-up of the Duma is shown in Figure 4.1. Both United Russia and A Just Russia are parties formed with Kremlin backing and can be relied on to support the executive's policies. The Liberal Democratic Party of Russia and the Communist Party of the Russian Federation are long-standing opposition parties. They present no serious threat to the regime. Their popular support is enough to show that opposition to the government is allowed, but not enough to get anywhere near power. Their leaders – Vladimir Zhirinovsky and Gennadii Zyuganov – have been in position since the end of the Soviet era. They appear to have reached an accommo-dation with the current regime, and lack the serious dynamic edge of effective opposition leaders. Indeed, Zhirinovsky's Liberal Democratic Party of Russia – a far-right nationalist party, despite its name – can usually be relied on to vote with the regime when required. It is probable that in the next few years one or both of Zyuganov and Zhirinovsky will move into political retirement. When this happens, the possibility arises that a new leader of either of these parties might wish to be more overtly combative in relation to oppos-ing the ruling regime, particularly if economic circumstances create fertile ground for such a stance.

Ideas in Russian politics – political forces in Russia today

While acknowledging the undemocratic nature of many aspects of contemporary Russia's political life, nevertheless, when it comes to assessing the broad political mood in Russia in recent years, the elec-tions for the lower house of the Russian parliament still provide a basic indication of the strength of the various streams of political thought, as represented by political parties, among the Russian people. Opinion polls confirm that the election results in Table 4.2 are a reasonably accurate reflection of how Russians said they would vote.

The clear winner in the 2007 parliamentary elections was United Russia, the party whose list of candidates was headed by President Putin, though Putin clearly had no intention of taking up his seat after the election. The political position of United Russia was – simply put – to support the policies of Vladimir Putin. These policies were

Figure 4.1   Distribution of seats in the State Duma, 2007 (percentages)

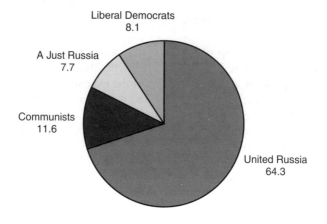

summed up as the 'Putin Plan', otherwise known as the 'Russia 2020' project to modernize the country, develop its infrastructure, diversify the economy, and produce an upturn in all indicators of social well-being. Medvedev committed himself to these goals on becoming president. United Russia's leaders style themselves as pragmatic managers, and certainly not politicians.

The United Russia party is the latest, most successful and longest-lasting of a constant phenomenon in post-Soviet Russia, the 'party of power'. This notion turns on its head the situation common in developed democracies, where the country's leader is in power because he or she has the support of their political party. With a 'party of power' the situation is reversed, and the party is in power because it has the support of the president. This is partly a result of the institutional situation in Russia in the 1990s, where a strong presidency was established before a party system was in place. It is partly too a result of a political culture that is used to following a single leader and to allowing position and power to trump political convictions.

The phenomenon was exemplified clearly in the Duma election of 1999. This election took place just before the end of Yeltsin's second term in office. It was clear that he would be stepping down, but it was unclear who would be succeeding him. Putin was an emerging figure, having recently become prime minister, but Moscow mayor Yurii Luzhkov looked a possible president too. The December 1999 elec-

Table 4.2   Percentage of votes on the party list ballot for the Russian
Duma, December 1999, December 2003 and December 2007

Party	1999	2003	2007
United Russia	–	37.6	64.3
Unity	23.3	–	–
Fatherland–All Russia	13.3	–	–
Communist Party of the Russian Federation	24.3	12.6	11.6
Liberal Democratic Party of Russia	6.0	11.5	8.1
Rodina ('Motherland')	–	9.0	–
A Just Russia	–	–	7.7
Russian Democratic Party 'Yabloko'	5.9	4.3	1.6
Union of Right Forces	8.5	4.0	1.0
Agrarian Party of Russia	–	3.6	2.3

Note: United Russia was formed by an amalgamation of, primarily,
Unity and Fatherland–All Russia. A Just Russia was formed partly out of
the Rodina ('Motherland') party.

tion result saw Putin's preferred party, Unity, finish second to the
Communists, but only seven seats ahead of Luzhkov's party,
Fatherland–All Russia. By the end of January 2000, Yeltsin had
resigned, and Putin had become acting president and the clear
favourite to be elected president in March. As a result, over thirty
Fatherland–All Russia Duma deputies simply left the party and
joined Unity instead. What mattered was not the party platform on
which they had been elected, but whether they were in the same party
as the next president, Putin. In other words, in a fine example of the
'party of power' principle at work, Unity became the most powerful
party because it had the support of the president, and not the other
way round.

The notion of parties being created from above, by the political
elite, rather than developing from below, by popular initiative, is one
that has been favoured by the executive in Russia under all three post-
Soviet presidents. Yeltsin, Putin and Medvedev have all had a neat
vision of a multi-party system, where two or three essentially loyalist
parties vie for power on the relatively narrow centre ground of poli-

tics. To be fair to them, this is the situation that applies in, for example, the United States, the United Kingdom, and many European democracies. The difficulty comes in trying to create it artificially in Russia, without allowing the potential destabilization that a genuine contest for power presents. The solution of each leader has been to attempt the creation of parties from above. Yeltsin supported the creation of centre-right and centre-left parties (Our Home Is Russia and the Bloc of Ivan Rybkin, respectively). Neither party exists today. Putin oversaw the amalgamation of Unity and Fatherland–All Russia into United Russia, and again attempted to create a centre-left party, A Just Russia, with limited success. Medvedev, within the first few months of his presidency, attempted to fill the gap on the liberal reformist right of the party spectrum by backing the creation of the Right Cause party.

There is therefore a clear awareness on the part of the executive of what broad political views exist in Russia, and of how they are represented – or not – in the party system. Away from the centre ground, the left and right have parliamentary representation via the Communists and the 'Liberal Democrats'. The pragmatic, less ideological, power-focused centre, which had significant public support while the economy was growing during Putin's presidency, is represented by United Russia and A Just Russia, with differences between them being over policy nuances rather than power. The major unrepresented group are the democratic liberals. Those who want a genuinely open and democratic Russia are against the current regime, and have policy preferences broadly in favour of a Russia that is like the rest of the democratic world – a free market, social welfare, civil liberties, open democracy, multi-party – and being a part of, or a broad supporter of, 'the West'.

Most of this chapter has focused on those in power in Russia. Let us now consider briefly the opposition forces in more detail.

The Communists and the Agrarians

After the collapse of the Soviet Union, the previously monolithic Communist Party virtually disintegrated and was banned for a brief period from the territory of the Russian Federation. By the time of the 1993 Duma elections, however, a Communist Party of the Russian Federation had re-emerged, rapidly becoming the largest party in terms of membership and votes received (see Table 4.1) with its leader, Gennadii Zyuganov, becoming the closest challenger to Boris Yeltsin in the presidential election of 1996 (see Table 4.3).

The Communists maintained a level of around a quarter of all votes cast in the party list ballot in the elections of 1995 and 1999, before falling to around half of that in 2003 and 2007 (see Tables 4.1 and 4.2). For much of this period, the Agrarian Party retained relatively close links with the Communists and shared some of the votes on the statist left, before splitting in 1999, when some gravitated towards what was to become United Russia while others remained with the Communists.

At their revolutionary peak, in the decades before and after their seizure of power in 1917, the Communist Party represented, above all, the young, industrial workers building and inhabiting the cities of the new Russia. By the 1990s, the Communists could be character- ized fairly accurately as the party of the elderly and the rural. They became the conservative option for those who had lost out in the upheavals of the 1990s. Increasingly, their ideas – at the electoral level, if not in the detail of party programmes – moved away from Marxism–Leninism and embraced Russian/Soviet nationalism. Zyuganov wrote repeatedly about the restoration of Russian power and pride, and ideas associated with the Communists included the alleged attempts of the West to destroy Russia through poor economic advice, military encirclement and 'cultural genocide'.

There is little doubt that, among the reasons for the Communists' relative decline in the elections of 2003 and 2007 – in which they none the less finished second – is the sense that, under Putin, as opposed to Yeltsin, the ruling regime was no longer wholly antago- nistic to the Soviet era, and was itself set on restoring national pride and great power status, as well as focusing its rhetoric repeatedly on the need to raise the standard of living of the Russian people.

Table 4.3   Russia's presidential election, second round, July 1996

Candidate	Percentage
Boris Yeltsin	53.8
Gennadii Zyuganov	40.3
Against both candidates	4.8

The Nationalists

For some time in the 1990s, the more alarmist observers predicted the emergence of an extreme nationalist regime in Russia. Analysts repeatedly raised the question of the 'Weimar syndrome' in Russia, drawing comparisons with the German state, which gave way to Nazism in the early 1930s. The similarities are clear – a great power humiliated, a (cold) war lost, and an economy in ruins. But the differences too are evident – in particular the lack of, indeed disdain for, ideology in the Putin/Medvedev regime. None the less, fears of fascism did not spring from nowhere. In 1993, in post-Soviet Russia's first democratic elections, the far-right – and misleadingly named – Liberal Democratic Party, led by Vladimir Zhirinovsky, gained almost a quarter of the popular vote (see Table 4.1). The Liberal Democrats' vote has fluctuated in subsequent elections (see Tables 4.1 and 4.2) but remains significant, though the sense of apprehension and fear surrounding its surprise appeal in 1993 has dissipated a little as Zhirinovsky has become to some extent a licensed maverick in the political establishment – expected to give the outrageous quote, occasionally assault opponents, but in the end to be essentially loyal.

Votes for Zhirinovsky's Liberal Democratic Party, with its somewhat eclectic platform and personalized nature, are by no means the only measure of the strength of nationalist ideas and their varying forms of expression in Russia today:

- Opinion polls show widespread xenophobic attitudes, a fairly entrenched level of support for broadly nationalist and authoritarian stances such as the need for a strong leader, and a rejection of 'Western paths' in favour of unspecified Russian variants.
- Violent xenophobic assaults and hate crimes are on the increase in Russia, with human rights groups noting 200 in 2005, resulting in twenty-five deaths, and 250 in 2007, resulting in over sixty deaths.
- During the past two decades, major contributions have been made to the literature on the Russian nation and its unique destiny in the world. Writers such as Aleksandr Dugin and Andrei Platonov have expressed extreme nationalist ideals in a literary and philosophical manner which feeds into deep-seated popular notions and builds on the difficulties experienced by many Russians in the post-Soviet era.

The Liberals

Liberal reformers, advocating Western-style democracy and economic reforms, were supposed to be Russia's future after the collapse of the Communist regime. Some would argue that they remain so, and that votes for United Russia and for Medvedev himself represent majority support for a democratic and economic path uniquely suited to Russia.

The argument is that the brash and ill-considered introduction of alien Western concepts to Russia in the 1990s not only did not work as well as predicted, but also attracted the opprobrium of the Russian people. 'Democracy' became a derogatory term, and, according to this view, leaders such as Putin and the apparently more liberal Medvedev represent the best that a supporter of market reforms and democracy can hope for in Russia at present. As the billionaire Mikhail Khodorkovsky wrote from his prison cell, where he awaited charges brought against him by the Russian state: 'Putin is, of course, not a liberal nor a democrat, but none the less he is more liberal and more democratic than 70 per cent of the population of our country.'

Such a view is borne out when considering the collapse of support for the overtly Western-orientated liberal forces in Russia in the 2003 and 2007 general elections. The two main liberal parties, Yabloko and the Union of Right Forces, both failed to garner enough votes to gain seats in the lower house of parliament in 2003. Partly as a result of this, their profiles diminished and support fell even further, until only 2.6 per cent of voters supported them in 2007 (see Tables 4.2 and 4.4). The Union of Right Forces disbanded itself in late 2008, with its leader, Nikita Belykh, accepting President Medvedev's invitation to become governor of Kirov Oblast, and a number of its senior members joining the newly formed, and Kremlin-backed, Right Cause party.

It is too soon, however, to say that liberalism is dead in Russia, and opinion polls assessing political attitudes remain ambiguous. For example, while some polls reveal a high level of xenophobia in Russia, others indicate that this stance is shifting among younger respondents. For a number of years, two features have been apparent in Russian opinion polls. First, respondents are more hostile to the abstract concept of 'democracy' than to specific democratic values, such as freedom of association or freedom of speech. Second, and to generalize, the older the respondent, the more illiberal the response.

Table 4.4   Party list votes for liberal parties in Russia's parliamentary elections (percentages)

Party	1993	1995	1999	2003	2007
Russia's Choice	15.5	3.9	–	–	–
Yabloko	7.9	6.9	5.9	4.3	1.6
Union of Right Forces	–	–	8.5	4.0	1.0

None the less, recent years have seen an increase in liberal supporters taking action outside the political system, in a manner akin to the dissidents of the Soviet era. The decline in support for liberal parties was caused to some extent by the denial of political space for them on the part of the regime, exemplified by Mikhail Kasyanov being barred from running in the 2008 election. At the same time, there has been an increase in authoritarian actions taken against opposition figures by the state in the form of the security forces. Arising from this situation, the group Other Russia has united liberal figures, such as Kasyanov and former world chess champion Garry Kasparov, with the extremist National Bolshevik Party, led by Eduard Limonov. Other Russia has organized demonstrations, which the authorities have broken up on the grounds that they did not comply with the law on demonstrations, and what they called an alternative parliament, the 'National Assembly' in St Petersburg in 2008. Kasparov in particular has proved to be an effective leader of Other Russia, appearing regularly in the Western media to condemn Russia's 'police state'.

5

The Economy

Chapter 4 considered Russia's political transition; here, we turn to an overview of the economic situation in contemporary Russia. There are in fact a number of cross-cutting themes and emphases evident in our assessment of Russian politics that are also apparent when looking at the economy.

First, both the polity and the economy can be considered within a straightforward transition framework. At the end of the Soviet era, Russia embarked on a process known as a 'dual transition': a political transition from totalitarianism to democracy, and an economic transition from a planned to a market economy. This framework is helpful up to a point, as it facilitates an understanding of policy steps taken initially and provides some broad targets against which to measure subsequent performance.

Second, as the analysis moves through the 1990s and into the twenty-first century, Russo-specific, informal cultural elements increasingly cloud the picture when it comes to assessing linear progress towards the simple transition goals of a liberal democracy and a market economy. The Russian elite becomes more firmly established, and less willing to simply follow Western advice and models. Instead, discussion arises, as we saw in the preceding chapter, concerning the need for Russian forms of democracy. This chapter demonstrates a similar process in relation to economic reform, as cultural differences with the West, or differences in terms of the structure of Russia's economy, are both cited – and disputed – as reasons for Russia to develop along its own path.

Third, comparisons with the Soviet era need to be treated with care. In Chapter 4 we noted a number of echoes of the Soviet political system in today's Russia, but emphasized that a more nuanced understanding requires awareness too of the substantial differences between the situation more than two decades ago and that which exists today. The same applies to the economy. While there is no doubt that in recent years the Russian state has taken control of some key areas of the economy – specifically, the energy sector and broader, state-led innovation initiatives – the institutional, international, financial and legal frameworks all differ significantly from the Soviet years.

Finally, as with the political situation, sweeping generalizations about whether policy has been a success or a failure are avoided here in favour of nuanced assessments. Judging the performance of the Russian economy as a whole is complicated by questions of periodization. Taking the years of the Putin presidency (2000–8), Russia's economy, as measured by its GDP, grew impressively, at a steady 6 per cent to 7 per cent per annum. Such a growth rate is particularly notable when set against the catastrophic decline in the size of the Russian economy by the same measure during the Yeltsin presidency (1991–9). Here, though, is the nub of the periodization question. The performance of the economy depends on where you are measuring it from. The analysis of this chapter balances assessments of the remarkable economic success of the Putin years – though in fact that particular economic growth spurt began during the Yeltsin presidency in 1999 – against the longer view, both backwards to the Soviet era, and projecting forward to consider Russia's economic plans to 2020 and the potential impact of the global economic downturn.

We begin with an overview of the nature of the Soviet economic system and the particularly difficult legacy it left for an independent Russia emerging in 1991. We then briefly map out the headline features of the Russian economy, over two distinct periods: the initial reform moves from 1992 to the financial crisis of 1998, and the years of impressive economic growth from 1999 to 2008. Having established our main themes, the chapter deals in more depth with key features of the Russian economy, namely resource dependence, the legal environment, trade, capital flight and foreign investment, before turning to the future and assessing Russia's economic prospects to 2020, with particular attention being paid to the impact of the global credit crunch on these prospects.

The Soviet planning system

The economic system adopted after Stalin's forced industrialization of the 1930s (see Chapter 1) was often termed 'command planning'.

The economic theorists, from Marx onwards, who had supported a planned form of political economy, had hoped that it would have a number of advantages (Brus and Laski, 1989). Rational economic planning would prevent the waste caused by cyclical variations in the market economy such as mass unemployment and machines sitting idle during recessions. Resources would no longer be frittered away on useless purposes such as advertising. Elimination of private ownership would mean the end of the 'exploitation of man by man' as unscrupulous capitalists appropriated surplus value for themselves. Planning would also ensure equitable distribution: 'From each according to his ability, to each according to his needs' would be the formula for distribution in a communist economy. Since their decisions would take all factors into account, planners would be able to ensure that the full costs of economic activity, including so-called 'externalities' such as pollution, would be taken into account in making economic decisions. There would also be important motivational effects: since people were working for the good of each other, rather than for the benefit of private individuals, they would work

---

Box 5.1   The main features of a planned economy

- State or collective ownership of almost all economic resources (some small-scale agricultural production for personal use was allowed on private plots).
- Production decisions made by state planners, with economic units (factories, farms and so on) given production targets, usually for quantity (gross output).
- Prices for all goods and services set by state planners.
- Distribution decisions also made by the planners – factories and farms instructed what to do with their output.
- A permanent bias to heavy industry, and in particular defence, and away from consumption – this was not, of course, a systemic requirement, but rather a policy decision sustained by the interests of powerful groups within the Soviet state.
- Largely monopolistic organization of industry in order to exploit economies of scale.

harder. Abolition of commercial secrecy and a more rational organization of production would both lead to greater efficiency. For all
these reasons, socialism would supposedly prove itself to be an
economic system superior to capitalism.

The reality of the planned economy represented an enormous
contrast to these hopes. Certainly, there were some benefits for both
the country and individuals. Prices for basic goods were low and
stable, and basic services were provided free of charge. The plan
proved a successful means of industrializing the Soviet Union rapidly
in the first place – albeit at great human cost – since it enabled
resources to be concentrated in the areas of priority to the state.
However, there were countless problems (see Box 5.2).

Economic decline

The Soviet economy had achieved impressive growth rates as it
industrialized in the 1930s, or in the reconstruction period after the
Second World War, but such growth was from a low base and was
achieved by putting resources into industrialization and reconstruction. By the 1970s, growth needed to be sought from innovation and
technological advance, both of which, as we have seen, were
hampered by the centralized plans of the Soviet system. According to
some estimates, 'the long-run context shows that from 1928 until
1973 the Soviet economy was on a path that would catch up with the
United States one day ... However, in 1973, half way through the
Brezhnev period, the process of catching up came to an abrupt end'
(Harrison, 2002).

The increased resources put into consumption meant that living
standards for many Soviet citizens did improve a little in the late
1960s and early 1970s. However, the absence of genuine structural
reform of an inefficient economic system meant that the transition to
a more intensive type of economic growth did not happen. Low fertil-
ity and increases in the mortality rate caused by difficulties in the
Soviet health system, as well as rising alcoholism, meant that population growth was minimal. Easily accessible sources of raw materials had largely been exhausted. Collectivized agriculture frequently
failed to produce enough food to feed the population, and grain had
to be imported from elsewhere. Attempts to keep up with the United
States militarily drained resources from civilian research and development (R&D), and diverted skilled workers into unproductive

Box 5.2   The problems of economic planning

- There was a constant problem of shortages. This was partly because, if one part of the plan failed to be achieved, knock-on effects followed. For much of the Soviet period, consumers had to suffer empty shops and long queues for the most basic necessities as a fact of everyday life.
- The plan, though designed ostensibly to foster continuing growth, was too static a conception of economic activity. A very difficult issue for planners to confront was how to manage change. Economic units altering processes or improving products takes time and is disruptive in the short term, which threatens plan fulfilment and consequent bonuses. There was little incentive to innovate arising out of the possibility of large profits accruing to individuals who think up something new (Schumpeter, 1934) and so the economy was inclined towards stagnation.
- Quality tended to take second place to quantity. Since it was the most measurable attribute, quantity of output tended to be the key target in plans. However, quantity is only one of a number of desirable features of production. Others include quality, range, style and so on. Too often plans were formally fulfilled, but the quality was so poor that consumers could not use what had been produced.
- There was a propensity to waste, as economic units had little incentive to economize on inputs of raw materials and labour. Ultimately, they were judged on whether they achieved their targets, regardless of how many inputs they used in order to do so. This contributed to the fact that, in the view of some economists, much Soviet industry, far from adding value, was in fact value-destroying, with the raw material inputs being worth more than the final product.
- Soviet industry could also be seen as value-destroying, because of irrational pricing structures. In the absence of markets, planners had no way of setting values for goods. Energy prices, for example, were very low in Communist countries compared to world market prices, which meant that much industry was highly energy-inefficient.
- International trade was neglected in planned economies. This was damaging because trade allows new technologies to spread rapidly, and also because of what economists term 'gains from trade', which arise from specialization suiting the particular strengths of individual economies.
- The gains that Communist economies had hoped to make as a result of increased worker motivation never appeared. The economic system was imposed by force, income distribution was never in fact egalitarian, and a low priority was put on meeting the needs of ordinary citizens. As the East European joke had it: 'Capitalism is the exploitation of man by man. Socialism is the reverse.'

employment. By the time of Brezhnev's death in 1982, economic growth had virtually ceased.

On coming to power in 1985, Mikhail Gorbachev became aware quite rapidly that piecemeal reform of the planned economy would not be enough to solve the economic difficulties, and that more radical steps would be necessary. Some measures were taken – for example, workers' co-operatives and so-called individual labour activity were legalized, creating a private sector in some areas of the economy. Gorbachev's policy was also to reduce the amount of planning that went on, thus giving managers more autonomy to make necessary decisions. Arms limitation agreements, it was hoped, would reduce the burden of military expenditure.

However, real structural reform and marketization of the economy did not occur in the 1985–91 period. For all their talk of restructuring the economy, and a plethora of alternative reform proposals, the Gorbachev years saw mere tinkering and talking in relation to the great economic problems facing the Soviet Union. It was these problems that were to dominate Russia's reform programme after 1991:

- The huge, monopolistic industrial monoliths, which dominated the economy, continued to operate in familiar ways, and continued to be subsidized by the state.
- There were so-called 'price reforms' under Gorbachev, but prices were still controlled.
- The refusal to allow unemployment meant that the labour market remained unreformed.
- No real competition was created, because the government failed to address issues of bankruptcy, or to create the conditions whereby non-state economic actors could enter markets and compete with state industry and agriculture.
- Accumulated savings that Soviet citizens had been unable to spend represented 'repressed inflation', and, in combination with the growing state budget deficit, meant that an inflationary surge was inevitable should real reform take place.

Overall, the Gorbachev period destroyed the effectiveness of the planned economy without replacing it with operative market mechanisms. When the Soviet Union collapsed and Yeltsin came to power in an independent Russia he proved himself willing to back real reform to address the economic crisis, rather than merely to vacillate.

Economic reform, 1992–8

The economic team created by Yeltsin was headed by the acting prime minister, Yegor Gaidar, and contained a significant number of younger, highly pro-market ministers, such as Anatoly Chubais, who was in charge of privatization. Many of them had knowledge of economics outside Russia, and were convinced that only market mechanisms could solve the deep economic problems facing the country.

None the less, Yeltsin's economic team was also very aware that, however essential the policy of marketization seemed to be to them, it would be a far from easy path to follow. Difficulties would come in the detail of the reforms and in their social impact. A common phrase used in the early 1990s to sum up the marketization of formerly centrally planned economies was 'shock therapy'. The therapy came in the treatment of what was deemed to be a terminally failing economic system incompatible with both a globalizing world economy and the new democratic polity being ushered in. The shock came in the inevitable hardships caused by inflation, unemployment, the closure of uncompetitive industries, the cutting of social welfare and so on.

As the 1990s progressed, the familiar – and heartfelt – comment to be heard was that Russia's economic reforms were 'all shock and no therapy'. And indeed, culminating in the financial crash of 1998, this broad overview seems to represent a pretty sound assessment of the situation. The population experienced great socio-economic hardship, as there was a reduction in state subsidies for social goods such as housing, transport and energy; inflation wiped out personal savings; unemployment rose; and wages went unpaid for months at a time in the state sector (for details, see 'Standards of living' in Chapter 3, pp. 64ff)).

However, dealing with the substance of the economic reforms, clearly some 'therapy' was taking place alongside the 'shock'. At first sight, it is hard to discern a consistent strategy for the Russian economy between 1992 and 1998. The frequent changes of government personnel and rhetorical shifts left observers baffled as to the real intentions of policy-makers. But despite the very different rhetoric of, for example, acting prime minister Gaidar in 1992, who was at the forefront of the push for rapid marketization, and the prime minister, Yevgeny Primakov, in late 1998, who took a more cautious approach, overall policy did not divert from the goal of marketization. However, because of the strength of political resistance to

> **Box 5.3   What is needed to turn a planned economy into a market economy?**
>
> After the collapse of communism, the countries of Eastern Europe and the former Soviet Union were attempting something without historical precedent in seeking to move from a system of command planning to a free market economy. There was no template to work from, but it was clear that the following reforms would be necessary.
>
> *Ownership changes.* In practice, state ownership had very often been the effective equivalent of no ownership. Managers and workers stood to gain little from committed work or forward thinking, and knew that loss-making enterprises would be bailed out by state subsidies, a situation referred to by the eminent Hungarian economist János Kornai as the 'soft budget constraint' (Kornai, 1992).
>
> *Privatization* of small-scale economic activity is relatively straightforward, but the privatization of whole industries is a different matter. How much are they worth? How will 'the people' participate in and benefit from the sale of what are theoretically their assets as well as the nation's? Should foreign ownership be allowed?
>
> *De-monopolization* to create the competition that is a central dynamic feature of a market economy and an incentive for efficiency.
>
> *Bankruptcy and unemployment.* Free competition means that loss-making enterprises are ultimately forced out of business. Russia's economic geography included a large number of company towns, where virtually all employment – as well as maintenance of housing stock, food supplies, holiday facilities, social services and so on – was dependent on a single employer. Closing a factory would cause serious damage to the entire community.
>
> *Price reform.* The rational allocation of resources in competitive markets arises through the interaction of supply, demand and price. Free

radical change, government strategies were couched increasingly in terms designed to mollify opposition.

Nevertheless, specific features of reform can be identified. The immediate freeing of prices, which led to initial rapid inflation, was designed to shift to a more rational price structure. In January 1992, 90 per cent of all retail prices were freed from the previous system, where the state determined the price of goods. The effectiveness of all other market reforms was predicated on this. Markets cannot be efficient without a system of prices determined by the interaction of supply and demand. In addition, there was a massive amount of 'spare' money in the system – that is, money that had been saved by pricing is a necessary component of the free market. Economic reform would require removing subsidies and increasing prices for many of the basics of life, such as staple foodstuffs, domestic heating and rents.

Monetary stabilization. The rouble as currency was not one in which citizens had much confidence, and it failed to act as a store of value in the way that harder currencies did.

The State Budget. Russia inherited public expenditure commitments far beyond levels that could be financed by taxation. Large budget deficits would have to be reduced by reducing state spending and increasing tax revenue.

Foreign trade and payments. Integration with world markets would enable mutually beneficial trade and facilitate foreign investment in Russia.

The infrastructure of the market economy. Developed market economies operate with sophisticated capital markets able to finance potentially profitable projects. The banking system was entirely undeveloped in Russia in 1992, and the legal basis for the operation of free markets (for example, contract enforcement and debt recovery) did not exist. A whole raft of new, and complex, legislation was required.

Federal aspects. Who owned economic assets: the central state; republics and regions; or cities and rural districts? How should resources be divided, and which levels of power were responsible for what? How should budgetary revenues, mainly collected locally, be divided up among the different levels of power?

The culture of capitalism. The dominant culture of the Soviet period was to see private ownership as an evil to be eliminated. The introduction of a private sector, and of, so to speak, official permission for private individuals to become rich, might cause reactions of extreme resentment and hostility.

citizens in a situation where its value was undermined by the lack of access to goods. Freeing up prices would absorb much of this monetary overhang.

In order to combat subsequent inflationary pressures, and to create a stable currency and real money, monetary policy remained at the forefront of policy decisions. By 1995, this had been sufficiently successful to make it possible to fix the rouble to a band of values against the dollar, in what became known as 'the rouble corridor'. Governments continued to attempt to ensure as stable a currency as possible, to control inflation, to increase domestic and international confidence in the state of the Russian economy, and to enable business to begin to make plans for the future with some degree of certainty.

In parallel, there was a process of opening up the Russian economy to the outside world, and by 1998 Russia was significantly more integrated into the world economy than it had been in 1992. This still did not represent free trade in key areas, with price distortions supported in some sectors by export quotas, high export duties, and import subsidies and controls.

A third strand of the reforms was the attempt to reduce the economic role of the state. Privatization took place in the mid-1990s, initially via the distribution to all Russian citizens of vouchers that could be redeemed for shares in newly privatized companies. Subsequently, it took place via auctions, and the highly controversial 'loans for shares' policy, where certain banks and industrial combines acquired shares in companies at prices far below their true market value in return for loans to the government.

The voucher privatization scheme was intended as an innovative way to solve the problem of selling off state-owned assets. By giving vouchers to all citizens, the question of the fair distribution of property among the population was addressed. In addition, it was hoped that voucher privatization would create, at a stroke, a nation of shareholders with a vested interest in the success of the economy. In addition to privatization by voucher, this stage of the process also involved giving shares in enterprises to their workers and managers.

Laudable though this approach might seem in theory, the results were not quite as anticipated in terms of a wide base of share ownership. Many small shareholders were persuaded to offload their shares to enterprise managers, either voluntarily or pressured by economic circumstances or managerial arm-twisting. In their turn, some such enterprises were sold on to Russia's larger business empires or, less often, to foreign investors. In thousands of cases too, the ability of shareholders to control companies was curtailed by the government retaining a controlling interest, having declared the need to do so because of the strategic importance of an enterprise to national security.

A related aspect of the attempt to change Russia's economic structure was the creation of a legal and regulatory framework for a market economy. Some aspects of this proved much more straightforward than others. The privatization programme, for example, was conducted largely by presidential decree. Bankruptcy laws were adopted with little resistance. However, laws on private ownership of land, foreign investment and taxation codes, to name just three, provoked notable disagreements between the government and parliament.

The results of these reform approaches were painful for both the Russian economy and the people. As Table 5.1 shows, Russia experienced dramatic and sustained economic problems in the 1992–8 period. According to official statistics, national output fell every year except 1997. By mid-1999, GDP was little over half its 1990 level. While not wishing to understate the degree of economic trauma that Russia experienced in the 1990s, it is likely that these official figures overstate the true decline in GDP, and consequently social welfare, for several reasons:

- In the planned economy, output figures were inflated. Since the structure of rewards was based on plan fulfilment and overfulfilment, economic units claimed to have achieved more than they in fact had.
- Some of the economic decline was made up of an end to the production of useless value-destroying items, as well as significant falls in previously excessive defence spending.
- Official figures do not adequately reflect the amount of economic activity that goes on informally outside officially monitored channels – for example, households growing their own food.

Table 5.1   Russia's economic indicators, 1992–8

	1992	1993	1994	1995	1996	1997	1998
GDP, % change year on year	–14.5	–8.7	–12.6	–4.2	–3.6	1.4	–5.3
Industrial production, % change year on year	–18.2	–14.2	–20.9	–3.0	–4.5	2.0	–5.2
Fixed investments, % change year on year	–40.0	–12.0	–27.0	–13.0	–18.0	–5.0	–12.0
Unemployment, % change year on year	4.9	5.5	7.5	8.2	9.3	9.0	11.8
Inflation %	2,520	842	224	131	22	11	84

In parallel with this rapid decline, the economy fundamentally changed its character in several important respects during the 1990s. Figure 5.1 shows how, in a very short period of time, Russia moved from being an economy dominated by industry to one where services predominated. Such a de-industrialization was a process experienced by many developed countries, in most cases perhaps two decades earlier than was the case with Russia.

This relative decline in industry and agriculture (see Box 5.4) was in part a consequence of Russia's increasing openness to the world economy, a trend visible in the sharply rising absolute volumes of exports and imports even against the background of overall economic decline. The sectors of the economy that were hit hardest by recession were in most cases subject to particularly strong foreign competition, such as clothing, agriculture and food processing, or industries such as electricity production or construction, demand for which directly reflects levels of output and investment. Similarly, the industries that

Figure 5.1   The structure of Russia's GDP, 1990 and 2003

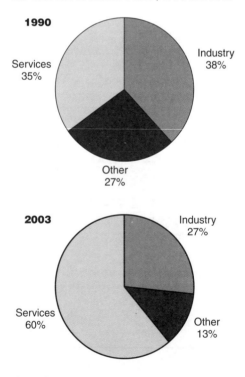

struggled least – oil and gas, basic metals and various other natural resources – were ones in which Russia is highly competitive on world markets.

The rise in the importance of service industries – both business and consumer – reflected a fundamental change in the nature of the economy. In a planned economy relatively closed off to the outside world, there was little need for accountants, management consultants, market researchers, advertisers, investment bankers and all the other job categories that help to make a competitive market economy function. The relative neglect of consumers in the planned economy meant that there was an insufficient supply of, for example, plumbers, electricians, travel agents, motor vehicle dealers, and many of the other providers of goods on which individuals might want to spend any surplus earnings. Between 1992 and 1996, the number of small businesses in Russia, according to Goskomstat, Russia's state statistical agency, increased from 560,000 to 840,000, with the true number probably higher because of the size of the shadow economy. A change in the economic structure also indicated an important shift in the political influence of various economic lobbies.

Of course, the decline of industry and agriculture was a shock that was also likely to have important electoral consequences. It is clear that opposition parties of both the right and the left had a base of support from workers and managers in declining parts of the economy and declining regions. The Agrarian Party of Russia reflected this in its very name (see Chapter 4).

This restructuring also had an important regional aspect. Regions that were relatively successful tended to be either resource-rich areas or metropolitan centres with good international transport connections able to act as entry points for international trade. Regions whose economy declined particularly seriously were often ones that were especially vulnerable to competition from imported goods, or agricultural republics that were already under-industrialized.

The crash of 1998

On 17 August 1998, the Russian government devalued the rouble and announced that it would no longer be able to pay much of its domestic debt and was imposing a moratorium on payment of much of its foreign debt. Prices rose rapidly, and, not for the first time in the 1990s, citizens who had deposited money in Russian banks saw their savings wiped out. The 35-year-old prime minister, Sergei Kirienko, who had only been in post a few months, was dismissed by President Yeltsin. Yeltsin, no economist himself, was a shrewd enough politician to realize that someone must be seen to be taking the blame and it had better not be him.

According to some observers, the 1998 crisis was basically a standard currency crisis. In other words, Russia's policy of achieving stability through a fixed – within certain limits – exchange rate backfired, since the rouble was overvalued. Government overspending meant that a large amount of debt accrued. Coupled with significant capital flight out of the country and an economy that was not growing – along with international unease following the Asian financial crisis of 1997 – the situation proved unsustainable. From a level of 6 roubles to the US dollar, the currency collapsed to 25 roubles to the US dollar.

This macroeconomic explanation is given more depth by bringing in developments – or rather the lack of them – at the micro level. According to a report by the Foreign Affairs Select Committee of the House of Commons in 2000, 'the crisis of August 1998 was above all the consequence of this contradiction: the macroeconomic stabilization achieved during 1995–98 was not underpinned by the micro-level structural changes needed to make it sustainable without considerable external financial support'. Using the exchange rate as the principal means of stabilization enabled the government for too long a time to avoid the necessary structural reforms and budget cutbacks. According to the International Monetary Fund (IMF), between 1992 and 1998 there was no sustained downward trend in the budget deficit. In essence, the subsidization of uncompetitive enterprises that had been a feature of the Soviet system, had continued – albeit hidden in a variety of procedures.

The 1998 financial crisis, however, seemed to act as a cleansing storm on the Russian economy. Two outcomes in particular proved to have positive longer-term effects. First, government policy after the crash was firmly orientated towards macroeconomic stability. The growth in exports following the August crash resulted in a rapid increase in money supply, and in normal economic circumstances unsustainably high levels of inflation would be expected to follow. However, the fact that Russia's industrial economy before then had been based more on barter and US dollars than on roubles meant that the growth in rouble supply was absorbed in the development of a financial sector, and the concomitant release of bank credits, which in turn boosted consumption. The second outcome worked in tandem with this growth in credits. The 1998 crisis meant that the cost of imported goods became too high for many to afford, and so domestically produced goods were more in demand, prompting an increase in output and competitiveness among Russia producers.

Economic progress, 1999–2008

In the nine years following the August 1998 financial crisis, Russia's economy saw strong growth. This coincided with the presidency of Vladimir Putin. In this section we assess the reasons for the impressive economic performance of these years, question to what extent that performance was a result of government policies, and analyse the impact of rising GDP on the underlying economic structure of Russia. To sum up before engaging with the details, economic growth in the period 1999 to 2008 was based overwhelmingly on high global prices for Russia's chief export goods – oil, gas and metals. The Putin regime's economic policies contributed to some extent, particularly during his first term, but increasing state control in key areas held back production growth, hindered foreign direct investment, and failed to promote sufficiently the innovation and diversification necessary to move the economy away from over-reliance on raw materials.

When Putin came to power in 2000, he declared in his eve of millennium address (Putin, 2000) that:

> It will take us approximately fifteen years and an 8 per cent annual growth of our GDP to reach the per capita GDP level of present-day Portugal and Spain, which are not among the world's industrialized leaders. If during the same fifteen years we manage to annually increase our GDP by 10 per cent, we will then catch up with Britain or France.

It is important to note that President Putin was talking about taking fifteen years to catch up with where Portugal and Spain were at the turn of the millennium. And if things went really well, then by 2015, Russia might reach the per capita GDP levels attained by Britain or France in 2000. Putin's realism was admirable, and in setting the target in such stark terms he sought to focus the minds of his ministers. Indeed, under Putin, there developed a focus on clear targets, with, for example, a rolling ten-year programme for doubling GDP each decade being put in place.

Between 1999 and 2008, virtually all of the key economic indicators showed positive trends (see Table 5.2), and real GDP in Russia grew by an average of 7.6 per cent per year. The strongest growth came in the export-driven industries, particularly in the oil sector, where high global oil prices proved crucial. In 1998, oil was priced just above US$10 a barrel; by early 2008 it was nudging US$160. Growth in this sector, however, is not the whole story, with the service and industrial sectors also growing, assisted by the knock-on effects of the oil price boom. Oil price rises were followed by increases in the price of gas and metals. Overall, during these boom years, the energy sector earned almost two-thirds of Russia's export income, which in turn made up about 40 per cent of public-sector revenue, and 30 per cent of national income.

There were positive trends in many key areas by 2008:

- Real wages, and disposable incomes, were well above the levels found before the 1998 financial crisis, with the number of people living below the official poverty line having fallen by around 55 per cent between its peak after the 1998 financial crisis and late 2007, when 15.7 per cent were officially living in poverty. A growth in consumer credit also increased both spending power and demand.
- Unemployment declined from 13 per cent in 1998 to just over 5 per cent in the first quarter of 2008 (though by the end of 2008, as the global financial crisis began to kick in, unemployment was nudging 8 per cent).
- The federal budget was in surplus every year from 2000 onwards, facilitating the establishment of a stabilization fund to meet budget needs in years when external factors, particularly low oil prices, might otherwise cause a shortfall. The stabilization fund amounted to over 10 per cent of GDP by 2008, when it was split into the Reserve Fund and the National Welfare Fund. Again, though, the economic crisis began to undermine this picture in the last quarter of 2008, when the federal budget slipped into deficit.
- Legislation was introduced to regulate and clarify activity in areas such as land ownership, labour, bureaucratic oversight and customs codes. Tax reforms saw the introduction of a low level of income tax, set at 13 per cent (the lowest level in Europe), with the intention of drawing many Russians out of the shadow economy and making them taxpayers.
- Investment grew even faster than GDP for much of this period, at around 11 per cent in 2004–5, though as a percentage of GDP,

Table 5.2 Russia's economic indicators, 1999–2008

	1999	2000	2001	2002	2003	2004	2005	2006	2007	2008
GDP, % change year on year	6.4	10	5.1	4.7	7.3	7.2	6.4	7.4	8.1	5.6
Industrial production, % change year on year	11.0	11.9	2.9	3.1	8.9	7.3	4.0	3.9	6.3	4.8
Fixed investments, % change year on year	5.3	17.4	10.0	2.8	12.5	11.7	10.7	13.5	21.1	19.0
Unemployment, % change year on year	12.4	9.9	8.7	9.0	8.7	7.6	7.7	6.9	6.1	5.8
Inflation %	36.5	20.2	18.6	15.1	12.0	11.7	10.9	9.0	11.9	12.7

investment in Russia has been lower than in many developed economies, let alone in those seeking to catch up.

- During the boom years of high oil prices, both Russia's current account and its foreign exchange reserves grew impressively. By mid-2008, Russia had currency reserves of almost US$600 billion. In 2006, Russia paid off in full, and early, the debts inherited from the Soviet Union that it owed to the Paris Club (a group of creditor governments from the major industrial nations). This payment amounted to US$22 billion, and represented the largest early payment of debts in the history of the Paris Club. Russia had total foreign debts of US$133 billion when Putin became president in 2000. By 2008, that figure was down to US$37 billion.

Box 5.4   Agriculture in Russia, 1992–2008

Only 13 per cent of Russia's land is used for agriculture, and 11 per cent of the workforce is employed in agriculture and forestry. In the Soviet era, all agricultural land was owned by the state, and farmed in state or collective farms. Agriculture was heavily subsidized by the state. In the years since 1991, reform efforts concentrated on the lowering of state subsidies, the liberalization of prices, and the gradual encouragement of private farming and land ownership.

Success has been mixed. State subsidies are low in comparison with the OECD countries. At the time of writing they amount to around US$2 billion per annum, though Russia's commitment to continuing and increasing this has been a stumbling block in negotiations to join the World Trade Organization (WTO). In terms of private farming and land ownership, 72 per cent of farmed land sits within large agricultural enterprises, and 28 per cent is farmed by households or individuals.

As with other areas of the economy, the 1990s was largely a decade of decline in the Russian agricultural sector, with 1998 being a particularly low point. In this year, there was a record low harvest, with production of many key crops (grain, potatoes, vegetables in general and sugar beet) being less than half of that in 1992. Over a similar period, meat production and livestock numbers also declined by more than half. Overall, between 1990 and 1998, agricultural production fell by 44 per cent in real terms. Russia came to rely increasingly on imports in the 1990s, particularly imports from the United States – becoming, for example, the top foreign market for US poultry exports. The issue of 'food security' became prominent in Russia, as food prices began to rise beyond the means of the poorest sectors of society, and senior political figures fretted about Russia's dependence on imports. Both the United States and the European Union sent substantial food aid to Russia in 1999 and 2000.

◗◗

In short, then, between 1999 and 2008 the Russian economy, in terms of most key indicators, flourished. It demonstrated a level of macroeconomic stability the country had not known for many years, evidenced and facilitated by impressive GDP growth, increased investment, a balanced budget and a current account surplus.

None the less, despite the clear progress made by the Russian economy since the financial collapse of 1998, there was still plenty of room for further improvement. As one observer put it in the early twenty-first century, with reference to the attractiveness of Russia for foreign investors, on a scale running from 'dreadful' to 'excellent', improvement thus far had been from 'very bad' to merely 'bad' (Hare *et al.*, 2004). Perhaps this should not be surprising, given the extent

---

After the 1998 financial crash, the Russian agricultural sector began to recover, helped by the high price of imports and the falling real value of debts. Agricultural output grew rapidly in 1999–2001, before settling down to lower but steady growth rates in subsequent years of around 2 per cent per annum. In 2008, Russia enjoyed the biggest grain harvest it had ever known, 112.5 million tons compared to 81.8 million in 2007. At the same time though, grain prices fell markedly, as the global grain harvest proved to be a bumper one. Consequently, farms had to rely on state subsidies to stay solvent, with the state buying up grain.

While state subsidies for agriculture have been cut in the post-Soviet era, direct and indirect subsidies still remain in place. According to the OECD, there is a tendency for these subsidies to prop up farms that have failed to reform since the Soviet years, whereas there exist a significant and increasing number of efficient and successful agricultural enterprises in Russia. Direct state support for farming is supplemented by the National Project for agriculture (noted in Chapter 3), the emphasis of which is on stimulating the development of rural areas and small farms, partly to combat depopulation, and partly to improve the state of farming equipment.

The right of private citizens to own land was established in the constitution of 1993, but for years the Duma refused to pass a law enabling this right. Finally, in 2001 and 2002, laws enabling the sale of, respectively, urban and agricultural land were accepted, with the latter law forbidding the sale of rural land to foreigners, though allowing foreign owners to have land on a long-term lease. Some estimates suggest that as much as 80 per cent of the population of Russia 'owns' land. However, the most prevalent form of land ownership is in the form of 'land shares' – paper entitlements to a proportion of land within large agricultural enterprises. Only about 1 per cent of those who hold land shares have ever actually received any land. In reality, private smallholders actually own very little land.

of the tasks necessary to transform a failing centrally planned economy into a successful market economy (see Box 5.3). As we have seen, the success of the Russian economy during the Putin presidency was based fundamentally on rising global energy prices – and specifically oil prices. In early 1999, *The Economist* magazine suggested that Russia's economic state was so bad that, instead of being in the club of the world's leading industrialized nations, it would perhaps be more at home with other war-ridden, poor, debt-encumbered and failing states such as Somalia, Sudan and the Congo. Even allowing for the slightly tongue-in-cheek nature of this comment, to many observers, the country was a basket-case in economic terms at the end of the last millennium. And yet, within a matter of years, Russia was booming and critics accused it of throwing its economic weight around like a global bully. What is clear is that this sudden transformation did not stem from a deep-rooted transformation or structural reform of the economy. It was too swift for that. Indeed, even Russia's leadership consistently acknowledged that the good times stemmed initially from high oil prices, and that the benefits they offered should not be squandered. To this end, the Russian state paid off debts, salted money away for when the downturn came, and began to make plans to diversify the economy and reduce its reliance on the production of raw materials.

Whether, despite all this, the boom years of 1999–2008 will still be looked back on as an economic opportunity largely lost is for history to judge. Critics claim, with some justification, that not only did the Russian economy fail to diversify substantially over this period, but also that some policy measures may well have hindered the modernization and development recognized by the state as being necessary. In particular, increasing state control over key sectors of the economy served to undermine ownership rights and hinder engagement with foreign investment. This in turn delayed or prevented necessary investment even in the core oil and gas sectors, let alone beyond that. Let us briefly consider some of these issues in more detail.

Resource dependence and the need to diversify

As noted earlier, Russia's riches in terms of natural resources – particularly oil, gas and metals – have been at the root of its economic recovery since the late 1990s. It is perhaps ironic, then, that this should be seen as a potential problem for the Russian economy, and indeed to have been termed by some observers a 'resource curse'. In what way might what seems to be a blessing turn out to be a curse?

The chief concern is that reliance on such natural resources makes Russia particularly vulnerable to fluctuations in the global market, particularly with regard to oil prices. In 2008, the oil and gas sector accounted for between 25 and 30 per cent of Russia's GDP. Clearly, then, Russia's economic growth is sensitive to fluctuations in energy prices. In addition, there are limits to the extent to which the export market for such resources can be expanded. Developed economies need only half as much oil per dollar of GDP now as was the case in the mid-1970s, and when oil prices are high there is more incentive for buyers to seek ways of using even less. In addition, oil and gas output growth in Russia are falling, and so there is no guarantee that export growth can continue. Finally, there is the question of the distortions that resource dependence may bring into an economy, supporting a strong currency, rising imports and decreasing exports.

Concern also exists that remaining a resource-based economy will condemn Russia to being in some way a second-rate economy, supplying the resources to richer nations as they press ahead with the technological advances at the forefront of economic development. After all, 'brain power and computer chips are supposed to be the fuel of the modern "knowledge economy" rather than oil' (*The Economist*, 21 August 2004). The Russian government's economic programme, looking ahead to the year 2020, places a good deal of emphasis on the need to diversify through innovation-based development. However, at present, the level of R&D-based innovation in Russia seems to be substantially behind other competitor countries seeking to reach the levels of development of the most advanced countries. In addition, the model of innovation introduced in Russia in recent years is predominantly 'top-down', apparently to be led by several newly created state holding companies. Such a model is in danger of promoting wasteful and misdirected state spending, rather than market-led entrepreneurial innovation.

The legal environment and state intervention

During the Putin presidency, the state took increasing control of key areas of the economy, particularly in the energy sector. From the point of view of both a transition to a market economy and the health of the economy itself, there are two big problems inherent in this process of increased state intervention. First, the question of the legal environment and whether it provides the certainty, transparency and fairness required for businesses – both domestic and foreign – to operate, plan and invest with confidence. Second, the fundamental issue of whether the Russian state is the best manager of the country's major companies, or is instead likely to lose sight of commercial aims within a wider remit of domestic and foreign policy priorities. Floating around these concerns there is also the problem of corruption in Russia. Transparency International's annual Corruption Perception Index for 2008 had Russia as the thirty-third most corrupt country out of the 180 on its list (Transparency International, 2008). Only Belarus in Europe was deemed to be – marginally – more corrupt.

It is clear that under Putin, Russia's energy complex was not to be used simply to boost the economy, but also as a tool in the restoration of Russia's state and its international standing. When Yukos's CEO, Mikhail Khodorkovsky, was arrested and imprisoned (see Chapter 3, Box 3.3), the state sought partly to reaffirm the message that the days of rich businessmen using their wealth to gain independent political power were over. To this extent, the constitutionally established state was being strengthened, albeit by a trial that was seen by most observers as corrupt. At the same time, the Yukos affair was about more than silencing Khodorkovsky; it was also about transferring the assets of Yukos to the state, in the form of state-owned Rosneft, and destroying any plans by Yukos to develop pipelines outside government control. Then, in September 2005, an oil billionaire who was more loyal to the Putin government, Roman Abramovich, agreed to sell Sibneft to state-run Gazprom. Foreign companies also came into the Kremlin's sights, with both Shell and BP being pressured to give up control of key elements of their operations in Russia.

Leaving aside moral questions for the moment, the lack of a stable and transparent legal framework to protect ownership rights and facilitate medium- and long-term planning is bad for investment. Russia's capital stock as a whole is getting old, and serious investment is needed to replace it. In the energy sector in particular there is a need for technologically sophisticated developments, which are best achieved in co-operation with leading global companies. When the state intervenes, it deters foreign investors. With regard to Russian owners, the notion grows that what they have could be removed by the state, and therefore the incentives are to keep their money abroad, to think in a more short-term way than they might otherwise have done, and to do what the Kremlin wants rather than what is best for business. So, for example, Gazprom has twice cut off gas supplies to Ukraine in what were ostensibly commercial disputes about gas prices. The Russian government conducted negotiations and directed policy in these cases, using a genuine commercial dispute to pursue political goals with regard to its relationship with Ukraine. From a commercial perspective, however, it may well have been detrimental to Gazprom's international image as a reliable supplier for negotiations to be handled in this way.

For many years, the working assumption of most observers is that no one who has made a lot of money in post-Soviet Russia has been able to do so while remaining untainted by corruption. A recent World Bank survey showed Russia ranking in the lowest 25 per cent of countries in terms of the rule of law and the control of corruption. Part of the reason for this has been that the legal framework for a market economy had to be created afresh in the 1990s, and therefore many areas of activity were unregulated. The piecemeal introduction of laws then led to legislative confusion, and the promotion of a culture where the law is considered to be neither effective nor relevant. To 'get things done' in the business world, it was often necessary to pay bribes and sweeteners. State officials themselves would supplement their wages by taking payment to register this item or vouch for that one. Such corruption has been particularly prevalent at the regional level, where the relationship between business and regional authorities can be especially close, and so regional legislation and practice has been used to provide advantages to favoured companies, and to restrict the activities of others. Both Putin and Medvedev have in turn proclaimed the fight against corruption to be a key element in their presidential programmes. That Medvedev had to do so in 2008 confirmed, as Putin himself admitted, that little had been achieved in this respect in the preceding years.

Engagement in the global economy

Russia's share in the structure of world trade has grown steadily in recent years, from around 1.5 per cent in 2001 to almost 3 per cent by the middle of the decade. In 2000, Russia's foreign trade amounted to US$176.6 billion, and by 2007 it amounted to US$671.32 billion, a rise of 280 per cent. The Russian government aims to continue this improvement by gaining membership of the World Trade Organization.

Russia applied to join the WTO in 1993, at a time when the WTO was emerging from the Uruguay round of the General Agreement on Tariffs and Trade as the new body overseeing global trade. More than fifteen years later, Russia still had not secured WTO admission. The WTO sits in judgement on international trade disputes. It sets the rules of trade and enforces them on its members. As an organization, its chief policy is one of trade liberalization, and membership for Russia would in the long term increase Russian access to global markets. In addition, the regulatory clarity required for WTO membership will provide a stability that should encourage foreign investment. In the short term, however, Russia's membership has been held up by, among other things, its reluctance to bring its trading regulations into line with WTO norms. In particular, this would require the removal of protectionist barriers in key sectors – such as banking, agriculture and metallurgy. When President Putin came to power in 2000 he brought with him a renewed vigour in terms of pursuing Russian entry into the WTO, and progress in this direction was helped by the firm support by Russia for the actions of the United States and its allies in its war on terrorism after 11 September 2001. Such initial vigour was followed by decreasing momentum on the part of Russia and some WTO member nations, as Russia's relations with the United States worsened and Russia's own economic development approach took on a more state-centric, internalized character. However, in the end, WTO accession is based on detailed negotiations about trade-related matters. In addition, the slight warming of relations between Russia and the United States – with new presidents Medvedev and Obama attempting to reset the relationship – means that Russian WTO membership was placed once again more firmly on the agenda in 2009.

At the same time as negotiating WTO membership, Russia is also seeking to develop a closer economic arrangement with a number of the states of the former Soviet Union within the Commonwealth of Independent States. In his 'state of the nation' address in May 2004, President Putin declared that 'our priority remains working on the deepening of integration on the territory of the Commonwealth of Independent States, including within the framework of the single economic space, the Eurasian Economic Community'. It is not clear precisely what Russia hopes to gain economically from this arrangement, and it may well be that the motivation for its development comes more from Russia's commitment to having a clear geopolitical sphere of influence, than from the expectation of great economic gain. Russia clearly sees this Eurasian Economic Community as being vital for regional and international stability.

As well as trading relations, two other indicators provide a useful assessment of confidence in the Russian economy as against the global economy as a whole – namely, capital flight and foreign investment.

Capital flight

Since the beginning of economic reform in the early 1990s, many Russians, quite understandably, thought it safer to convert their money into foreign currency and get it out of the country as quickly as possible. For much of the transition period, such 'capital flight' was estimated to be around US$15 billion a year, though precise figures are difficult to find. In some years, the figure was far higher, and even official government data listed capital flight in 2000 as US$24 billion. These government figures then showed a reduction as the state of the Russian economy improved, with capital outflows estimated as US$16 billion in 2001 and a little over US$11 billion in 2002. The economic crisis of 2008 onwards resulted in record levels of capital flight, with Russia's finance minister giving a figure of US$200 billion for the period from October 2008 to February 2009. Whatever the precise figure, the point is that huge amounts of money have left the Russian economy since the late 1990s – often in semi-legal ways – instead of being invested, spent, saved or taxed in the domestic economy.

Foreign investment

Capital outflow is obviously offset by capital inflow, and a major part of this is foreign direct investment (FDI). Taking the post-Soviet years overall, FDI into Russia has been at a relatively low level, with a lack of confidence in the business environment and concerns over the future development of the economy deterring would-be investors. Before the 1998 crash it was around US$5.3 billion per annum, and by 2002 the post-crash recovery had only brought it back to around US$4 billion. Such figures include the return of capital flight from abroad (much of it held in Cyprus). During the period 2000–3, FDI was around 1 per cent of GDP, but as the Russian economy grew, so FDI increased to remain around the 2–3 per cent mark in 2005–8, before slumping during the subsequent economic crisis.

A number of key foreign investors in Russia have suffered high-profile difficulties in recent years, serving as a warning to other would-be investors. For example, the joint venture between BP and the Russian company TyumenNefteGaz, much trumpeted when signed in 2003, hit all sorts of difficulties stemming from what many saw as Russian attempts to take overall control of the business by administrative means, with the support of the state. Shell similarly experienced problems in its joint project with Gazprom to develop the Sakhalin II gas fields, eventually ceding control to its Russian partner.

While the energy and raw materials sector is an important element in FDI, much investment into Russia has been predicated on selling goods and services to Russian consumers – the high-profile examples of McDonald's and IKEA being illustrative of a wider phenomenon.

Conclusion

Russia's economy, as it entered the difficult period of global recession from 2008 onwards, had enjoyed almost a decade of growth. Towards the end of the Yeltsin era, when Russia's economic news was consistently bad, there was much discussion among analysts as to the role that Western advisers and the international financial institutions had played in Russia's transition. One view, shared by many in Russia, was that the advice given by Western specialists had been inappropriate. According to the chief economist of the World Bank, Joseph Stiglitz, writing shortly after the 1998 crash, standard Western advice wrongly took:

> an ideological, fundamental and root-and-branch approach to reform-mongering as opposed to an incremental, remedial, piece-meal and adaptive approach ... Some economic cold warriors seem to have seen themselves on a mission to level the 'evil' institutions of Communism and to socially engineer in their place the new, clean and pure 'textbook institutions' of a private property market. (Quoted in Lloyd, 1999)

Others argued that the trouble was not the Western advice itself, but the fact that it was not followed, and that despite this the IMF kept granting money to shore up a Russia reluctant to undertake the necessary root-and-branch reforms.

Such heated arguments faded in the twenty-first century, as the Russian economy began performing well on many indicators. A stronger Russia paid back foreign debt, saw capital return as investment, and began to rebuild its infrastructure. As with political reform, the Russian economy today does not look exactly like that envisaged by the purist reformers of the immediate post-Soviet era. It remains far removed from the Soviet legacy of 1992, and yet has not thrown off every last structural and behavioural vestige of that era. In particular, the role of the state has once again been called into question, as the state has established control over the major energy companies in particular. By the time Medvedev became president in 2008, economic growth had become the norm and the state was setting out plans for the future; plans to use the proceeds of growth to develop Russia, to improve state provision of education, housing and health care, and to diversify the economy to avoid so much depending entirely on high oil prices and the continued exploitation of raw materials. These plans remain in place for technologically driven diversification, even as the economic downturn hits Russia. However, the economic crisis has meant renewed debate as to the role the state should play in future developments. The outcome of this debate will decide the nature of the Russian economy in the coming years.

6

Rights, Freedoms and Civil Society

This chapter briefly explores the Soviet legacy regarding the application of law and the rights and freedoms enjoyed – or not enjoyed – by Soviet citizens. We then turn our attention to rights and freedoms in contemporary Russia, focusing on freedom of speech, freedom of the press, freedom of worship, and Russia's human rights record as seen through international eyes. Such rights and freedoms are, of course, essential if a thriving civil society – itself seen as a prerequisite for genuine and lasting democracy – is to thrive.

Today's Russia is a signatory to the major international human rights conventions; is a member of the Council of Europe, with all the human rights requirements which that entails; and has constitutional guarantees for a whole raft of normative rights and freedoms. At the same time, though, reports of the denial of certain rights and freedoms, and at times of more serious human rights abuses, are still heard about Russia. Is this just a matter of Western sensitivities from the Cold War era creating extra vigilance with regard to Russia's record in this area? Or are there serious grounds for stating that Russia reins in the rights and freedoms expected of a democratic nation?

To those with a knowledge of how the law was applied in the Soviet Union, and to a lesser extent in the post-Soviet era, this description of the 'privatization' of the law rings true. The behavioural legacy of the Soviet period presents a challenge that twenty-first-century Russia has to overcome if a truly law-based state is to be created.

The Soviet legacy

The Soviet Union had a developed legal system, backed by a Constitution outlining the rights and obligations of its citizens. (After the founding Constitutions of Soviet Russia (1918) and the Soviet Union (1924), the USSR had two further constitutions, the Stalin Constitution of 1936 and the Brezhnev Constitution of 1977.) As Mark Sandle puts it, 'the basic ethos was that the rights of the individual were state based and were then delegated to the individual from the state' (Sandle, 1998). In practice, this meant that the authorities were above the law. Cases, particularly cases of political importance, would be decided not on judicial grounds alone, but as a result of what became known as 'telephone law'. The party and the judicial authorities would consult, and decide what the verdict and the sentence should be. As the Khodorkovsky case demonstrates (see Chapter 3, Box 3.3), at the highest level such 'telephone law', albeit now termed 'Basmanny justice', still exists in the sense that the authorities are able to obtain a court verdict in their favour in circumstances where this is deemed to be essential.

If 'telephone law' was the practice at the higher end of the scale, it was mirrored in the experience of many citizens in their dealings with the law, where judicial criteria might be secondary to other factors such as political reliability, favours to be granted, scores to be settled, or bribes to be paid. During the last years of the USSR, Soviet leader Mikhail Gorbachev (1985–91) tried to create a 'law-based state', which he described as being essential to the stability of the Soviet Union. However, the ideological, institutional and constitutional confusion of the Soviet endgame did not allow for the clear development of this concept, nor its embodiment in the behaviour of the authorities.

Gorbachev had been working towards the enactment of a new Soviet Constitution. With the Soviet Union no longer existing after 1991, the task became the development of a new Russian Constitution. As noted in Chapter 1, arguments over the nature of the Constitution and questions of how and by whom Russia should be ruled eventually led to military action on the streets of Moscow in October 1993, and the forcible dissolution of parliament by troops loyal to President Yeltsin. We turn now to a discussion of the 1993 Russian Constitution, which still serves as the fundamental law of the Russian Federation.

Constitutional rights in contemporary Russia

The Russian Constitution was adopted by national referendum on 12 December 1993. A constitution can perform a variety of functions, setting out the rules of the game for political engagement, the institutional arrangement of power, the 'mission statement' of a state, the division between central and devolved powers, the limits of the state and so on. In different chapters of this book we deal with different aspects of constitutional provision (in particular, Chapter 4 covers the institutional arrangement of power). Here, though, we are concerned with what the Russian Constitution says about individual rights and freedoms, and the supremacy of law.

Before tackling this topic in any detail, it is worth pointing out that, to many people, the Russian Constitution's position on the supremacy of law was compromised before the Constitution was ever adopted because of the circumstances surrounding its adoption. We outlined in Chapters 1 and 4 the events that led to armed conflict in Moscow between supporters of the president and the parliament in 1993. The key point for our purposes here is that the dissolution of parliament by the president in September 1993 was not allowed under the Constitution then in force. In other words, whatever the current Russian Constitution says about the supremacy of the law, it was adopted on the back of a fundamentally unconstitutional act, namely the dissolution of parliament by the president.

There is of, course, a counter-argument to this view, which is that the Constitution still in force in September 1993 was void of real authority and served as a barrier to the democratic development of Russia. It was the 1978 Constitution of the Soviet-era Russian republic, and had been amended so many times that it could scarcely be called a fundamental law any longer. Though this argument is correct so far as it goes, the fact remains that, from a legal-technical point of view, the dissolution of parliament in 1993 was not lawful.

Despite its provenance, the Russian Constitution provides an apparently firm foundation for the provision of human rights. We have noted that, under the Soviet system, individual rights were subsumed by the needs of the state. This Marxist–Leninist conceptualization of rights is replaced in the current Constitution by a liberal approach, with Article 2 declaring that 'the individual and his rights and freedoms are the supreme value'. An entire section of the Russian Constitution is then devoted to 'human and civil rights and freedoms', which are guaranteed within 'the generally recognized principles and norms of international law'.

Among the rights and freedoms to be guaranteed by the Russian Constitution are all those that might be expected in a liberal democracy, including:

- equality before the law;
- inviolability of the home and the person;
- the presumption of innocence;
- freedom of conscience;
- freedom of thought and speech; and
- the right of association.

There are also a number of rights and freedoms that carry specific echoes of the Soviet era. Some of these involve statements of rights that were often infringed during the Communist years, such as the right to travel and to live where one chooses, the right to privacy of communication, and the right to own property. Others involve guarantees reminiscent of the broad social welfare provisions claimed by the Soviet state; for example, guaranteed provision of pensions, certain social security benefits, housing, and education; the right to a decent environment; and the constitutional statement that 'the development of physical culture and sport ... are encouraged'.

It is clear, then, that the Russian Constitution provides a substantial legal underpinning of the rights and freedoms to be enjoyed by the citizens of the Russian Federation. The Constitution is the fundamental law of the state, and all other laws must be in accordance with it. As we shall see, though, the mere statement of something in a constitution does not in itself mean the application of that provision. After all, the Constitutions of the Soviet era were in many ways splendid documents. It was the fact that they were not reflected in much of everyday life that was the problem. A key question to ask, then, is whether the legal guarantees of the current Constitution have resulted in a change of behaviour on the part of the state. Does the state now act in confirmation of the view that individual rights take precedence? Or does the old view that the state is more important still hold sway?

We must also bear in mind that the provisions of the Constitution are broad-ranging, and many of them require a detailed working out in law before they can be applied. For example, the Constitution guarantees the right to buy, sell and own land. However, it is clear that the division and sale of state- and co-operative-owned land presents a complex situation for which detailed law-making is required. If, however, there is a reluctance among law-makers to pass laws on land ownership, as was the case in Russia for the first post-Soviet decade (see Chapter 5, Box 5.4), then the application of this constitutional provision becomes problematic.

A similar example is discussed later, in our consideration of freedom of worship. The Russian Constitution declares that potential conscripts into the military have the right of alternative service. Despite this, the lack of a law defining how such alternative service might be undertaken meant that, until such a law was finally passed in 2002, this provision was very difficult for private citizens to enforce. The lack of such 'enabling legislation' hampered several areas of constitutional provision in the years after 1993.

Having considered the fundamental constitutional guarantees of rights and freedoms offered in Russia today, let us look more closely at their application in practice. We shall look at two examples of long-standing importance in both the Soviet era and today – namely, freedom of information and freedom of worship – before considering Russia's record on the provision of rights and freedoms as seen through the eyes of the international community.

Freedom of information

The deterioration of press freedom during the first decade of the twenty-first century has been a widely discussed issue almost ever since Putin's accession to the presidency in 2000. In 2003, the international 'democracy rating' organization, Freedom House, downgraded its evaluation of the Russian media from being 'partly free' to being 'not free' in its annual Press Freedom Survey, a position in which it has remained in subsequent surveys. Such a negative evaluation is, broadly speaking, the result of the closure of numerous commercially owned media outlets and the exertion of an array of pressures on the Russian media in recent years.

In the twenty-first century, the concept of freedom of information has a wider application than ever before. Here we are talking of freedom of the press and broadcast media. We are also talking about state control over and surveillance of telephone conversations, e-mails, and the World Wide Web. In Russia, one in every three people has a computer at home, and that proportion is rising. Governments across the developed world are wrestling with the questions of how and to what extent to control information flows. Putin noted this fact in his first public statement as acting president in 2000, placing 'landslide developments in information science and telecommunications' in the front rank of issues which bring both hope and fear to the twenty-first-century world. Fittingly, this first public statement was published on the presidential website.

Let us deal with the more specific question of media freedom, and build up a picture of the historical context within which today's Russia must act. The Soviet era as a whole was marked by the most severe state control over newspapers, television and radio. This extended beyond the stringent editorial vigilance exerted by the Communist Party and the KGB, to an information blockade designed to prevent access to all forms of Western media. Radio broadcasts from the West were habitually jammed by the authorities, and the importing of most Western newspapers into the Soviet Union was illegal.

This control of information by the Soviet authorities was more effective than is sometimes believed. Of course, there were ways in which it was undermined. Many families owned short-wave radios on which, for example, the BBC Russian Service or the US-funded Radio Liberty could be heard. Furthermore, there was a widespread scepticism among the intelligentsia, at least about the reliability of Soviet media, and an almost ubiquitous lack of belief in the existence of anything approaching objective media. Despite this undermining of Soviet censorship, however, the control of information was broadly successful in terms of its aims. Nearly all Soviet citizens received their daily knowledge of world affairs through the state media, and where there was intelligent scepticism it often extended to Western information sources too: 'We tell our story, they tell theirs; the truth is somewhere in the middle.' Knowledge of the West was similarly sketchy.

All this, of course, began to change under Gorbachev, whose most important policy shift, among a number of fundamental changes, was surely that of *glasnost'*. *Glasnost'* has often been translated as 'openness', but is more accurately rendered as 'public transparency'. The introduction of this policy under Gorbachev in 1987 represented a step towards freedom of the press and free speech in general. However, *glasnost'* was not free speech *per se*, and had a clear functionalist role in the reform process. It appears to have been conceived initially as a weapon to be used by Gorbachev and the reformers against conservative opponents in the Communist Party. If the press was more open about, for example, corruption in the Party, then a reformist mood would be fostered and encouraged among other party members and the public at large against the practices of the Party conservatives.

Similar but wider possibilities presented themselves in other spheres. The more openness there was about the problems facing the Soviet Union, the more people would realize the necessity of Gorbachev's reform programme. So, instead of the 100 per cent positive view of life in the USSR that had been the staple of the Soviet media for decades, there began to appear what were at the time startling revelations about, for example, the existence of prostitution in the Soviet Union, the danger of AIDS and so on.

At first, then, *glasnost'* was as much a policy of state editorial control as what had gone before, albeit with more varied content. There were '*glasnost'* newspapers' such as *Argumenty i fakty* ('Arguments and Facts') and the glossy weekly *Ogonyek* ('Little Light'). All publications remained under state ownership but, as the control of the state, and particularly the leadership of the Party, became more and more fragmented, distinct publications could be identified increasingly as reformist or conservative. By the end of the Soviet era, what had begun as a functionalist state policy had developed into the widespread existence of journalistic freedom. Independent newspapers began to be established, the availability of Western media was less and less controlled, and the liberation of access to previously suppressed information and to a kaleidoscope of different opinions contributed massively to the heady atmosphere surrounding the Soviet collapse of 1990–1.

In the 1990s, freedom of the press flourished relatively unchecked in Russia, as the media landscape was transformed by the rise of the super-rich oligarchs, the withdrawal of state funding for many publications, and the endeavours of journalists revelling in new-found freedoms. Of course, this statement represents a broad overview, and the decade of the 1990s was not all rosy for the journalistic profession. As in other areas (for example, freedom of worship, discussed elsewhere in this chapter), the time between the collapse of the Soviet system and the normalization of the current Russian system towards the end of the 1990s presented opportunities and freedoms that were later reined in to some extent. That short period in the early 1990s, when the state still funded much of the media and yet its ability and willingness to exert editorial control had vastly diminished, is looked on by some observers as the heyday of press freedom. Gradually, as the 1990s progressed, several factors began to influence journalistic freedom.

In particular, as a few individuals gained control of a number of the main media outlets in the 1990s, editorial freedom began to diminish. Many of the newspapers that emerged out of the Soviet collapse tried to establish themselves as truly independent, but increasingly economic reality blocked their efforts as they lacked the financial resources to continue. Consequently, several businessmen who had grown very rich very rapidly in the aftermath of the Soviet collapse began to acquire media assets.

The first such Russian 'media baron' was Vladimir Gusinsky, whose 'Most' group was built up to include a major national newspaper, *Segodnya*, and the national TV network NTV. He was soon followed by Boris Berezovsky, who gained effective control over a similar profile of media outlets, including the newspaper *Nezavisimaya gazeta*. He also became known as the key figure of influence behind the major national TV station ORT, which, while 51 per cent owned by the state, was largely managed by men close to Berezovsky. A number of other businessmen acquired media holdings, as did the Mayor of Moscow, Yurii Luzhkov. Clearly, with the acquisition of broadcast and print media resources, Gusinsky, Berezovsky and others were able to gain a measure of control over editorial policy.

The 1996 presidential election represented a key point in the development of media-political relations in Russia. At the beginning of that year, incumbent president, Boris Yeltsin, languished in the opinion polls, having just seen his main rivals – the Communists – emerge from the parliamentary election of 1995 as the biggest party in the Duma. On the basis of poll evidence alone, the possibility that Yeltsin might lose the presidency to his Communist rival, Gennady Zyuganov, seemed very real. None the less, the months preceding the presidential vote in June 1996 saw concerted support for Yeltsin across virtually all of the main print and – of particular importance – broadcast media. The big three national TV channels (ORT, NTV and the wholly state-owned RTR) all produced coverage heavily supportive of Yeltsin, who, of course, eventually won the election.

Yeltsin's victory in 1996, and the vital role of the media in achieving it, had two particular effects of relevance to media freedom:

- First, it created an expectation among the media magnates that they would be rewarded in some way for supporting the regime, thereby strengthening the links between media control and political influence.

- Second, the remarkable rise in popular support for Yeltsin in the first half of 1996 emphasized the power of the media. In doing so it increased the determination of other businessmen in the large 'financial-industrial groups' which controlled the commanding heights of the Russian economy to build up their media holdings.

Similarly, and particularly towards the end of the 1990s and into the Putin presidency, the state began to regain control of key information media. In 1998, a state holding company was created which controlled the national RTR TV channel, as well as nearly seventy regional TV stations and a large number of transmitters across the country. The following year, President Yeltsin created a Press, Television, Radio Broadcasting and Mass Communications Ministry, to develop a state policy on advertising and oversee the auction of broadcast licences. Many observers saw this as an attempt by the Yeltsin regime to ensure that support for his chosen successor in the 2000 presidential election would match the backing he had received in 1996.

The election campaign of Yeltsin's anointed successor, Putin, in 2000 did by and large enjoy the support of the media. The situation, however, was slightly different from that in 1996. At that time virtually the entire media establishment – owners and journalists alike – had felt justified in supporting Yeltsin as the only candidate capable of beating the Communist Zyuganov. After all, the Communists were scarcely known as defenders of media freedom. By 2000, the prospect of a Zyuganov victory seemed less likely, and the retirement of Yeltsin led a number of the political and business elite to back potential successors other than Putin. By early 2000, a Putin victory, partly on the back of positive war-reporting from Chechnya, seemed assured. None the less, Gusinsky's media outlets were markedly less supportive of either the Chechen conflict or of Putin than were the other main media outlets.

An editorial in the London *Times* newspaper in July 2000 declared that 'a healthy and vigorous press was Yeltsin's proudest legacy, the best guarantee of democratic pluralism'. While we have expressed specific reservations about the freedom of the media in the Yeltsin era, this statement still holds. It is equally clear that, since the end of the Yeltsin presidency, press freedom in Russia has declined.

As noted above, serious concerns about attacks on press freedom were raised in the summer of 1999 when Prime Minister Putin created a new Press Ministry under Mikhail Lesin. The aim of this ministry was to increase central state control over the media, and while the comparisons with the Soviet-era 'Main Administration for Literary and Publishing Affairs' (*Glavlit*) made at the time may have been exaggerated, events since certainly seem to indicate a new, firmer attitude toward the media in Russia.

Some of the examples of state control over the press since the summer of 1999 are familiar from earlier in the 1990s. In particular, reporters' access to Chechnya during the war there from 1999 onwards echoed similar restrictions that applied during the conflict of 1994–6, and bias in coverage of the parliamentary election of December 1999 and the presidential election of March 2000 was similarly familiar from the corresponding elections of 1995 and 1996. By the time of the elections of 2003 and 2004 such a bias in media coverage had worsened, though even then it was rarely crude and simplistic, manifest rather through shorter amounts of time and more negative coverage given to opposition candidates on the national TV channels. By the Duma election of 2007 and the presidential election of 2008, such media bias in election coverage was almost taken for granted.

A poll taken in 2007 revealed that almost all regular TV watchers paid little attention to coverage of politics, believing it to lack objectivity. In the 2008 presidential campaign, it was taken for granted by most voters that Medvedev would win, and television coverage reflected this. Medvedev himself refused to participate in television debates, as if setting himself apart from the grubby business of actual campaigning and arguing for his programme. The two main opposition parties – the Communist Party of the Russian Federation and the Liberal Democratic Party of Russia – filed a complaint with the Central Electoral Commission alleging that state-owned Channel One and Rossiya TV, and Moscow city-owned Centre TV, gave Medvedev 85 per cent of their election coverage, and an independent media research company similarly stated that over 80 per cent of television coverage was devoted to Medvedev. The only national TV channel that appeared to give a more balanced view of the campaign was Ren TV, a channel that habitually attracts only around 10 per cent of the audience.

What, then, was it that changed almost immediately after Putin became president to make journalists from across a range of Moscow-based newspapers publish twice in 2000 an *Obshchaya gazeta* ('common newspaper') aimed at defending press freedom? First, the attitude of the state had toughened markedly. In February

2000, a Russian journalist, Andrei Babitsky, working behind the lines in Chechnya for the US-founded Radio Liberty was arrested by the Russian authorities and handed over to the Chechen forces in exchange for five Russian POWs. The complex tale led eventually to the release of Babitsky and his return to Moscow. Shortly after these events, the then acting-president Putin had a book published ('First Person'), consisting of detailed and frank interviews about his life and political views. The portrait of Putin in this book was, as would be expected, a sympathetic one. None the less, the one point where Putin's responses seem the most intemperate concern the Babitsky case. Putin describes Babitsky as a traitor, working for the enemy and justifying atrocities. He is, in Putin's eyes, 'not a Russian journalist', and, most revealingly for our discussion here, Russia's president states that: 'what Babitsky did is much more dangerous than firing a gun . . . We interpret freedom of expression in different ways and if you mean direct complicity in crimes, I will never agree to that.'

Second, the trend towards increasing state control over the media, which we noted as gathering pace from 1998 onwards, developed into a campaign in the summer of 2000. President Putin had, to the approval of many observers in both Russia and the West, declared his intention to clamp down on the influence of the mega-rich businessmen who dominated much of Russia's domestic politics in the Yeltsin era.

Within months of winning the presidential election, the state in various guises began to bring under its control the media empires of Gusinsky and Berezovsky. The cases differ slightly, in that Gusinsky's Media Most group were openly critical of Putin, whereas the Berezovsky-controlled media were broadly – though certainly not uniformly – supportive. Gusinsky was arrested briefly on suspicion of fraud, but eventually charges were dropped, allegedly on condition that he facilitated the transfer of his media holdings to the huge state-controlled gas company, Gazprom, to whom Media Most was in any case in substantial debt. Berezovsky apparently voluntarily began negotiations to transfer his holdings in the ORT channel to the state, though ORT was similarly in substantial debt, in this case to a state-controlled bank. Since 2000, all the national television channels in Russia have been under the control, either directly or indirectly, of the state – while Gusinsky and Berezovsky have been living in exile in Europe in fear of prosecution should they return to Russia.

Under state control, television news coverage has become more uniform and more supportive of the ruling regime, with the state bringing the television companies demonstrably back into line on occasions when they are deemed to have overstepped the mark. One such occasion was the Moscow theatre hostage crisis of October 2002, after which President Putin criticized coverage which he claimed undermined the anti-terrorism operation. It was clear that NTV's coverage upset the authorities – though whether the blame should be laid with them, or with those military authorities that allowed TV crews into the immediate environs of the siege is debatable – and within three months the head of NTV, who had himself been seen as a government placeman on his appointment, was removed from his post. It was notable too that during the key hours of the culmination of the siege, the feed of Western news coverage from, for example, CNN and BBC World, was turned off in a number of central Moscow hotels.

In 2000, Russia's Security Council produced an 'information security doctrine'. It had been worked on for some time, including during

---

Box 6.1   Deaths of journalists

According to the International News Safety Institute, an international coalition of news organization and journalists, Russia ranks second in the number of journalists killed on duty in the decade from 1997 to 2007. The deaths of journalists is commonly tied to criticisms of media freedom in Russia, the most prominent example being the murder of campaigning journalist Anna Politkovskaya in 2006.

Politkovskaya had gained a reputation for fearless reporting from Chechnya, reporting abuses by Chechen rebels and the Russian military alike. She was also critical of the Putin regime. Her writing gained her many enemies. In October 2006 she was shot dead in the block of flats where she lived. Three Chechen men were charged with her murder, but acquitted by a jury in Moscow in February 2009.

Precise figures on the deaths of journalists are difficult to establish and interpret. In particular, it is difficult to make clear connections between the number of journalists who die while carrying out their work, and the degree of media freedom in a country.

The Centre for Journalism in Extreme Situations, founded in 2000 as a human rights organization within the Russian Union of Journalists, reports – according to the Russian press – that 156 journalists died in Russia between 2000 and 2007, but of these most died in accidents or of natural causes, and only five can definitely be said to have died as a result of their work. For the preceding seven years, during the Yeltsin presidency, when Russia's media was freer than during the Putin era, the Centre for Journalism in Extreme Situations cites a figure of eleven journalists killed as a result of their work.

Putin's tenure as chief of the Security Council. Though a vague document in itself, this draft backs up the conclusions we draw here about media freedom in Russia. The Russian state sees the media as a legitimate object of state intervention, and the strengthening of state control over the media as essential to national security. At the same time, though, both Putin and Medvedev have repeatedly given verbal backing to press freedom. The draft information security doctrine asserts these two positions, and only in the detail are the apparent incompatibilities of these two positions tested. As in many countries, the fight against terrorism has been a key battleground for the question of media freedom. In 2006, a law on countering terrorism was eventually passed by the Duma, but only after particularly stringent restrictions on media reporting had been removed from the bill – including a provision that at terrorist incidents journalists had to remain in a special zone and could only report official information, not their own impressions.

Freedom of worship

According to the Russian Constitution of 1993, freedom of worship is guaranteed in the Russian Federation. To enshrine this right in the country's fundamental law marked a clear break with the past, and particularly with the Soviet era, when the persecution of religious believers had been continuous and widespread. The situation for religious believers in the Soviet Union had begun to improve under Gorbachev's leadership, particularly from 1988 onwards. This was the year that marked the millennium of Christianity in Russia, and it was officially celebrated across the country, with the atheist Communist leadership even sanctioning the production of postage stamps marking the occasion.

In 1990, the Soviet Union introduced a Law on Freedom of Conscience and Religious Associations, which was the most liberal religious law of the twentieth century in Russia. It declared the fundamental right of freedom of conscience, the equality before the law of believers and non-believers, and the right to freely choose, hold and disseminate religious or non-religious convictions. As we noted when considering media freedom, the period of the 1990s was freer and more open than the situation that applies in Russia today. Old laws and practices had been swept away, and there was a sense of intoxication with new freedoms.

What did these new freedoms mean for religious believers? At the most basic level, believers of all faiths could begin to attend church (or mosque, synagogue, temple and so on) more freely and openly than before. They were able to obtain religious literature (particularly Bibles) with increasing ease, religious groups were able to engage in charitable work and in the expression of their faith, and there was more contact with fellow believers abroad. This latter point meant a growth in overt evangelistic activity by different religious groups on the streets or through the media.

In short, the official recognition of religious freedom brought a surge of religious activity across a range of faiths. The Russian Orthodox Church, which still sees itself as the carrier of the faith of the Russian people, was by no means excluded from such activity. Indeed, it enjoyed the full range of rights, and began to enjoy financial benefits from the state, the return of property confiscated by the Communist regime earlier in the twentieth century, and an increasingly prominent position alongside the state machinery. For example, the Patriarch of Russia began to participate in state ceremonies, such as the inauguration of the president, and the Russian Orthodox Church once again had official links with the Russian armed forces.

As the 1990s progressed, however, there was something of a backlash against this burst of religiosity. In particular, nationalist, anti-Western elements within federal and regional government, and within the hierarchy of the Russian Orthodox Church, began to object to the activities of what they termed 'non-Russian religious sects and cults'. Several streams of thought came together in this view. There was an element of the idea found increasingly in other policy areas as the 1990s progressed, that Russia should not simply accept what the West had to offer, but should build on its own traditions and civilization to find its own Russian path. There was also a fear expressed, particularly in the Orthodox Church, that the Russian people might be 'led astray'. The argument was that, after decades of atheistic propaganda, the Russian people might slake their spiritual thirst on whatever was put before them, without having the depth of knowledge necessary to discern between the various faiths on offer. The existence of certain extreme cults in Russia backed up this fear, but also led to almost anything that was not Russian Orthodoxy being branded as a cult. Confessions that had existed since at least the early years of the century in Russia and persisted throughout decades of Communist persecution (such as the Baptists or the Pentecostals) often found themselves referred to in this way and accused of being 'Western' faiths.

These fears surrounding the growth of religious freedom found an echo among a good proportion of the Russian population, and gradually regional leaders began to promulgate laws that restricted the activities of 'non-Russian' religious groups and, in doing so, often ran counter to the provisions of the Russian Constitution.

In 1997, then, after a couple of failed attempts, the Russian parliament finally passed a law on religion which the president signed. The provisions of the 1997 law 'On Freedom of Conscience and Religious Associations' were a step backwards from the 1990 Soviet-era law in terms of religious freedom, and they also appeared to contradict the Russian Constitution. In its preamble, the 1997 law singled out Russian Orthodoxy as making a 'special contribution' to Russia, and then gave respect to those faiths that form 'an inseparable part of the historical heritage of Russia's peoples', naming specifically Christianity, Islam, Buddhism and Judaism. According to the Constitution of Russia, no faith is to be preferred by the secular state. While the 1997 law's preamble makes no specific provision for preferable treatment to be given to the religions there named, the singling out of Russian Orthodoxy as the foremost faith of Russia reflects the general attitude of the authorities.

The most substantive part of the 1997 law with regard to the practice of religious freedom came in the differentiation it makes between different types of religious association. According to the Constitution, all religious associations are equal before the law. The 1997 religion law, however, declared that religious associations fall into two categories – they are either religious organizations, which are registered and have the full rights of a legal personage, or they are religious groups which are not registered and do not have those rights. Religious groups are therefore, among other restrictions, not able to own property, establish and maintain buildings, employ people, or issue invitations to foreign citizens.

The process of registration is a complex one, and those groups that have had the most difficulties are faiths with links or origins outside Russia. To facilitate registration, many smaller groups have had to place themselves within larger 'umbrella organizations', because belonging to a centralized religious association makes registration easier. Furthermore, the passing of the 1997 law on religion appears to have been seen, particularly by regional authorities and certain elements in the Orthodox Church, as authorization of the harassment of non-Orthodox groups. There are still fairly regular reports from Russia of church groups being evicted from buildings, of evangelistic meetings being broken up, or of foreign missionaries and priests being denied visas.

In the early twenty-first century, the Roman Catholic church in particular seemed to have problems with visas for its clergy. In a number of such cases, lawyers operating on behalf of church groups have appealed successfully against the actions of officials. None the less, it is clear that a group that has been denied registration will have less of a case in law than does a registered association, and that while the situation is vastly improved from the blanket persecution of the Soviet era, it is too early to talk of the firm establishment of freedom of worship in Russia. In recent years this situation has also been exacerbated by the passing in 2002 of a law on extremism, under the provisions of which some Islamic literature has been judged, with no justification, as inciting religious extremism, leading to the authorities harassing or prosecuting its authors and distributors.

Wider human rights and civil society issues

From our examples of media freedom and freedom of religion, we can discern a pattern in relation to rights and freedoms in Russia that is familiar from other areas of discussion in this book. The pendulum of reform swung out widely in the early to mid-1990s, and then began to swing back again. For example, despite massive progress in democratization in the 1990s, there was no full transition to a normative Western liberal democratic system, let alone the consolidation of such a system, and in the twenty-first century Russia has become less democratic, although again not undergoing a full reversion to the situation existing in the Soviet years.

Looking at human rights in general, with particular reference to Russia's place in the international sphere, we can note that Russia is a signatory to the six core UN Human Rights treaties. It has also accepted the human rights obligations of the Council of Europe. None the less, despite these binding assertions, which take precedence over Russian law, concern has been expressed in the West about aspects of Russia's human rights record. In addition to the questions surrounding media freedom and freedom of worship, the main areas of concern are freedom of speech, individual rights within the 'closed institutions' of the military, the health service, and the Russian prison system, and the area which has attracted the most international attention, the conduct of military action against the Chechen Republic.

We shall deal with these issues in order. First, freedom of speech. There have been several cases that have gained international attention, the most noteworthy of which were the separate cases of the environmental activists Aleksandr Nikitin and Grigory Pasko. Both of these men were charged with espionage after revealing details of the environmental impact of Russia's nuclear naval facilities. The fact that they were investigated by the FSB (the KGB's successor) and charged in this manner provokes comparisons with Soviet-era practice, and campaigners on their behalf have made much of this. However, there is a key difference: both men have at different times been acquitted by Russian civil courts, in the Nikitin case at the very highest level of the Supreme Court, though Pasko was subsequently imprisoned under the jurisdiction of a military court and not released until January 2003.

Just as in the religion-related cases noted above, the decisions of the courts have shown that – in these specific instances at least – officials are not always above the law. However, other cases demonstrate that freedom of speech is not defended consistently by the legal system. The US State Department and Amnesty International have both expressed serious concern over the treatment of Igor Sutyagin, an academic who was arrested in 1999 for allegedly passing classified information about Russia's nuclear weapons to a London-based firm. Sutyagin was sentenced in 2004 to fifteen years in prison. There are serious doubts over this conviction, since he claims never to have had access to secret material, and concerns about the harsh nature of his sentence and conditions of confinement.

Allegations of human rights abuses in the Russian military, health system and prisons relate largely to the poor conditions in these institutions. Lack of resources in the military have led in recent years to poor standards of nutrition, substandard accommodation and frequent training accidents resulting from ill-maintained equipment and insufficient expertise among the troops. The loss with all hands of the nuclear submarine *Kursk* in August 2000 appears to be the most obvious example of failings in military training and equipment. In addition to these difficulties caused largely by lack of funding, the 'tradition' of systematic bullying of conscripts entrenched in the Russian armed forces has also led to deaths, protests and the desire to avoid being drafted into the armed forces under Russia's system of universal conscription. In 2008, the period of conscription was reduced from two years to one, partly in an attempt to break the cycle of bullying based on a hierarchy of conscripts, and partly to edge Russia a little nearer to having professional armed forces.

Russia has the second-highest prison population per capita rate in the world, at about 650 per 100,000 population. In this prison system, according to human rights group Amnesty International, over a million prisoners endure conditions which are 'cruel, inhuman and degrading'. Much of this results from a lack of resources, which leads in particular to severe health problems, the most worrying of which is a new and virulent strain of tuberculosis (see Chapter 3). There are also stories of torture and ill-treatment of those held in police custody. In terms of the health service, human rights groups have throughout the 1990s raised concerns about the treatment of the mentally ill and, to a lesser extent, the disabled, particularly children, within Russia's system of state orphanages.

As noted above, the biggest single human rights issue with which the West has been concerned in relation to Russia in recent years is the conduct of war in Chechnya in 1994–6 and again from 1999 to 2009. In both of these periods, Russian armed forces have attempted to subdue separatist guerrillas by the wholesale 'invasion' of Chechnya. (Though of course, this is not an invasion in terms of international law, as Chechnya remains officially part of the Russian Federation.) Critics of Russian action argue that, in waging war in Chechnya, Russia has targeted civilians, mistreated prisoners, sacrificed its own conscript soldiers, harassed independent media, and denied access to international bodies such as the International Red Cross and the OSCE.

As a result of Russia's conduct of its war in Chechnya:

- the European Union limited the funds earmarked for the promotion of democracy in Russia and transferred uncommitted funds to humanitarian assistance for refugees from the conflict area;
- the Parliamentary Assembly of the Council of Europe stripped Russia of its voting rights, and declared 'totally unacceptable' the failure of the Council of Europe's Committee of Ministers to denounce Moscow's conduct of the Chechen war; and
- President Putin was widely criticized by the international community for his conduct of the war, and President Bill Clinton of the USA even used a speech to the State Duma in Moscow to urge a re-think of policy in Chechnya.

Despite all these actions by the international community, support for Russian action in Chechnya remained fairly solid among the Russian population, albeit with some notable exceptions – such as the

Committee of Soldiers' Mothers. This is partly because media coverage of the war largely supported the Russian position. It has also resulted from widespread anger and horror at terrorists attacks within Russia.

After the terrorist attacks by Al-Qaeda on New York and Washington on 11 September 2001, President Putin, and indeed the Chechen rebels, increasingly sought to 'internationalize' the discourse around the Chechen conflict. For Putin, the conflict in Chechnya was part of the global war on terrorism, and this interpretation was to some extent accepted by some Western governments. (For more details on Chechnya, see Chapter 2. For more discussion of how the war in Chechnya fits into the larger picture of Russia's place in the international community, see Chapter 8). President Medvedev formally announced an end to counter-terrorism operations in Chechnya in March 2009.

A weak state and securitization

A key to understanding rights and freedoms in contemporary Russia is knowledge of the historical background. This applies not only to an awareness that authoritarianism and even totalitarianism dominated Soviet society during the twentieth century, but also to a knowledge of more recent post-Soviet history. In particular, we have noted a shift from the beginning of the Putin presidency in 2000 towards more state control, and a rolling back of previous advances in terms of democracy and certain aspects of rights and freedoms. An adequate understanding of the Russian government's policies in these areas requires recognition of the 'weak state hypothesis'.

A consensus began to develop at the end of the Yeltsin era among observers of contemporary Russia that the central political issue to be dealt with was the weakness of the Russian state. As an explanatory framework for what happened in Russia in the 1990s, stalled state-building explains a great deal. The essence of the problem was the heavily presidential nature of the Russian state under Yeltsin and its role in hindering the development of democratic institutions and behaviour, thus creating a weak, personalized state. Under Yeltsin, the Russian state could not collect taxes, pay wages, keep order on the streets, rule its regions, provide adequate health and education services, and perform many other functions of a state.

When Putin came to power in 2000, a degree of consensus existed among observers and the new regime alike; the state strengthening agenda headed the list of tasks facing the Russian government at the turn of the millennium. The policies of Vladimir Putin with regard to state strengthening included bringing all regional laws into line with federal legislation, reforming the tax system with a 13 per cent rate of income tax applicable to all, and undermining the influence of 'oligarchs'. These are policies that addressed in a straightforward manner the widely acknowledged problems Russia was facing at the end of the Yeltsin era. Switch the discourse a little, however, and a focus on Putin's approach can bring a different interpretation.

For some observers it was enough to put 'former KGB colonel' and 'strengthening of the state' together to conclude that Putin's aim was for Russia to become more authoritarian. To add more fuel to the fire, Putin's two key phrases with regard to state strengthening echoed the communist past. In place of the Marxist 'dictatorship of the proletariat' promised by Lenin, Putin promised a 'dictatorship of the law'. And instead of Stalin's infamous declaration during his rural terror campaign of the 1930s that he would 'liquidate the Kulaks as a class', Putin said that he would get rid of 'the oligarchs as a class'.

As we have seen, with regard to the rule of law, the record in terms of high profile cases is mixed. Courts make decisions based on legal rather than political considerations in less high profile cases, but this is a hit and miss affair. In cases such as the attempt to ban the Salvation Army in Moscow – on the grounds that it was a 'paramilitary organization' – or the prosecution on spying charges of environmental campaigner, Grigory Pasko, the message was confused, with courts variously striking down and restating earlier decisions. In other cases, such as that of the academic Sutyagin charged with spying, legal procedures were far from ideal, and the suspicion that the Russian security service (the FSB) had undue influence is held by many observers.

Similarly, with regard to the liquidation of the oligarchs as a class, again the picture was mixed. The three best known oligarchs – Vladimir Gusinsky, Boris Berezovsky and Mikhail Khodorkovsky – now either live in exile (Gusinsky and Berezovsky) or in prison (Khodorkovsky). However, the motivation on the part of the Russian regime for their removal from having any influence was identified by many observers as the desire to place their vast media holdings in the hands of the state, and to remove a source of funding and support for opposition groups, rather than to clean up politics.

Whatever the interpretation put on these developments, it can be argued that there has been a process of 'securitization' going on in

Russian life since the end of the 1990s, in two senses. First, in the technical, political science sense of 'securitization', policy decisions have been made for avowed reasons of state security. This is not a phenomenon unique to Russia, and indeed the 'war on terror' has been a justification for policy decisions the world over since 2001. In the Russian case, decisions such as halting the direct election of regional leaders in 2005, harassing certain religious groups for the possession of extremist literature, and limiting the media and electoral space of opposition voices have all been justified by reference to state security.

Second, the term 'securitization' can be used to refer to the increasing role of the security services in Russia since 2000. Indeed, it could be argued that such a process began under Yeltsin, as three of his last four prime ministers had backgrounds in the security services. Certainly there is a group of influential figures in Russian politics today known as the *siloviki*, which is the Russian term for men with career experience in the force ministries and security services. While there may be arguments over the precise make-up and role of this group, the term has come to be used to signify those who prefer state control and lean towards authoritarian over democratic means. They do not dominate Russian politics unchallenged – and indeed President Medvedev himself does not really fit into this group – but they are undoubtedly a powerful influence. Aside from, or perhaps alongside, the *siloviki* as a political force, the presence of the FSB (the domestic successor to the KGB) in Russian life has also become more pronounced, with media, NGOs and business circles among others regularly reporting that an awareness of potential FSB attitudes to their activities has influenced their behaviour. While being some way from the KGB-dominated state of the Soviet years, again the pendulum has swung back from the weakened and demoralized state of Russia's security services in the 1990s.

Civil society in Russia

The American analyst, Gordon Hahn, stated at the beginning of Putin's second term in 2004 that Russia had a regime which could not be classified as democratic, but was rather a 'soft authoritarian' regime. If your starting point for comparison is the Soviet era, then Russia has become markedly more liberal; but if your comparison is with the somewhat anarchic liberties of the first half of the 1990s, then state-strengthening has been accompanied by an increase in authoritarianism. Making inter-state rather than temporal comparisons provides a further option, but this approach has been complicated somewhat by the 'global war on terrorism', which has shifted some perceptions of the ways in which states can justifiably act.

Broad conclusions become problematic, but in the case of Russia today the concept of 'snatch-squad control' offers a helpful framework. The analogy is straightforward. When policing a crowd, a snatch squad may identify particular individuals, move in and arrest them, but leave the vast majority of the crowd alone. In Russia, beginning with the law on religion of 1997, and progressing through laws on social organizations, political parties, extremists, migration, foreigners, the media, information security, and NGOs, there are sufficient regulations in most cases for the state to move with a legal basis against groups or individuals that might be considered in some sense a threat. In particular, the minutiae of registration regulations and the ill-defined catch-all nature of some provisions – for example, the ban in the law on extremism of 'the propaganda of exclusiveness, superiority or inferiority' – mean that, for groups making up civil society, transgressions of the law, deliberate or not, are relatively straightforward to allege or identify.

A healthy civil society is a sign of a consolidated democratic system. In contemporary Russia the development of civil society has been hampered by several factors. First, the registration processes noted above, where the state's desire to control society impinges on the freedom that would facilitate it. Second, the lack of a strong base for civil society, largely a legacy of the Soviet years, when no organization officially existed without it stemming in some way from the Communist Party of the Soviet Union. Research by Marc Morjé Howard (2003) found that, of all the post-Communist countries, Russia had the weakest civil society in the 1990s, and the desperate economic straits in which most Russians found themselves in those years left little energy and motivation for doing much beyond devoting oneself to earning a living. Third, the development of civil society in Russia became caught up in the increasing anti-Westernism and securitization of the second Putin term in particular. Many NGOs were considered to be tools of foreign influence by the FSB, and, more broadly, the state wished to develop a native Russian civil society, not one shaped externally. Such thinking influenced changes to the laws affecting NGOs in 2006, resulting in more stringent and intrusive registration requirements, particularly with regard to groups based abroad.

So, the situation in civil society to some extent mirrors that in other spheres of Russian socio-political life. Great strides were made in the 1990s towards the democratization of Russia, and yet the ideological commitment of the regime to democracy remains uncertain. There was freedom for all sorts of groups to establish themselves in the 1990s – albeit that those with Western support, particularly financial, flourished most readily – but now there is greater control and a small percentage of religious organizations, political parties and other elements of civil society have had action taken against them on the basis of the registration laws in place. The Russian regime seeks, primarily, a manageable state. Whether there is motive enough for a deeper democratic shift now that such a state has been achieved is doubtful, but not beyond the realms of feasibility.

7

Ideas and Culture

There are few countries in the world where the concept of a 'national idea' is quite as strong as it is in Russia. Nor perhaps are there many countries where arguments are so fierce over precisely what makes up this idea, and how important it is. In this chapter we explore the question of the Russian Idea, as a precursor to a discussion of the importance of ideology and identity in Russian life. In order to understand a little about how Russians live, it is essential to know something of the shared experiences and narratives that shape national consciousness. We consider the story that Russia's rulers tell about their country today.

We investigate too the place of culture in contemporary Russia, looking at the role played by literature, music and other art forms in illuminating our understanding of the Russian nation and its people. The nation that gave the world great writers such as Pushkin, Tolstoy and Dostoevsky, and great composers such as Tchaikovsky and Shostakovich, has an impressive heritage on which to draw. While the post-Soviet era has not been an easy time for the identification of contemporary literary and musical greats, the twenty-first century is beginning to highlight names known both in Russia and beyond. We consider briefly too the place of sport in the life of Russia, and Russians, today.

The Russian Idea

A glance at the titles of a number of academic books written about Russia in recent years reveals that there are elements of commonly acknowledged Russian-ness that go beyond political and socio-economic explanations to touch something deeper: *Russia and Soul, The Agony of the Russian Idea, Russian Messianism, Night of Stone: Death and Memory in Twentieth Century Russia, Russia in Search of Itself* – all these are academic books published in the past few years from a range of disciplines, which have in common an awareness of distinctive elements of the Russian identity.

The Russian Idea is, at its broadest, the sense that there is a destiny and identity inherent within Russian-ness that is not Western, that has different cultural roots and different core values. It is the idea – or perhaps more accurately, the myth – that Russians are less materialistic, less individualistic, and less shallow than their Western counterparts, and instead have a greater commitment to spiritual values, egalitarianism, community, and the deeper mysteries of faith and eschatology.

As discussed in Chapter 2, the empirical evidence for such claims is weak, but the strength of these claims comes in their widespread acceptance. Russians go to places of worship and become involved in the collective institutions of civil society far less than do – in this order – Americans, Western Europeans, and even, as Marc Morjé Howard found out in a recent study (Howard, 2003), the inhabitants of other post-Communist states. None the less, such hard data as church attendance figures and engagement in civil society do not measure a more elusive inner sense and self-perception. Indeed, an authentically Russian response might be to deem as typically Western and materialist any attempt to measure the inchoate depth of such concepts as community, togetherness, spirituality and national identity.

It is perhaps difficult to talk about a vague 'Russian Idea' without falling into clichés and generalizations. As Dale Pesmen points out in her book *Russia and Soul*:

> Some Russians and others dismiss Russian soul as a hackneyed notion irrelevant to tough millennial post-Soviets. Some mourn it, implying that whatever it was died. Some figure good riddance. In all these cases, Russian soul's vitality is assumed to have disappeared. Russian soul was certainly a myth, notion, image, consoling fiction, trope of romantic national self-definition, and what romantic foreigners came to Russia for. (Pesmen, 2002)

Pesmen's research notes that many Russians are themselves aware of the myth-like elements of the Russian Idea, and talk of it in self-mocking, satirical terms. And yet, as noted in many places in this book, there is a reality to the generalizations that finds outlet in political debate, policy formation, international relations and so on.

James Billington (2004) identifies three forces that give Russian culture its distinctiveness:

- *A traditional religious base.* During the 1990s – with the loss of the certainties of communism – the Russian state, and arguably its people, sought to define a national idea. Indeed a state-sponsored competition was held, with a prize awarded to the essayist who best summed up what it meant to be Russian. Almost without fail, writers and politicians – atheists and believers alike – settled on Russian Orthodoxy as a key locus of Russian identity. Russian Orthodoxy celebrates the mystery of faith, ahead of the intellectual explanations of Western Protestants. It promotes a community of believers ahead of the hierarchies of Roman Catholicism. Politicians of the left, right and centre frequently seek to portray themselves as supporters of Orthodoxy, since nothing else better serves to identify them with Russia, its uniqueness, its history and its people.

  Religion in Russia, however, is not just about nationalism and Orthodoxy, or even about nationalism and Islam. There is a tradition of an openness among the Russian people to spirituality, as opposed to organized and doctrinally precise religion. Russian peasant faith often drew from diverse sources, including Asiatic shamanism and paganism. Within such a setting, superstitions, premonitions, curses, blessings and ecstatic experiences all had a place. As too did the figure of the 'Holy Man' or 'Holy Fool', archetypically a bearded, somewhat wild, mystical figure who might live apart from society and be called upon as an adviser and healer. Grigory Rasputin, the womanizing Siberian monk who wielded significant influence in the court of the last Tsar, is a version of this figure. Such spiritual and mystical elements of life do not by any means belong solely to Russia's past; they remain part of the experience of many Russian citizens today (Lewis, 2000).
- *Periodic borrowing from the West.* As noted in Chapter 1, the question of 'catching up' with the West is a recurrent feature in Russian history. Such borrowing entails an ambiguity, with a desire to take the best that the West can offer while retaining a Russian identity and resisting the overwhelming of Russian culture. Russia since the later 1990s has demonstrated this ambiguity in many areas, with a broad opening up to the West resulting in the cautious

embrace of many of the facets of 'globalization', combined with a determined resistance to what the more extreme opponents of Westernization have called 'cultural genocide'.

- *A special feeling for land and nature.* Russia was urbanized more recently than most other European nations, and in most families it is only a matter of a generation or two at most before rural, predominantly peasant, roots can be found. Furthermore, the vast expanse of Russia's territory means that it contains some of the most sparsely populated areas on earth. Nature and the land continue to play a part in many lives, even for urban inhabitants. The celebrated *dacha* (summer house) beyond the boundaries of the cities is the destination for millions of Russians in the summer months.

  Trips to the countryside to pick berries and mushrooms in season are regular motifs in Russian literature, and continue to be regular occurrences for many Russians. At the *dachas*, and even within the environs of the cities, private plots where vegetables and fruit can be grown are common – indeed, there is strong evidence to suggest that such private agriculture kept the Soviet Union going when the official state-administered agricultural industry failed.

  This feeling for the land has made particularly controversial the recent post-Soviet reforms seeking to open up the market for buying and selling land (see Chapter 5, Box 5.4). At some deep level, the sale of land taps at the root of the cry of peasant revolts across Russia's centuries – 'the land belongs to the people'.

Alongside the elusive questions of the Russian soul and the Russian Idea, it is also possible to point to identifiable experiences in history and repeated features of everyday life that help to explain contemporary Russia's cultural identity.

Death and martial culture

The experience of violent death and social chaos marked the Russian people as a whole in the twentieth century. From the First World War in 1914–18, followed by revolution in 1917 and the civil war of 1918–20, with its attendant shortages and famines, through the largely self-inflicted famine of 1932–3, and the mass arrests and executions of the Stalinist terror – over 30 million Russians died prematurely even before the Second World War began. Between 1941

Illustration 7.1   Martial culture, Red Square, Moscow, May 2008

Preparations for the Victory Day parade, to commemorate victory over the Nazis in 1945.

and 1945 the war claimed a further 28 million victims, far more than in any of the other combatant nations. Soviet military losses alone were over 8 million, when US military losses were under 350,000 and British losses nearer to 300,000.

Such experiences cannot but leave an impact on the Russian people. No family remained untouched by the devastation of war. In comparison, the second half of the twentieth century was relatively less traumatic, with the war in Afghanistan (1979–88) being the only major conflict of note. None the less, some observers have portrayed the upheavals of the 1990s as being of significant magnitude. The British historian, Christopher Read, wrote tentatively of the difficulties involved in comparing the political mass murders of the Stalin years with the 'economic mass murder' of the 1990s (Read, 2001).

The impact of the Second World War on the Russian nation is difficult to overstate. If the veneration of veterans is noteworthy in, say, Great Britain or the United States, then it is doubly so in Russia, which has, of course, a particularly Russo-centric view of the Second World

War. The Great Patriotic War, as Russia terms this war, started for the Soviet Union when Germany invaded in June 1941, and ended with the German surrender on 9 May 1945. Little mention is made of the pact between Germany and the Soviet Union in 1939, which led directly to the occupation of a divided Poland by invading Nazi and Soviet forces and left Great Britain standing alone against Hitler's forces in Europe. Nor is much made of the continuation of the Second World War outside Europe until victory over Japan was achieved in September 1945. For Russians, 'Victory Day' is 9 May, which remains a universally celebrated public holiday in Russia. In 2008, the Victory Day celebrations were given even greater status than they had been for most of the post-Soviet era, with the restoration of a major military parade through Red Square in Moscow.

During the atheistic rule of the Soviet Communist Party, elements of reverence for the military provided key unifying features where perhaps religion might previously have played a role. For example, the tradition developed that, on their wedding day, couples would follow a civil ceremony with a visit to the local war memorial, where photographs would be taken. This practice continues today.

Of course, the martial culture of Soviet society was enhanced because:

- the Soviet Union's superpower status depended above all else on its military strength, especially its nuclear arsenal;
- military training formed a compulsory element of the school curriculum; and
- conscription into the armed forces was also maintained.

In contemporary Russia, conscription remains in place, but the majority of potential conscripts manage to avoid it by taking advantage of the variety of exemptions and loopholes available. As already noted in Chapter 6, the period of conscription was reduced from two years to one in 2008. This was partly designed to discourage such draft avoidance, and included the closure of a number of loopholes which had previously facilitated this practice. Military training was dropped as part of the school curriculum in the immediate post-Soviet era, but by the end of 2003 a new education bill that was to reintroduce it was given its first reading in the Russian parliament. Broad support for this move reflects the widespread respect for the armed forces that still exists in Russia, where post-Soviet opinion polls have long shown the army to be the second most-trusted public organization after the Russian Orthodox Church.

Physical expression of respect for these pillars of Russian identity can be seen in the new developments in Moscow under Mayor Luzhkov from the mid-1990s onwards. In 1995, in time for the fiftieth anniversary of the end of the Second World War, a vast new memorial, 'Victory Park', was opened – though its accompanying metro line was not completed until some seven years later. In 1996, a statue of the most famous Russian commander of the Second World War, Marshal Zhukov, was erected near the entrance to Red Square. Perhaps the most noticeable new addition to the Moscow cityscape in recent years has been the Cathedral of Christ the Saviour, built between 1995 and 1997 in time to mark the somewhat contrived celebratory anniversary of 850 years since the foundation of the city.

Russian self-conceptualization – *byt*, *sobornost* and literary models

The Russian word *byt* expresses the concept of life as it is lived, those features of everyday life that are common and recognizable to most as elements of daily existence. The very prevalence of such an idea as *byt* demonstrates an awareness among many Russians of elements in national life that are sufficiently common to count as communal experience. *Byt* stands in opposition to the soul, in that it tends towards the negative side of life, those things that drag people down. This sense of an everyday life that burdened all was perhaps particularly marked in the Soviet years, when the ubiquity of the Party's rule and its fetish for conformity, order and controlling the lives of its citizens meant that the inhabitants of Minsk would readily recognize the lives lived by the inhabitants of Vladivostok, thousands of miles to the east.

In the first decade of the twenty-first century it is difficult to identify precisely those elements in Russia's identity and everyday life that owe their existence simply to the Soviet experience, and those that are part of some deeper Russian-ness. For example, the root Communist ideal that the workers of the world would unite was sown in fertile ground in Russia, where the concept of *sobornost* – a mystical unity – was central to national Orthodox identity. Similarly, the workers' councils, or *soviets*, of the Soviet era could build on the tradition of the peasant village council, or *mir*.

And what about the ubiquitous influence of bureaucracy in Russia? Anybody doing business in Russia today will complain about the difficulties imposed by often contradictory regulations, unknown to the many, but zealously applied by the few. But how far back can we trace this element of Russian life, which so readily feeds into the corruption virulent in contemporary Russian officialdom? It is easy to see the roots of bureaucratic power in the deadening hand of the Soviet centrally planned economy, with its oversight of the most minuscule details across the length and breadth of its vast empire. None the less, a cursory glance at some of the classics of pre-Soviet nineteenth-century Russian literature reveal that the overweening bureaucrat did not spring newly-formed from the flames of the Communist revolution. Nikolai Gogol's comedy, *The Government Inspector* (1836), is based on the premise that such people wielded inordinate influence in Russia, and was written almost a century before the centrally planned economy was established.

As we note later in this chapter, Russia has traditionally, since the Enlightenment, maintained a strong intellectual and literary tradition. Indeed, the very word 'intelligentsia' is Russian. At the turn of the millennium, another nineteenth-century literary model was recognized by a number of observers as the Yeltsin presidency gave way to that of Putin. Ivan Goncharov's novel of 1859, *Oblomov*, told the story of a fat, lazy Russian landowner – the eponymous central character of the novel – who scarcely ever got out of bed, from where he conducted whatever business he could be bothered to conduct. Juxtaposed to Oblomov is the German estate manager, Stolz, who is hard-working, businesslike and efficacious. In this model, Yeltsin was Oblomov, given to excessive drinking and being regularly absent from his office for long periods, seemingly incapable of doing much beyond talking about Russian greatness, as his 'estate' – that is, Russia – fell into debt and disrepair. Putin was the efficient and pragmatic Stolz, an identification facilitated by the fact that Putin speaks fluent German and had served as a KGB officer in East Germany for several years in the late 1980s. Under Putin, Russia began to take decisive action to reverse its decline. This literary analogy is one that fits well with the narrative of national identity created by the Putin regime in the first decade of the twenty-first century.

Putin's political narrative and the use of history

Throughout the Putin presidency and beyond into that of Medvedev, Russia's ruling regime has put significant effort into the construction

Illustration 7.2   Contrasting influences on the official narrative of contemporary Russia, Red Square, Moscow, May 2008

A Russian Orthodox icon of Christ is visible behind a temporary standard erected to commemorate Victory Day, marking the end of the Second World War. Note that this standard includes the Cyrillic letters, 'CCCP', meaning USSR.

of a national narrative that would make sense of the historical development of Russia, explain current policies, and develop a national idea suited to contemporary Russia. National identities arise partly from below, from 'the people', and are created partly from above, by the rulers. Both of these elements draw on history and notions of national consciousness. To understand contemporary Russia, it is vital to know what it says about itself, or, more precisely, what its leaders say to its people.

During the Yeltsin presidency (1991–9), the regime had failed in its attempts to build a Russian national identity. In terms of drawing on history and notions of national consciousness, there were three particular problems. First, Yeltsin's national identity narrative was polarizing, not unifying. It centred on a wholesale rejection of the Communist past – a stance particularly evident in the pivotal presidential election of 1996, when Yeltsin was presented as the only hope to prevent a return to communism. Second, symbols are key in the creation of national identity, and the Yeltsin regime struggled to find appropriate ones. At the 2000 Olympic Games in Sydney, when Russia's gold medallists stood on the podium, they had no recognizable national anthem to sing. Russia under Yeltsin had adopted a far-from-rousing provisional anthem called 'Patriotic Song', written in the nineteenth century by composer Mikhail Glinka and lacking in words. Nor did the new national holidays of that era strike many Russians as appropriate symbols for national celebration – Constitution Day (12 December) marked 1993's flawed constitutional referendum; and Independence Day (12 June) marked Russia's break with the Soviet Union. The very newness of such symbols meant that they had shallow roots in the national consciousness. Third, the narrative and symbols around the Russian national identity in the Yeltsin years came to mark a period of national decline. They became associated not with Russian greatness but with poverty, lawlessness, a weak pro-Western foreign policy and a corrupt elite.

President Putin's central narrative of power sought to define his period in office positively against the failures of the Yeltsin years. The key *leitmotifs* of Putin's national identity discourse became stability, unity and the notion of Russia as a great power. These themes have been to the fore since the beginning of Putin's presidency in 2000, and have developed in substance and prevalence in official discourse.

Perhaps the first issue in the Putin regime's narrative was the question of what was to be done with the Soviet years. Too often in the Western media, the impression is given that in some way contemporary Russia is, for want of a better word, 're-Sovietizing'. In other words, becoming increasingly like the old Soviet Union. We have argued in several places in this book that many developments – centralizing the government, reducing space for opposition and civil society, creating uncompetitive elections, believing that Russia should have a sphere of influence in international relations – have echoes of Soviet era practices. Let us be clear, though, that such practices are not exclusively Soviet in character. More importantly, when it comes to the core element of the Soviet regime – namely a belief in the Communist ideology – the Russian government has no time for that at all.

At the beginning of his presidency, Putin's 'eve of millennium' address tried to explain the balance he sought in dealing with the

Soviet past. On the one hand he talked about the 'outrageous price our country and its people had to pay for that Bolshevik experiment', and the 'historic futility' of Communism's 'blind alley ... far away from the mainstream of civilization'. At the same time, though, he refused to deny the 'unquestionable achievements of those times'. In a speech to the State Council in December 2000, Putin addressed the question of state symbols and called on the members of the Council:

> not to burn bridges, and not to split society once more. If we accept the fact that in no way could we use the symbols of the previous epochs including the Soviet one, then we must admit that our mothers and fathers lived useless and senseless lives, that they lived in vain. I can't accept it either with my mind or my heart. There was already a period of time in our history when we rewrote everything anew. We can act in the same way today, too. We can change the flag, the anthem and the coat of arms. But in that case it would certainly be right to call us rootless creatures. Let us direct all our tireless energy and our whole talent not to destruction but to creation.

The symbols that were adopted achieved Putin's desired effect admirably – the coat of arms from the pre-imperial era, the flag from the imperial period, and the Soviet anthem, but with new words. These were a symbolic representation of the commitment to unity, stability and Russia's great-power status, which we have noted as the *leitmotifs* of the official Russian identity today. The early years of Putin's presidency demonstrated a commitment to this version of national identity. Unity as a theme was encapsulated in the notion of trying to heal the breach in Russian history caused by the Communist revolution of 1917. Putin made a point of visiting communities of Russian émigré families who had fled the Bolsheviks. At an émigré cemetery in Paris in 2000, he declared that 'we are all children of Russia' and that the time had come to unite. In Russia, the political vehicle created to back Putin in parliament was given the name Unity, and later, United Russia. The rhetoric of stability is related to that of unity. In his first public statement as acting president on the eve of the millennium, Putin declared that the Russian people had had their fill of cataclysmic events and radical reforms; he promised to bring stability. In addition, Russia's place as one of the world's great powers has been emphasized by Putin and by his successor, Medvedev.

These early symbolic statements and gestures set down the base on which the revived concept of Russian national identity was to be built in the Putin era. Its content was then developed by Putin and his colleagues through engagement with Russian history and philosophy, and an ever-widening public promotion of a Russian national identity that embraced the Tsarist era, lauded those who fought against communism, and yet refused to reject entirely the experiences of the Russian people during the Soviet years. Russia's national identity discourse now celebrates those who actively fought for the Whites against the Communist Reds in Russia's post-revolutionary civil war (1918–22). In October 2005, Putin attended the reburial in Moscow of General Denikin and the philosopher Ivan Il'in. Denikin was a leader of the White armies in the civil war, and Il'in an anti-Bolshevik philosopher expelled from Russia by Lenin in 1922. Il'in was much quoted for a time by Putin and Russian government ministers, as were other anti-Bolshevik professors of the revolutionary era, such as the legal scholar Lev Petrazhitskii and the historian Vasilii Klyuchevskii.

The Slavophile notion of a distinct Russian civilization that differs from 'the West' is prevalent in the philosophy of Ivan Il'in, who is lauded as the Russian philosopher so sure that communism would collapse that he wrote about what Russia would require once this happened. His emphasis on a 'Russian democracy', suited to the circumstances of Russia, found echoes in Putin's reactions to criticism from the West that he was taking Russia down an anti-democratic path. There are also strong elements of morality and opposition to corruption in the writings of Il'in, which have been cited by Putin. In his 2007 presidential address to parliament, Putin repeatedly made reference to the importance of Russia's historically moral and spiritual character.

The emphasis on a 'Russian way' is not supposed to be isolationist but rather, in line with declared Russian foreign policy, to demonstrate that Russia is a strong sovereign nation and will engage in the global community as such. Again, historical figures are used to make the point. Foreign Minister Lavrov has lauded the contribution of Fedor Golovin, the late-seventeenth-century chief minister to Westernizing Tsar Peter the Great. Golovin played a key role in expanding Russia's international influence by diplomatic means. Another historical figure resurrected by official discourse during the Putin presidency was Aleksandr Shtiglits, a nineteenth-century state official, banker and philanthropist who provides in some ways an ideal type for contemporary Russian officials. He was connected to both the state and the world of business and finance, and is portrayed as having used his wealth and influence for the good of those who were less well off.

The starkest symbolic break with the Communist era made by President Putin was the abolition in 2004 of 7 November as a national holiday. During the Soviet era this date was Revolution Day, the main Soviet holiday and symbol of Soviet power, with its massive military parades through Red Square in front of the Party leadership. Under Yeltsin, the day remained on the list of national holidays, although in 1996 Yeltsin had renamed it the Day of Reconciliation and Accord. Under Putin, 7 November was removed completely from the list of official holidays, and National Unity Day on 4 November replaced Revolution Day. National Unity Day commemorates the liberation of Moscow from the Poles in 1612. This event ended the civil war and foreign intervention of the 'Time of Troubles' and ushered in the Romanov dynasty, which remained in power until the revolution of 1917.

When National Unity Day was first celebrated in 2005, television programmes were broadcast explaining the significance of this day. Clear parallels were drawn between the civil conflict and crisis of the early-seventeenth-century 'Time of Troubles', and the 'time of troubles' experience by Russia in the 1990s. The implication was that, just as the Romanov dynasty brought stability in 1612, so the Putin era had brought stability after the chaos of the Yeltsin years. Other elements were also woven into the narrative around National Unity Day. It celebrates a Russian victory over Western domination, symbolized by Orthodox Russia beating Catholic Poland. Its instigation also facilitated a dig at the oligarchs, who flourished under Yeltsin. The 'seven *boyars*' who reputedly sought their own personal interest, wealth and power in league with enemies of Russia abroad in the seventeenth century stood as types for the 'seven bankers', the seven major oligarchs of the Yeltsin era, broadly accused of the same behaviour. For a regime that had identified oligarchs such as Berezovsky and Khodorkovsky as its chief opponents, such a narrative around Russian national identity was seen as being particularly helpful.

The process of re-creating a narrative of Russian national identity involves symbols, discourse and a good deal of official effort in creating national holidays, propagandizing a particular version of history through speeches, ceremonies, books and the media, and organizing international conferences and cultural events. The result is a narrative that is in line with the broad policy statements of the current regime. However, this focus on national identity does not have a straightforward political effect. Very little of the effort expended in crafting official narratives around historical figures, philosophical treatises and civilizational dialogues has any direct impact on the mass of Russian people. Television programmes on National Unity Day can cleverly set out comparisons between the Yeltsin years and the 'Time of Troubles', but this does not mean that people will watch them, let alone take in their nuanced message. Polls in 2005 showed that 63 per cent of Russians disapproved of the decision to stop celebrating Revolution Day.

The discourses of Putin's national identity project are too neat for the complexities of everyday political life. They contain ambiguities and tensions around issues such as the lack of progress in fighting corruption, whether Russia is competing with or working alongside other major powers, and the disjunction between overlapping notions of the West, the USA and Europe. One such ambiguity often picked up on by Western observers relates to the place of Stalin in Russian history. As we have noted, the narrative of Russian identity developed during the Putin years seeks to distance itself from the political elements of the Soviet era while acknowledging that not everything that happened during those decades needs to be disparaged. So, for example, Putin's Soviet heroes are not Communist leaders, but men such as cosmonaut Yurii Gagarin, Second World War general Georgii Zhukov, and dissident author Aleksandr Solzhenitsyn (see Box 1.2). At the same time though, we have seen the central place in Russian identity of the Second World War and its continued position as the key national holiday in Russia. The clear difficulty is that Russia's leader in this great victory was also its most brutal Communist dictator, Josef Stalin.

Ideology

We have dealt so far in this chapter with the realm of ideas and the cultural currency of contemporary Russia. In any country there exists a storehouse of assumptions, commonplace attitudes, clichés, humour and shared experiences. A lack of awareness of these will swiftly identify an outsider, and it is part of our task so far in this chapter to touch on some of the central elements of this common existence, as well as identifying what the regime says about itself. The chapter will conclude with an overview of key elements in Russian culture and popular life (literature, film, music and sport). Before that, however, let us consider briefly the role of ideology in shaping contemporary Russia.

There has been no state in history to which ideology has been more important than it was to the Soviet Union. As noted in our discussion of *byt* above, the Soviet state demanded conformity, and this conformity extended to the opinions expressed by both state and people. The very legitimacy of the state depended on acceptance of its central idea, and the resources of the state were applied to propagandizing this idea in everyday life. So predominant was the state's ideological nature that the Russian Constitution of 1993, still in force today, felt it necessary to ban the state from ever again having an ideology. The Yeltsin, Putin and Medvedev regimes have all tried to build up a national idea or narrative, but none of them have sought to impose an ideology. It is for this reason, among others, why talk of a 'new Cold War' between the West and Russia is questionable. During the Cold War, the opposing sides did not just have divergent interests, they had fundamentally opposed world views. That is no longer the case.

However, the ideological legacy of the Soviet era still has an impact in Russia today, almost two decades after the collapse of communism in Russia. The Soviet regime based its legitimacy on the ideology of Marxism–Leninism. Of course, as with all regimes, other legitimating factors came into play, but underpinning all these factors was the supreme legitimation of ideology. Put starkly, the only justification the Soviet regime could put forward for its seizure and retention of power in 1917–18 was belief in the correctness of Marxist ideology. Were the question to be asked of the regime at any point in the Soviet Union's history, 'Why are you in power?', the only answer that could be given was that Marxist ideology correctly interpreted the world, that the building of communism was the goal of history, and that the Communist Party of the Soviet Union was at the vanguard of history. Little wonder, then, that the Soviet authorities set such store throughout the USSR's existence in propagandizing its ideology.

The Soviet people as a whole were heavily politicized. Marxism–Leninism formed a compulsory element of the university curriculum, as well as being proclaimed in work places across the land. Consequently, as the Soviet Union collapsed and the Russian state was re-established, democratic institutions were not planted on virgin political land but in one of the world's most politicized countries. The nature of the politicization of the Soviet people tended towards duality and polarization. The propaganda of Marxism–Leninism revolved around the clash of two systems, capitalism and communism, engaged in a zero-sum game. In this black and white conceptualization, little room existed for shades of grey, for compromise, for the borrowing of ideas, or for cooperating with ideological opponents.

The consequences of both these factors – politicization and polarization – can be discerned in Russia today. Having for all of their lives been obliged to participate in some form or other in political life, many Russians now enjoy the freedom not to be involved in politics. This 'anti-politics' attitude is built on a distrust of political parties in general, and, fuelled by the corruption of the post-Soviet years, on a distrust of politicians and of political ideologies. Consequently, Russia's biggest party, United Russia, boasts of its lack of an ideology, and proclaims itself to be a party of managers rather than politicians. Within its ranks it has people with all sorts of differing political approaches, brought together predominantly by access to power. The calculation is clear. To a sufficiently large proportion of people in Russia 'politics' and 'ideology' are dirty words. In twenty-first-century Russia, the anti-politicians have come to power.

Culture and contemporary reality

The importance of literature and art in the lived experience of educated Russians was heightened during much of the twentieth century by the strict censorship that the Soviet authorities exercised in these areas. State control of literature, music and art in order to force it into the straitjacket of service to what was a fundamentally utilitarian, anti-spiritual and philistine regime affected the intellectual psyche of the Russian people.

To love art forms for their own sake was to defend a small area of personal independence from the authorities. Literature and music were used to express subtle – and not so subtle – dissatisfaction with the dominant ruling party, and to interpret these messages required a high-level of artistic literacy. Intellectual debates still rage, for example, over the precise meaning of passages in Shostakovich's symphonies. In the Soviet era, the heavy literary journals would regularly sell out on publication, and people would pass round carefully copied typescripts of banned works. The word *samizdat* (literally 'self-published') became – like *glasnost'* several years later – a term sufficiently well-used to be understood by many in the West, referring as it did to illegal literature of all forms, from heavyweight novels, through political statements against the regime, to religious tracts.

Although strong state censorship was in place for most of the Soviet era, the state education system none the less helped to produce a highly literate population that knew not only the Russian classics of Pushkin, Tolstoy and Dostoevsky, but also a range of foreign classics. Russian knowledge of, and respect for, the works of Shakespeare, for example, can often seem to exceed that in England. In the early 1990s, as the Soviet Union dissolved itself and censorship disappeared, many Russians avidly snapped up those works that had previously not been available. Multi-volume sets of the works of dissident Soviet authors such as Solzhenitsyn, Pasternak and Bulgakov appeared on the bookstalls swiftly set up around the Moscow metro system, alongside complete works of other literary giants, copies of the Bible, and the ubiquitous 'Teach Yourself English' courses that were increasingly *de rigeur* for Russians seeking to make a life for themselves in the uncertain new world of the market economy.

If at first in the post-Soviet era the bookstalls and kiosks of Moscow reflected the relatively highbrow tastes of the intelligentsia and focused on Russian works, they swiftly branched out as the almost anarchic freedoms of the early 1990s took hold. Pornography began to be sold openly on the streets of Moscow, attracting such crowds of browsers that stallholders began to charge for leafing through the merchandise at the stall as well as for the actual purchase of it. Kiosks selling pirate video copies of the latest Hollywood blockbusters appeared, often able to provide purchasers with films within days of release. Similarly, pirate CDs of the work of previously unobtainable Western and Russian musicians became easily available. Back on the bookstalls, things were also changing, with classic literature giving way to detective stories, thrillers, science fiction and fantasy. Russian translations of Western bestsellers such as Agatha Christie and Tom Clancy elbowed the more highbrow literature out of the way.

As the 1990s progressed, however, the somewhat naïve excitement of the first flush of cultural liberty began to give way to a more sophisticated and unique popular culture. The clichés of the late Soviet period revolved around the supposed desire among young Russians for anything Western – scarcely a Western traveller to the Soviet Union in the last decades of its existence was sent off without being advised to pack an extra pair of Levis for selling on arrival – and the apparent preoccupation of Russians with outdated Western music, notably the Beatles and 1970s heavy rock bands. President Medvedev embodies this latter cliché, with a genuine and much publicized devotion to the music of English rock band Deep Purple, who played a private concert for his benefit in the Kremlin in early 2008, forty years after the band was formed.

Whatever truth exists in these clichés, the younger generation of Russians swiftly blew it away in the 1990s. Russian youth movements emerged with a distinctly indigenous edge; literary genres and musical styles alike drew on Western examples and swiftly added Russian ingredients. Russian detective writers found plenty of material in the crime-ridden business culture of the new Russia, and other genres too (notably fantasy and science fiction) soon identified their own authors instead of merely accepting translations of Western bestsellers. A similar process of adoption and adaptation occurred across musical genres, culminating in the unprecedented – and short-lived – dominance of the UK and European pop and dance charts for several weeks in 2003 by Russian artists, the teenage faux-lesbian duo Tatu. Tatu were also trail-blazers for Russia in the Eurovision Song Contest, finishing third in 2003. Russian singer Dima Bilan won the Eurovision Song Contest in 2008, a victory considered to be highly prestigious in Russia, and granting Moscow the right to stage the contest in 2009.

Literature

As with any country, Russia's literature reflects the state of the nation. The great novels of Tolstoy and Dostoevsky in the second half of the nineteenth century addressed the 'accursed questions' of the human soul, alongside the questions of Russia's place in the world and the social divisions within Russian society. We have mentioned already in Chapter 1 the prescience of Chekhov's play, *The Cherry Orchard* (1904), closing with the sound of an axe striking a tree, symbolizing the blows being struck to the old social order as the revolutionary twentieth century dawned.

During the Soviet era, the Communist regime sought to subjugate literature to its own demands and ideas. The genre of 'socialist realism' told stirring tales of devotion to work and building the new industrialized Soviet state; for example, in works such as Nikolai

Ostrovsky's *How the Steel Was Tempered* (1934). The official policy was that literature should be positive and optimistic. The counterpart of socialist realist literature in painting and sculpture was the healthy, well-proportioned, musclebound worker, sleeves rolled-up, a smile on the face, and a hammer or sickle (sometimes both) raised aloft. Such images fitted the self-conceptualization of the Communist elite, which incidentally happened to control all publishers, exhibition halls, concert venues and so on.

Of course, the best artists and writers, almost by their nature, are most unlikely to shape their output in line with such crass strictures. Pasternak and Solzhenitsyn were both awarded a Nobel Prize for Literature, though the Soviet regime persuaded Pasternak to decline his award. Both smuggled their greatest works, respectively *Dr Zhivago* and *The Gulag Archipelago*, to the West for publication and were vilified by the authorities at home. Pasternak remained in the Soviet Union until his death in 1960. Solzhenitsyn was exiled until finally returning to Russia in 1994, where he was lionized by successive presidents. He died in 2008, shortly before his ninetieth birthday. Other writers, such as Yury Trifonov (1925–81), succeeded in remaining within the pale of official Soviet literature and yet touch on topics which, so far as their readers were concerned, were much more 'realistic' than socialist realism's tales of building communism. Trifonov wrote, earlier than most but relatively obliquely, about the difficulties of the Stalin years.

From the 1960s onwards, fiction dealing with the more risqué topics – such as the purges, the drudgery of modern urban life, and the double domestic/professional burden carried by Soviet women – became increasingly common. While the state sought to control and guide the content of literature throughout the Soviet era, the degree of artistic licence that was allowed ebbed and flowed at different times. There was a cultural thaw in the Khrushchev years (1953–64), and in the late 1960s and early 1970s more controversial works, such as Solzhenitsyn's devastating labour-camp critique, *One Day in the Life of Ivan Denisovich*, were published in the Soviet Union, before later being banned.

As the Soviet era came to an end and censorship disappeared, it was something of an irony that the state of Russian literature can be said to have declined somewhat. There were two main reasons for this:

- the new freedoms meant that many readers turned to what had previously been unavailable – the banned works of Soviet dissidents, Western literature, and the less highbrow genres of fantasy, crime and thrillers; and

- the removal of the dead hand of the state from its monopoly control of publishing meant an end to the focus on more literary works – albeit of varying quality – which the Soviet system encouraged.

For most of the 1990s, then, pulp fiction became the dominant force in Russian literature, with a number of authors selling books in their millions, producing novels at a great rate, and being paid royalties far below what would be paid to authors in the West. The stories of Aleksandra Marinina, Viktor Dotsenko and many others are set in the world of the mafia and criminal gangs. Liberally sprinkled with the jargon of that milieu, such works do not shy away from the sex and violence associated with the lives they portray. Set all of this within a fast-paced and tightly plotted story, and the sales follow. The very best-selling authors are set apart from their competitors by the creation of strong hero figures who became the centre of their novels, such as Marinina's female detective, Anastasia Kamenskaya.

The literary purists bemoaned such a state of affairs, as Russia became far more like the rest of the world in its dealings with literature. No longer were writers quite so venerated and so much a part of public and political discourse as they had previously been, and in many ways the Russian people's special relationship with literature has gone – or at the very least, been put on hold. None the less, the literary scene in contemporary Russia has gradually regained strength in recent years, helped to some extent – certainly in terms of publicity – by the establishment of prizes such as the Russian Booker Prize, the Big Book Prize (with a generous cash award, partly funded by the Russian state), and the National Bestseller Award. Several themes are apparent in contemporary Russian literature. Some writers, such as the 2006 Russian Booker winner, Olga Slavnikova, and former Soviet dissident, Vladimir Sorenko, have written novels assessing the state of contemporary Russia and imagining a dystopian future of political violence and authoritarianism. Others have tended to look back, for example, to the great literature of Russia's past. The prolific Dmitrii Bykov has not only written biographies of Boris Pasternak and the author and singer Bulat Okudzhava, but also refers back to the writings of Gogol in his work. Alexander Ilichevsky, the 2007 Russian Booker winner, and Zakhar Prilepin, winner of the National Bestseller Award in 2008, both received recognition for novels that present realistic and uncompromising portrayals of life and poverty in post-Soviet Russia.

Indeed, it is this world which, in different ways, is also reflected in the writings of Viktor Pelevin, whose prose reflects the chaotic Russia he portrays. Pelevin's writing shows a nihilistic world infused with materialism, Buddhist philosophy, drug-taking, computer games, advertising slogans and violence; he writes in a style that is cinematic, episodic and impressionistic. In this approach, Pelevin certainly taps into and reflects a particular strand in Russian literature, his writing in places being reminiscent of Dostoevsky's psychological portraits, such as *Notes from the Underground*, or Pilnyak's portrayal of post-revolutionary Russian in 1919, *The Naked Year*.

Though Pelevin and his fellow literary authors have to some extent become known outside Russia, such fame has been among those who follow Russian literature rather than among the Western reading public in general. Boris Akunin, however, has made the breakthrough that Pelevin and others have not, and is a Russian author – although born in Georgia, he has lived in Moscow for over half a century – who publishes and is a bestseller in both Europe and the United States. Akunin writes detective thrillers, but of a slightly more genteel type than the blockbuster mafia novels discussed above. Instead, Akunin's stories are set in the nineteenth century, with his hero, Erast Fandorin, owing more to Sherlock Holmes than to contemporary movie heroes.

Film

As with so much in contemporary Russia, the world of film follows a pattern from the late 1980s to the present day of liberalization, Western influence, and then a rebirth of a more distinctly Russian approach. In the last years of the Soviet era the most noteworthy films were those that began to break the taboos imposed by state censorship. *The Cold Summer of '53* (1988) dealt with the labour camps and Khrushchev's decision in 1953 to release large numbers of criminal – as opposed to political – inmates; and *Little Vera* (1988) tackled the social problems of the late Soviet period, becoming renowned both for this and for breaking taboos by its inclusion of a nude scene.

When the Soviet Union collapsed, so too did its state-controlled, and therefore state-funded, studio system, known as Goskino. This meant that funding for Russian films became increasingly scarce. At the same time, Russia opened up to Hollywood blockbusters. Many of the new glossy magazines that began to appear carried the sort of gossip and tittle-tattle surrounding the lives of American film stars that is familiar in the West, and the cinemas showed American films on global release, dubbed into Russian. This state of affairs continues today, but at the same time indigenous film-making has recovered to some extent.

In the 1990s, Nikita Mikhalkov's *Burnt by the Sun* – an account of the brutalities and betrayals of Stalin's terror – and Sergei Bodrov's *Prisoner of the Caucasus* (*Prisoner of the Mountains* in its Western release) were both critically acclaimed and funded by private investors, but made next to no box office impact in the West. *Burnt by the Sun* won an Oscar for best foreign film, and *Prisoner of the Caucasus* was nominated in the same category. Mikhalkov and Bodrov were both nominated again for best foreign film at the Oscars in 2008, with *12* and *The Mongol*, respectively. In a similar vein, in the early years of the twenty-first century, Aleksandr Sukurov's *Russian Ark* (2002) received rave reviews for its cinematographic brilliance. Lavishly costumed and filmed in the Hermitage Museum in St Petersburg, this sweep through 200 years of Russian history is the first full-length feature film ever to be composed of a single unedited shot running uninterrupted from beginning to end. Once again, though, artistic acclaim did not lead to box office success.

However, as Russia's economy grew in the 2000s, so the Russian film industry flourished. The popular basis for this came on the back of growing audiences, as 2007 saw a record of over 100 million cinema tickets sold in Russia, and a number of multi-screen complexes built in Russia's major cities. Though it was foreign films that dominated audience figures, none the less the number of Russian films on general release by 2008 was around a hundred a year, more than double the figure of ten years earlier. What is more, films such as *Night Watch*, by promising director Timur Bekmambetov, showed that Russian films could also be box office hits.

Music

Most of the big names in Russian popular music are little known abroad, with the exception, as noted above, of the duo Tatu, who briefly shot to the top of the European charts in 2003. It is fair to say, however, that an essential part of understanding the cultural make-up of Russians whose formative years were the 1960s and 1970s is an awareness of the icons of Soviet popular music. Two names in particular stand out – Vladimir Vysotsky and Alla Pugacheva. Vysotsky was a gravel-voiced, hard-living, maverick actor turned singer-song-writer, in some ways a Soviet Bob Dylan, in that he played guitar, had a highly distinctive voice, and – most significantly – wrote lyrics that were a literary and poetical comment on the world around him. Vysotsky died aged only 42, in 1980. In his lifetime his politically 'unreliable' lyrics meant that none of his songs were officially released, and his following was built on unofficial cassettes of his music, and *samizdat* publications of lyrics. Pugacheva, on the other hand, was a more traditional figure. She enjoyed official approval in the Soviet era, becoming the Soviet Union's first and greatest pop star. During her career she has sold over 200 million albums, and has made the transition successfully to the post-Soviet era, enjoying a legendary status among Russian citizens and émigrés alike – of a certain age.

In the sphere of classical music, Russia's ability to produce some of the world's finest performers continues unabated. In the Soviet era, the likes of the dissident cellist Mstislav Rostropovich or the pianist Sviatoslav Richter achieved global fame for their virtuosity. Today Russia can continue to boast some of the greatest of contemporary musicians, such as the conductor Valerii Gergiev, who has a famed commitment to Russian music, the young pianist Boris Berezovsky, and the violinist judged by many to be the world's best, Maxim Vengerov.

Sport

The Soviet Union devoted impressive resources to the development of leading sportsmen and women, seeing international success as a sign of the supremacy of the socialist system. This socialist supremacy was apparent in some sports more than others, notably gymnastics and athletics. The tradition created in these sports contin-ues today, and in addition new areas of excellence are springing up. What is more, the Russian state, is – like other states – once again using sport as a platform for proclaiming its standing in the world. The 2014 Winter Olympics are due to be held in Sochi, in southern Russia, near the now-disputed border with the Georgian region of Abkhazia, which Russia has recognized as independent since summer 2008. The Sochi Games have already become a totemic event in Russia, spoken of as a key political marker in Russia's continuing development as a world power and vested with such significance that the authorities dare not let anything go wrong in the preparation for these Games.

In the 2008 summer Olympic Games in Beijing, the Russian team came third in the medals table, behind China and the United States, with seven athletics gold medals, including a second Olympic gold for the remarkable Yelena Isinbayeva, the first woman to pole-vault over 5 metres. Russia will continue to be the foremost European power in athletics for many years to come. Since the collapse of the Soviet Union there is one sport where Russia has become increasingly dominant, but which scarcely featured in the Soviet Union's list of sporting achievements. That sport is tennis, and women's tennis in particular. Of the top ten women's players at the beginning of 2009, five of them were Russian. At the 2008 Olympics, all three medallists in the women's singles were from Russia – namely, Yelena Dementieva (gold), Dinara Safina (silver) and Vera Zvonareva (bronze).

In terms of spectator sports, football remains the most popular game in Russia, though Russian teams have rarely enjoyed huge success either internationally or in European club competitions over the years. Again, however, as Russia's economy improved, so did Russia's standing in European football, boosted partly by major clubs having the wealth to sign foreign players and to pay sufficient wages to retain – at least longer than previously – home-grown talent. In 2005, CSKA Moscow won the UEFA Cup, and in 2007 the traditional dominance of Moscow-based clubs was broken by Zenit St Petersburg (owned and funded by the giant gas company, Gazprom), which won the Russian Premier League and followed that up in 2008 by winning the UEFA Cup and UEFA Super Cup, beating Manchester United in the latter.

A final area of traditional Russian excellence is chess. The world game has been dominated by Russian players and administrators for decades. Only the American Bobby Fischer in the early 1970s briefly interrupted a continuous list of Soviet and Russian world chess champions in the post-war era. The World Chess Federation, FIDE, is headed by the president of the Russian republic of Kalmykia, Kirsan Ilyumzhinov. In the 1990s, the chess world was split, as world champion Garry Kasparov refused to recognize FIDE's authority and created his own world championship, which was won in 2000 by Vladimir Kramnik. In 2006, the World Chess Championship was once again reunited, and Kramnik became undisputed champion until being beaten by the Indian Viswanathan Anand in 2007.

8

Russia and the World

The most significant developments in contemporary Russia's policies in recent years have come in the arena of international politics. During Vladimir Putin's second term as president (2004–8) and in the first year of Dmitrii Medvedev's presidency (2008–9), Russia's foreign policy became more activist than in the previous decade or so, and Russia took an ever more independent line in relation to the major Western powers. The conflict with Georgia in August 2008 demonstrated Russia's increasingly active international agenda in action. It demonstrated too the complexity and contradictions inherent in Russia's international policy.

To some observers, the Georgian conflict was a return to traditional Russian/Soviet imperialism, with Russian troops invading the territory of a neighbouring country for the first time since the Soviet invasion of Afghanistan in 1979. As we have argued repeatedly throughout this book, however, contemporary Russia is not the Soviet Union, and comparisons – even where appropriate – take us only so far. In the case of the Georgian conflict, this was not an invasion of a neighbouring country designed to occupy it and take it over. We consider the conflict in more detail later in this chapter, but for now it serves to highlight some of the key issues facing Russia in the world today.

Russia considers itself a great power, with a geographical sphere of influence it believes the rest of the world should accept. But Russia has also made an avowed commitment to the upholding of international law. In terms of its own interpretation of international affairs, Russia is strongly in favour of a multi-polar world, that is, a world where the United States does not dominate, but instead other poles of influence – such as Europe, China, Russia itself – take decisions. At the same time, Russia does not want to be isolated, but rather to be part of a new world order in which it has friendly, albeit competitive, relations with other countries.

This set of beliefs, set out by President Medvedev in September 2008, form the basis for understanding Russia's place in the world from a Russian perspective. They are not as straightforward as they might at first appear . The vision of a world in which 'great powers' have 'spheres of influence' is central to official Russian perceptions, but can be seen as an outdated echo of imperialist thinking. Taking this line might not always sit well with holding to a commitment to international law. What if countries that Russia deems to be within its sphere of influence do not want to be designated as such, as exemplified by Ukraine and Georgia, to name just two cases in recent years? Similarly, is it possible to act as a pole of global influence, able to take key decisions in relation to a sphere of influence, at the same time as not being isolated from other major powers, who may well not accept this conceptualization of the twenty-first-century world?

The notion of a sphere of influence also interacts with relations between Russia and the West. Positive relations – for example, Russian membership of the G8 group of leading nations, or the establishment of the NATO–Russia Council – are undermined from the Russian perspective by a sense of grievance that NATO's and the EU's eastward expansions impinge on its regional interests. Using the Georgian conflict of August 2008 as an example again, while this conflict had specific causes related to the independence or otherwise of South Ossetia and Abkhazia, Georgia's desire to join NATO had already played a key role in souring relations with Russia. As a corollary to this, Russia's relations with NATO – and so with 'the West' more generally – had also been undermined, as NATO was perceived as wanting to encroach on Russia's backyard.

This penultimate chapter considers the question of Russia's place in the international arena against the background set out above. Chapter 1 used as an organizing theme the duality present in Russian history with regard to relations with the West. The influence of this on Russian domestic affairs has been apparent throughout this book. Let us now return in a sense to where we started – where does Russia fit into the twenty-first-century world? The starting point for answering this question is context, or, to put it more simply, Russia's history and geography.

Geopolitics and echoes of empire

Russia's self-conceptualization as a 'great power' with a legitimate sphere of influence stems from many of the factors explored earlier in this book – its size, its evolution into the Russian and then the Soviet empires, the 'Russian Idea' with its connotations of messianism and civilizational uniqueness, and its geographical and historical place not only in Europe but also in Asia. The Soviet Union's superpower status drew on a number of these factors, and added some of its own:

- Military – during the Cold War, global international relations were dominated by the existence of two great opposing military blocs – the Warsaw Pact and NATO. Their military pre-eminence came from their capability of fighting an all-out nuclear war, the consequence of which would be global annihilation. Nuclear weapons were essential for superpower status, but attention was also given to the development and production of conventional weapons. Developments in military technology, from the 1980s onwards in particular, meant that quality of weaponry became increasingly important, whereas Soviet conventional strength had traditionally been built on quantity.
- Imperial – the Soviet bloc (those countries whose political systems were installed and maintained by the USSR) reached into the heart of Europe and, after 1979, the Soviet empire had begun to extend southwards by means of the eventually doomed invasion of Afghanistan. Furthermore, as the leader of one pole of a bipolar world, the Soviet Union had significant influence with allies across the globe, notably in South-East Asia, the Middle East, Africa and Central America.
- Ideological – the USSR was an ideological state. Its self-legitimation came from a belief in Marxism–Leninism, and the presumption that the Communist Party of the Soviet Union led the world on the path to communism and workers' power. Though easy to dismiss today, such an ideological underpinning strengthened and guided the international policies of the Soviet leadership. It provided a sense of mission and influenced the decision of some client states to ally themselves with the USSR.
- Economic – despite the Soviet economy was failing rapidly by the early 1980s (see Chapter 5), trade relations played a key role in giving substance to the ideology of international relations. Towards

the end of the Soviet period some two-thirds of the country's foreign trade was with other socialist countries. Furthermore, the Soviet Union strengthened ties with key countries by subsidizing arms exports. In the Gorbachev years (1985–91) only a third of arms exports were paid for directly; the rest were sold under advantageous credit conditions, subsidized massively, or given away free of charge.

The bipolar world of the Cold War era finally collapsed in 1989–91. Anti-Communist revolutions in Eastern Europe broke up the Warsaw Pact, the nations that had made up the Soviet Union became independent, and the USA led a coalition of forces from across the developed world to victory in the short war with Iraq in early 1991, leading to talk of a 'new world order' and a unipolar system, with the United States being the sole superpower.

It was into this world, and with the legacy of the superpower status outlined above, that Russian foreign policy emerged. There are a number of key ways in which Russia's international relations since 1991 have been shaped by aspects of the USSR's standing in the world. On the break-up of the Soviet Union, Russia became the official successor state to the USSR, and therefore took over one of the five permanent seats on the United Nations Security Council, as well as accepting primary responsibility for fulfilling treaty obligations and taking over the institutional structures necessary for the conduct of foreign policy (for example, the MFA, embassies and the Foreign Intelligence Agency).

Russia identified itself immediately as one of the 'great powers', and at the time of the Soviet Union's break-up there was little international surprise at, or argument with, the assumption of succession on the part of Russia. In the West, this process alleviated concern that the disintegration of a superpower, to be replaced by fifteen independent states, would lead to massive instability, particularly with regard to the proliferation of nuclear weapons. Among the clear majority of the 'successor states' themselves there was a recognition that only Russia had the capability and standing to take over the USSR's role on the international stage.

Identification as one of the UN 'permanent five' fitted the continuing insistence in Russian foreign policy that Russia is indeed a great power and should be treated as such. On becoming acting president on millennium eve 1999, Putin declared, in 'Russia at the Turn of the Millennium', his belief in the greatness of Russia: 'Russia was and will remain a great power. It is preconditioned by the inseparable characteristics of its geopolitical, economic and cultural existence. They determined the mentality of Russians and the policy of the government throughout the history of Russia.'

Russia's 'sphere of influence' and the Commonwealth of Independent States

Russia's increasing insistence since the late 1990s on having a 'sphere of influence' in terms of international politics raises the immediate question of how far this influence should extend. In the Soviet era, it could be seen as having a core, an inner ring and an outer ring. The core was the Soviet Union itself, which broke up into the fifteen independent states in 1991. The inner ring was the 'Soviet bloc' consisting of those Central and Eastern European countries with Communist governments, under Moscow's control until 1989. The outer ring was a looser and more fluid grouping of countries around the world that relied on Moscow for military, economic and political support. Contemporary Russia's policy of seeking a clear 'sphere of influence' has been manifest in several ways, primarily focusing on the core of former Soviet states, but also exhibiting a degree of grievance that the countries of the former Soviet bloc have now clearly aligned themselves with Western Europe.

In the immediate post-Soviet years, the formation of the Commonwealth of Independent States (CIS) represented a solution to the problem of how to organize (most of) the states that had made up the Soviet Union. Russia's decidedly pro-Western foreign policy during these years, under foreign minister Andrei Kozyrev (1990–6), gave way in Yeltsin's second term as president to a broader and more pragmatic 'Russia first' foreign policy. Then, as Russia grew stronger during the Putin presidency (2000–8), this 'Russia first' stance widened to promote the idea of Russia as regional leader.

Drawing on the historical and geographical context set out above, it is easy to understand why Russia's initial priority in terms of regional leadership is those countries that were formerly part of the Soviet Union. This is not a view based wholly on grand perceptions of geopolitics and great-power status. It also had a basis in the objective realities of economic and military infrastructures remaining from the Soviet era, and in the moral claim to influence given by the existence of a Russian diaspora up to 25 million strong in the former

Soviet states in 1989. Such realities, however, diminished over time, and most of the Russians who wanted to have returned home (see Chapter 2). None the less, the desire to retain influence over most of the former Soviet states remains at the top of Russia's foreign policy agenda today.

Of the successor states to the Soviet Union, eleven of these, along with the Russian Federation, have made up the CIS for most of the post-Soviet era. The three Baltic republics of Estonia, Latvia and Lithuania declined to join the CIS on the break-up of the Soviet Union, and consistently pursued membership of NATO and the EU, gaining both in 2004. In 2005, Turkmenistan changed its CIS status to that of associate member. In 2008, Georgia announced, after the August conflict with Russia, that it was leaving the CIS.

In the short term, immediately after the collapse of the USSR, Russia and the other post-Soviet states were faced with concrete issues of disentanglement and the reorganization of relations that inevitably result from the fracture of what was one country into fifteen. Military deployment had to be disentangled, property had to be shared appropriately – leading, for example, to disputes over the Black Sea Fleet in Ukraine and the Baikonur space-launch facility in Kazakhstan – independent currencies were established, and even such apparently minor matters as representation at the 1992 Olympic Games and the establishment of national football teams involved careful negotiation, resolved by the creation of interim CIS teams. There has never been any serious suggestion that the other former Soviet states would re-unify, with the exception of Belarus, which since 1996 has been negotiating – with very little progress other than a formal agreement – a union with Russia.

The CIS was formed in December 1991 and included most of the states emerging from the Soviet Union. From its very inception some members – Russia in particular – saw it as a means of holding on to some aspects of the Soviet Union, while others saw is as a means of achieving a 'civilized divorce', a dividing-up of what once belonged to the Soviet Union, before the newly independent states went their own ways. The CIS is not itself a state, and the non-Russian CIS is no monolith. It rests on a mix of formal multi-lateral treaties and a network of more substantial bilateral agreements between Russia and individual states. Each member state has interests that deviate to different degrees and at different times from those of Russia. There are complicated dynamics in a series of relationships, and any attempt by Moscow to make the CIS a tighter organization would risk its disintegration through centrifugal forces. For simplicity's sake, the CIS countries can be represented as an inner core of countries that want closer ties, and an outer ring joined primarily by the desire for greater freedom from Russian influence, and indeed from the CIS itself (see Box 8.1).

If the short-term difficulties of imperial break-up are complex and fraught with tension, they are at least readily identifiable. The longer-term legacy has been a forced retraction of the Russian sphere of influence. What were republics within the Soviet Union are now independent countries, and therefore subjects of international law and objects of international relations. If the Russian Federation were to

---

Box 8.1   The Commonwealth of Independent States

- The closest formal relationship is between Russia and Belarus, who are committed to a treaty on the formation of a Union State, though with little sign of anything of real substance coming of this in the near future.

- The rest of the inner core consists of Belarus, Kazakhstan, Kyrgyzstan, Russia and Tajikistan, which make up the Eurasian Economic Community, founded in October 2000.

- Armenia and Uzbekistan join this group in the Collective Security Treaty Organization (CSTO), founded in September 2003 on the basis of the remaining signatories to the Tashkent treaty of 1992. In 2008, Russia proposed that the Georgian Republics of Abkhazia and South Ossetia, which Russia recognizes as independent states following the conflict in August of that year, become part of the CSTO.

- The outer ring was made up for a decade of a loose, semi-official grouping of states, known by the acronym GUAM (Georgia, Ukraine, Azerbaijan and Moldova), and founded in 1998. This group had originally included Uzbekistan, which withdrew in 2005 and moved closer to Russia in terms of its external relations. Georgia, on the other hand, moved in the other direction and announced its intention to leave the CIS. GUAM's aim has been to avoid Russian dominance of the regional agenda, while at the same time maintaining friendly relations with Russia. (This conceptualization of the CIS as an inner core and outer ring is useful, but does not convey the full complexity of relations between the twelve independent states.)

- The Shanghai Cooperation Organization (SCO), founded in June 2001, consists of China, Kazakhstan, Kyrgyzstan, Russia, Tajikistan and Uzbekistan. It has become increasingly active, developing co-operation on a range of security issues.

engage in expansionist policies, these are now front-line countries to be expanded into, rather than launching pads for further aggrandisement. With the exception of the Georgian conflict in 2008, the blame for the initiation of which is disputed, Russia has shown little inclination for military expansion, compared to the expansion of influence. The post-Soviet equivalent of the Soviet Union's war with Afghanistan (1979–88), in terms of the attempt to secure Russia's southern flank, has been two wars with the Chechen Republic, which is not even one of the post-Soviet states but legally a component of the Russian Federation. When Russia has wanted to base troops in surrounding republics, it has had to do so after careful negotiation, combined with activities such as peace-keeping and border guarding, with the exception again of the incursion into Georgia in 2008 in response to Georgian troops' actions in South Ossetia and Abkhazia. Furthermore, it is not only Russia that has stationed troops in the former Soviet republics. During its invasion of Afghanistan in 2001, the United States established a military presence in Kyrgyzstan, Uzbekistan, Tajikistan and Georgia.

Clearly, therefore, Russian foreign policy has become more closely focused on a reduced sphere of influence compared to that of its Soviet predecessor. This provided something of a post-imperial psychological shock for Russia's policy-makers. The very idea that, for example, Ukraine is a foreign country, was a difficult conceptual leap for elite and masses alike to make, as was made dangerously clear when Russia allegedly attempted to interfere in Ukraine's presidential election in 2004. The term 'near abroad' is still widely used in Russia to refer to the former Soviet republics, as if to reinforce the fallacy that these countries are in some way not quite abroad. From the perspective of the other independent states that once made up the Soviet Union, this term is, of course, pejorative.

It seems clear that the future of the CIS, so far as its European members are concerned, is tied in with the success of their attempts to become more closely integrated into pan-European structures. By the end of 2004, the determination of Russia to hold on to, or indeed to re-create, its influence in Europe's second largest country, Ukraine, became evident in its initially staunch support for the more pro-Russian candidate, Viktor Yanukovych, in Ukraine's disputed presidential election. Yanukovych's eventual concession of defeat to Yushchenko – amid charges of electoral fraud and dirty tricks, including the serious poisoning suffered by Yushchenko – represented a serious error of judgement on the part of President Putin and Russia,

Box 8.2   Estonia's Bronze Soldier

The Russian view that the former Soviet states are clearly within their sphere of influence is perhaps most problematic when it comes to the Baltic states of Estonia, Latvia and Lithuania – always the most independent-minded of Soviet republics, the first to declare independence from the Soviet Union, and all now NATO and EU members.

Russia's stance in relation to these countries is particularly difficult, because they are both formerly Soviet and yet indisputably now part of 'the West' in terms of institutional allegiance. Given this, formal relations are for the most part remarkably good, helped by the rapid withdrawal of Russian troops from the Baltic states in the early 1990s. None the less, occasionally events reveal underlying tensions stemming from differing identities and perception.

In 2007, the Estonian government agreed to the dismantling and relocation of the Bronze Soldier of Tallinn, a memorial to Soviet soldiers who died in the Second World War.

To Estonian nationalists, this was a memorial to the troops who had brutally and illegally occupied their country, and a number had complained that this was akin to having a statue of a Nazi soldier in their capital city.

To Russians, and the many ethnic Russians living in Estonia, the government was removing a memorial to the men who had liberated Estonia from the Nazis. Indeed, the site was more than a memorial, since the remains of a number of Soviet soldiers were buried there.

On the removal of the Bronze Soldier there were several days of rioting in Tallinn, loud condemnation from the Russian government and parliament, and reports of a 'cyber attack', allegedly originating from Russia, that affected the operation of key Estonian institutions including the parliament, banks and broadcasters.

serving only to emphasize Russian impotence in its supposed sphere of influence.

The events in Ukraine in 2004 became known as the 'Orange revolution', after the colour adopted by the Yushchenko campaign. The 'colour revolutions' – chiefly Ukraine's Orange revolution and Georgia's 2003 'Rose revolution'– are seen by Russia's ruling regime as Western-inspired provocations, designed to undermine Russia's influence in its 'near abroad'. From the Western perspective, support given to the 'revolutionaries' in these cases is less controversial, sitting within the concept of the promotion of democracy.

Russian defence and security doctrines have consistently taken the line that the Russian Federation has key security interests in the CIS. Involvement, for example, in the civil war in Tajikistan in the 1990s was justified partly by the assessment that the Russian Federation could be destabilized by Islamic extremists. Moscow has deployed peace-keeping troops in Georgia and Tajikistan, and in Moldova, where the Transdnestr region continues to represent a potential source of regional instability.

Russia has also sought to exercise its influence within the CIS through the use of energy resources. On two occasions – 1 January 2006 and 1 January 2009 – Russia cut off gas supplies to Ukraine. Ostensibly, and to a large extent genuinely, the disputes leading to the cutting off of gas supplies have been commercial in nature. In 2006, Ukraine had refused to accept the new price set by Russian supplier Gazprom, which was significantly higher than the previously subsidized rate. In 2009, there was again a failure to agree prices, coupled with Gazprom's demand that Ukraine pay off the debts it owed for gas already supplied. The commercial nature of these disputes was, however, clearly augmented by political factors. Gazprom's majority shareholder is the Russian state, and, particularly in the 2009 dispute, Russian Prime Minister Putin appeared to go out of his way to demonstrate that he was issuing instructions to the company. The not-so-subtle political messages in these disputes were twofold. First, that if Ukraine wanted to move politically Westward and out of Russia's sphere of influence it should not expect any help from Russia in doing so, be that in terms of subsidized energy prices or long credit lines. Second, and directed not just at Ukraine, that Russia saw its strategic control of energy companies as a significant tool in international relations. There is a balance for Russia to strike, however, in using such a tool, between short-term political gain and a longer-term commercial loss of confidence on the part of customers. In the case of gas supplies to Ukraine, customers affected included many European countries, for whom Ukraine is a transit company for supplies from Russia. Incidents such as these serve to increase efforts on their part to find alternative suppliers and supply routes.

Russia, the West and beyond

The preceding two sections have concentrated on the contextual underpinning of Russia's foreign policy, and on setting out the notion of a Russian sphere of influence. We now widen our view beyond Russia's immediate neighbours to consider relations with the West. Since the collapse of the Soviet Union and the implementation of a truly independent Russian foreign policy, the main dividing line between Russian politicians has been the extent to which the Russian Federation should conduct a pro-Western policy. In the initial flush of post-Soviet euphoria, the first Russian foreign minister, Andrei Kozyrev, took an openly Westernizing stance. He spoke of Russia becoming a 'normal' country, by which he was understood to mean a Western-type country, economically prosperous, democratic in the Western liberal sense, and unencumbered by prescriptive ideology. In foreign policy terms this would mean co-operative participation in the major international organizations, an end to the divisive competition of the Cold War, and the opening-up of Russia both economically and culturally to Western involvement; the West, and in particular the United States, would be an ally, not an adversary. Eventually, Russia might join NATO and the European Union.

In opposition to this Westernizing stance, however, came the views of those, often termed Eurasianist, who see Russia's destiny as being separate from that of the West. This broad distinction between Eurasianists and pro-Western 'Atlanticists', was widely applied in the 1990s and is useful as a basic concept. However, contemporary Russia's attitude to the West is far more nuanced than a simple 'pro' or 'anti' label allows. The most well-known statement of Russian foreign policy in recent years was made by President Putin at the Munich Conference on Security Policy in 2007. Here he attacked the United States as showing disdain for the basic principles of international law and, alluding to the US-led invasion of Iraq in 2003, for militarily overstepping its national borders without the support of the United Nations. This stance is one that seeks to present the United States, and not Russia, as out of step with 'normal' rules of international behaviour. Russia was not alone in taking this view, and indeed had joined with France and Germany among other European nations in opposing the Iraq war.

Russia's official attitude to 'the West' has shifted several times since the late 1990s. The Westernizer versus Eurasianist division first became apparent in Russian foreign policy almost immediately after the collapse of the Soviet Union. In 1992, the control of foreign policy became a matter of contention between the Ministry of Foreign Affairs under Kozyrev, and the Security Council under Yurii Skokov. The main area of debate was over the formulation of an official foreign policy concept, and it was the Security Council that eventually took the lead in drawing this up. The resultant document took a more Eurasianist stance than that taken by the Ministry. It asserted

Russia's 'great power' status and made particular reference to its sphere of influence in the CIS.

By the second half of the 1990s, President Yeltsin's administration, having followed policies in line with Western priorities, turned to a more critical stance, encapsulated in strong opposition to NATO action against Serbia during the Kosovo crisis, particularly while Yevgeny Primakov was foreign minister (1996–8). There are several overlapping explanations for the rise of a less pro-Western foreign policy in these years in Russia, notably public opinion; disappointment with the results of pro-Westernism; the perception that Russia was being treated as a 'junior partner' in international affairs; the desire for a multi-polar world; and Russia's role as a regional leader.

When President Putin came to power in 2000, Russia shifted initially towards a more pro-Western stance. Putin's first foreign trip as president was to the United Kingdom, he established good relations with Western leaders, and post-9/11 he was strongly supportive of the US in its 'war on terror'. On 11 September 2001, when New York and Washington were attacked by Al-Qaeda terrorists, President Putin was the first world leader to offer his sympathy and support to President George W. Bush. The strength of this support, at that time and subsequently, took many observers by surprise, and brought Putin some criticism at home, especially from within the military.

Relations with the United States

Why, then, did Putin respond so favourably to the US 'war on terrorism' in the aftermath of 11 September 2001? First, it is important to note that while 11 September provides a useful point from which to date a shift in policy, there were already signs of such a shift before then. That the Islamic terrorism of Osama Bin Laden was a mutual threat to Russia, the United States and Europe had certainly not escaped the attention of policy-makers across these areas, and there had reportedly already been discussions about possible joint action against Al-Qaeda before 11 September 2001. Second, in his letter to President Bush immediately after the attacks on New York and Washington, Putin stated that the Russian people, perhaps above others, could empathize with the United States, having experienced terrorist attacks on their capital city. It was exactly two years earlier that terrorists – allegedly Chechens – had blown up two apartment blocks in Moscow, killing hundreds. Russia had been engaged in a second brutal war in Chechnya since then, in the face of much

Western criticism. Throughout that time the line taken by Putin had been that Russia was defending Europe against Islamic terrorism. After 11 September, Putin's views were listened to more in the West rather than dismissed out of hand, and Western criticism of Russian action in Chechnya decreased.

In the early years of the presidencies of both Vladimir Putin and George Bush, which almost exactly overlapped chronologically, relations between the two leaders were good, symbolized by Bush's famous statement after their meeting in Slovenia in 2001, that 'I looked the man in the eye. I found him to be very straightforward and trustworthy and we had a very good dialogue. I was able to get a sense of his soul.' The difference between the meeting in Slovenia in 2001 and that in Slovakia in 2005 was marked. By his second term as president, Putin had turned on the United States for its support of the Orange and Rose revolutions and continuous criticism of Russia's internal affairs. By the time of Putin's Munich speech of 2007 (see above) the United States' plans to site missile interceptors in Poland and a radar system in the Czech Republic had further aggravated US–Russian relations. The rhetoric of confrontation was not just ratcheted up by Russia, however, with Vice President Cheney delivering a blistering attack on Russia in a speech in Lithuania's capital, Vilnius, in 2006, the year before Putin's Munich speech. Cheney accused the Kremlin – with particular reference to the Orange revolution and the gas dispute with Ukraine in January 2006 – of 'blackmail', 'intimidation', 'undermining the territorial integrity of its neighbours' and 'interference in democratic processes'.

Dmitrii Medvedev's first trip abroad as president was to Kazakhstan and China, reflecting Russia's emphasis on the CIS and support for a multi-polar world. None the less, President Medvedev has previously been less belligerently anti-Western than most of his colleagues, and in 2008 he gave his own speech in Germany on foreign relations, which was far more conciliatory than that given by his predecessor the year before. The near-overlap of presidential terms in Russia and the United States at present has meant, seemingly fortuitously, that Russia's new president came to power in 2008 just a few months before the United States' new president, Barack Obama. This has enabled both parties, in the words of Vice President Joe Biden, to 'press the reset button' with regard to their relationship. The metaphor is revealing, in that it suggests that differences between the US and Russia, while substantive, have not been fundamental. In other words, there is no great ideological divide between the two

Box 8.3   Russia's foreign ministers

Andrei Kozyrev	November 1991–January 1996
Yevgeny Primakov	January 1996–September 1998
Igor Ivanov	September 1998–March 2004
Sergei Lavrov	March 2004–

states, but rather a series of specific disputes aggravated by differing approaches. The button can be reset in terms of tone and approach, and this may facilitate a resolution of a number of these disputes. The strength of the US–Russia relationship has waxed and waned in the two decades since the Soviet Union collapsed. This can be explained by the fact that, for every area of disagreement and antagonism, there is an area of mutual interest, such as preventing terrorism or, as the two major nuclear weapon states in the world, ensuring non-proliferation of such weapons and therefore acting together in relation to the intentions of countries such as Iran and North Korea in this regard.

Disappointment with the West

As noted earlier, the broad aim of pro-Westernism in the early 1990s was that Russia would become part of the Western community, fully involved in international organizations and, more abstractly, in the building of the new post-Cold War world order. At the popular level, closer links with the West would surely bring economic benefits and a rise in living standards towards Western levels. As time went on it became apparent that the perceived benefits of a pro-Western policy were not appearing as rapidly as had been anticipated. The economic situation is discussed in Chapter 5. In the international arena, Russia felt itself and its sensitivities to be increasingly ignored. A major example of this was the conflict in former Yugoslavia in the 1990s, where Russia's sympathies towards Serbia clashed with the notion of a pro-Western foreign policy. Increasingly, instead of co-operating with Western policy, the Russian Federation took a pro-Serbian line, and by the middle of 1995 the MFA was asserting that NATO action against the Bosnian Serbs exceeded the United Nations' mandate and could lead to 'genocide'.

This pro-Serbian stance led to a widening gap between the West and Russia, as NATO prepared for and fought a war against Serbia in 1999.

The beginning of NATO's bombing campaign against Serbia provided an illustration of the poverty of the relations between Russia and the West by the end of the 1990s. Yevgeny Primakov, by that time Russia's prime minister, was informed of the bombing when halfway across the Atlantic en route to a meeting with US Vice President Al Gore. He immediately ordered his plane to turn around and return to Russia.

To be in Moscow at this time was to be aware of strong anti-Western feeling and deep anger, expressed in the media by many otherwise pro-Western politicians as well as by the more nationalist-minded. This anger sprang from a variety of sources: a feeling of kinship with Russia's Slavic and Orthodox brethren in Serbia; a fear that, in the same way as action was being taken to protect the Muslims in Kosovo from Serbian armed forces, NATO might take action to protect the Muslims in Chechnya against Russian forces; and most of all, a feeling of impotence, that Russia no longer mattered and that NATO could wage war in Europe irrespective of Russia's feelings. However unrealistic these views might seem from the point of view of the West, they were widely held.

The apparent lack of interest in Russian sensitivities over Serbia on the part of NATO represented just one of several disappointments. Membership of the Council of Europe was delayed until early 1996 because of concerns over Russia's commitment to human rights, and Russia's voting rights in the same body were removed during the second Chechen war (from 1999 onwards). Even the Partnership and Co-operation Agreement signed between the EU and the Russian Federation in June 1994 was not fully implemented, as a sign of the EU's displeasure at the first Chechen war, 1994–6. The real impact of these measures was not great, however, and did little to curb Russian actions in Chechnya or indeed to harm longer-term relations with the EU.

Perhaps the most significant issue to foster Russian disappointment with the West was the question of NATO expansion. The decision by NATO countries to expand the alliance eastwards disappointed Russia's Westernizers, who saw it as a betrayal of their avowedly friendly stance, and confirmed the suspicions of Eurasianists, who believed that the West was determined to gain maximum advantage from its post-Cold War strength, and Russia's post-Cold War weakness.

Russia's initial post-Soviet hopes were that an entirely new European security architecture could be built. Indeed, this remains Russia's hope today, as exemplified by President Medvedev's 2008 speech in Berlin, where he proposed the drawing up of a new

European Security Treaty. However, the notion of a new European security architecture was not to be in the 1990s, and instead of diminishing in importance, NATO began to talk of expansion eastwards. As the leading Russian observer of international affairs and former deputy chair of the Duma International Affairs Committee, Aleksei Arbatov, by no means a hard-line nationalist, put it:

> While Moscow was agreeing to the reunification of Germany and to having that country stay in NATO, to disbanding the Warsaw Pact and then the very Soviet Union, to deeper reductions of nuclear and conventional forces than in the West, to the hasty withdrawal of half a million troops from comfortable barracks in Central Europe to tent camps in Russian fields – while Moscow was agreeing to all of these things, nobody took the trouble to warn Russians that NATO, the most powerful military alliance in the world, would start moving toward Russian borders. (Alexei Arbatov, 'As NATO Grows, Start 2 Shudders', *New York Times,* 26 August 1997)

Of course, this is a one-sided view, nevertheless it is representative of views widely held in Russia, particularly after the 1997 NATO Madrid summit, at which the Czech Republic, Hungary and Poland – the latter bordering the Russian territory of Kaliningrad – were invited to join NATO.

Proponents of expansion, however, saw things differently. NATO declares itself to be a purely defensive alliance. The key right and obligation of member states is that of collective defence, and therefore any state can be invited to join, so long as it is willing and able to meet the obligation of collective defence, and other member states are willing to accept its right to belong to the organization. Under these terms, the Russian Federation has nothing to fear from NATO, and – more pointedly – why should Russia have any say in whether independent states in East–Central Europe are able to join a military alliance or not? Russia in turn recognizes the validity of these arguments, but argues that NATO enlargement does not reflect the new security realities of the contemporary world. None the less, the Putin regime was content merely to disagree with NATO expansion, and not to try actively to stop the second wave of 2004, which included countries that had formerly been part of the Soviet Union, namely Estonia, Latvia and Lithuania (see Box 8.4).

Throughout the process of NATO enlargement, the Russian Federation took a stance based on the belief that Russia was a 'great

---

Box 8.4   NATO expansion

1999	**2004**
Poland	Bulgaria
Hungary	Estonia
Czech Republic	Latvia
	Lithuania
	Romania
	Slovakia
	Slovenia

---

power' and should be treated as such. This can at least be seen to have produced some benefits, in the form of the Russian–NATO Founding Act of May 1997, which set up a Permanent Joint Council (PJC) to provide a forum for consultation between Russia and NATO.

The optimism of the 1997 Founding Act was soon blown away by tensions over the Kosovo conflict, and Russia withdrew from regular PJC meetings. However, it was another international crisis and conflict – the terrorist attacks on New York and Washington on 11 September 2001 and the subsequent NATO-backed war in Afghanistan – that for a short time put Russian–NATO relations on a stronger footing than ever before. Russian support for the US-led, NATO-backed war against terrorism led to Western efforts, headed by the United Kingdom in the form of Prime Minister Tony Blair and NATO Secretary General Lord Robertson, to reward Russia with greater integration into NATO by the creation of a NATO–Russia Council in 2002. The difference between the PJC and the NATO–Russia Council lies in the latter's ability to provide genuine joint decision-making across a range of security issues, rather than NATO simply reaching agreement and using the PJC to present Russia with a *fait accompli*. Like its predecessor, however, the NATO–Russia Council has been suspended in protest at military action – this time NATO withdrawing for a period after Russian action in Georgia in 2008.

Russia's sense of grievance

The Russian Federation is one of the five permanent members of the United Nations Security Council. It has its own council with NATO, the aim of which is to ensure consultation and co-operation. Not only is Russia a member of the G8 group of leading industrial nations – a status that does not match its economic performance – but in 2006 Russia also held the G8 presidency, and President Putin hosted the annual summit that summer in the splendour of St Petersburg. None the less, these apparent signifiers that a 'great power' is being dealt with have not, certainly in the eyes of Russia's leaders, always been matched in the world of events and decision-making. Again, a sense of grievance has developed – some would say, has been nurtured – since the later 1990s at the supposed isolation of Russia from the high table of world affairs.

This sense of grievance has been expressed in several ways over recent years. As the 'Russia first' policies of the late 1990s developed it became a central element of Russian foreign-policy thinking. In August 1998, the United States launched missile strikes against suspected terrorist bases in Afghanistan and Sudan. It had long been Russian policy to stand shoulder to shoulder with the USA and other world powers engaged in the fight against terrorism. On this occasion, however, President Yeltsin issued an unexpectedly firm denunciation of American action. By the end of the year, such firm denunciations of American, and British, air strikes were to become commonplace, as the short Anglo-American bombing campaign against Iraq began in December 1998. President Yeltsin charged, in words very similar to those that President Putin would use in his Munich speech almost a decade later, that the USA had 'crudely violated the UN Charter and the generally accepted principles of international law'.

NATO action against Serbia in 1999 and US-led invasions of Afghanistan and Iraq in 2001 and 2003, respectively, increased the sense in Russia that certain Western powers, most significantly the United States, were prepared to ignore Russian wishes and sensitivities. The question for Russia was, what could be done about it? On one level, speeches could make this point, as could gestures such as the temporary withdrawal of ambassadors from Washington and London in 1998, and the resumption of bomber flights close to NATO airspace during Putin's second term as president. As relations with certain Western countries, particularly the United States and the United Kingdom, became progressively worse during these years, a number of events occurred which, although not foreign relations *per se*, certainly were seen by some as a message of Russian anger towards these states (see Box 8.5). What Russia did in terms of a broader foreign policy approach was to concentrate its diplomatic efforts increasingly on attempts to create a multi-polar world, in

Box 8.5   UK–Russian relations in the 2000s

Relations with the United Kingdom became particularly tense and difficult during the first decade of the twenty-first century. This was partly
a factor of the UK being seen as the United States' most loyal ally, and
therefore serving as a proxy state for Russian displeasure. However, it
was mainly related to specific UK–Russian disputes.

Russia wanted to extradite a number of its citizens from the UK,
including advocates of Chechen independence and 'oligarchs' from the
Yeltsin years, but these requests were rejected by the UK courts, who
granted political asylum to a number of figures who were viewed as criminals or even terrorists by the Russian authorities. London came to be
seen as a refuge from the Kremlin for many opponents of the Putin
regime, or – as the Kremlin might have put it – enemies of Russia. While
the UK government explained that it could not influence the decisions of
the courts, the Russian leaders found this hard to believe, perhaps because
such influence over their own courts would have been easy for them.

Those granted political asylum included a former KGB officer,
Aleksandr Litvinenko, who had made enemies in the Russian secret
service, and had accused some of its officers of being behind the
Moscow apartment bombings of September 1999, which had been
blamed by the authorities on Chechen terrorists. In 2006, Litvinenko
died of polonium poisoning in London and the British media, with the
odd exception, implied that the Russian state, or even Putin himself,
was behind this death. A police investigation led to the UK requesting
the extradition of a suspect from Russia. This was refused by Russia,
on the grounds that the Russian Constitution did not allow for such an
extradition. The UK government found this hard to believe.

In Moscow, the Russian authorities launched raids on the offices of
the British Council, alleging financial irregularities, and the British
ambassador experienced regular harassment by a political youth organization loyal to the Kremlin.

There were a number of other disputes involving the refusal of visas
to British businessmen, mutual accusations of espionage, and commercial disputes, all of which served to deepen the crisis in UK–Russian
relations.

contrast to what was widely perceived to be a unipolar world dominated by the United States.

A multi-polar approach

Russia effectively adopted a policy of 'counter-hegemony' in foreign
affairs from the second half of the 1990s. While such a
policy need not by definition be an anti-US policy, its aim was never-

theless to build up other poles of influence and power in order to rein in US hegemony. Foreign Minister Primakov's Eurasianism led to his favouring the building up of a tripartite alliance in Asia, and so Russia's relations with China and India increased in significance, both in diplomatic terms and in practical terms – for example, in the increased arms trade between these powers. The development of the Shanghai Cooperation Organization (SCO) in the first decade of the twenty-first century has taken the creation of another pole of influence still further. The SCO is made up of China, Russia, Kazakhstan, Kyrgyzstan and Tajikistan, with Iran, Mongolia, India, Pakistan, Afghanistan and Turkmenistan having observer status. In 2007, the SCO conducted military manoeuvres, and some in Russia see it as potential counter to NATO as a military alliance in the longer term.

When President Putin came to power in 2000 he proved himself to be far more of a foreign policy activist than his predecessor. Within a year of succeeding Boris Yeltsin, he had visited the United Kingdom, Germany, France, Italy, Spain, China, Japan, Mongolia, the two remaining Marxist–Leninist countries – Cuba and North Korea, and the CIS states of Belarus, Ukraine, Azerbaijan, Uzbekistan, Turkmenistan and Kazakhstan. There was concern in some quarters in the West – the United States in particular – that Putin was creating a pole of influence out of those states that had long-standing quarrels with the USA. Russia's closer relations with North Korea, Cuba, Iran and Iraq led to talk of an 'alliance of the aggrieved'. Such a stance was again apparent in 2008, when President Medvedev visited Cuba and Venezuela in 2008.

Both Putin and Medvedev, on the other hand, have also declared Russia's foreign policy to be Eurocentric, again raising the possibility that a wider Europe might increasingly represent a separate pole of influence in a multi-polar world. Finally, even the poles have become a source of multi-polar thinking. Russia is at the forefront of those nations who are seeking to claim areas of the Arctic as their own territory. In 2007, a submarine expedition saw the much publicized planting of a Russian flag under the sea at the North Pole, as part of Russia's claim to a vast territory under the ocean, on the grounds that it is a continuation of the Siberian continental platform.

Public opinion

The concept of anti-Westernism is deep-rooted in Russian political discourse, from the Slavophiles versus Westernizers debate of the nineteenth century, to the Cold War of the twentieth century. As such, it is an easy concept for politicians to use and the public to understand. Populists and nationalists find anti-Westernism a particularly attractive notion, and it has been useful to recreate the sense of a strong, independent Russia in recent years. Ancient, buried emotions can easily be brought to the surface by the idea of, for example, a NATO threat to Russia.

The Putin administration set itself up as returning Russia to stability and strength after the chaos and weakness of the Yeltsin years. The serious economic difficulties experienced by the vast majority of Russians in the 1990s were seen by many to stem from the adoption of a Western market democracy. In simple terms, the attitudes of the Russian public towards the West can be said to have hardened as official relations have cooled. Surveys carried out by the Russian Academy of Science's Institute of Sociology show that, in 1998, only 4 per cent of Russians saw NATO as a threat, but by 2007, the word 'NATO' provoked a negative response from 76 per cent of respondents. In 1995, attitudes among Russians to the United States were 77 per cent positive and 9 per cent negative. By 2007, they were 37 per cent positive and 45 per cent negative.

However, popular attitudes to the West can be assessed on a deeper level. When Russians are asked whether they are closer to the West or to the East in terms of their culture or their economy, they identify more closely with the West. Analysing the Russian public's attitudes towards the West shows that the notion of anti-Westernism is more complex than its use in the media or in political debate often allows.

What is 'the West'? During the Cold War it was clear that East and West were separate power blocks, defined by competing ideologies. It is less easy to define 'the West' today. There is no doubt that the United States is 'the West' in most Russian minds, but the situation with regard to Europe has become less clear. The run-up to the Iraq war saw Russia, France and Germany aligned against military action, with the United Kingdom, Spain and Italy in favour. The European Union would seem obviously to be in 'the West' as an entity, but many Russians do not instinctively consider new member states such as Bulgaria, Poland and Romania to be Western. Indeed, the existence and expansion of the European Union has complicated Russian attitudes to Europe. In the 1990s, the view that Russia is a part of Europe was more commonly held than it is now, since contemporary attitudes confuse the notion of Europe as a geographical and cultural identity with that of Europe as in the European Union. 'Europe' as an entity is still viewed positively in Russia, but the percentage expressing this positive appraisal has slipped a little, from 83 per cent in 2000 to 72 per cent in 2007.

Conclusion

This chapter has presented an overview of contemporary Russia's place in the wider world which reveals the multi-faceted approach taken towards external relations by the Russian Federation. As all states do, Russia draws on its history, traditions, economic interests, geopolitical situation, public opinion and cultural values in its inter-action with other countries. Russia, though, is not like the vast major-ity of states. Its recent history is as a global superpower. Its traditions are imperial. Its economic interests affect vital energy supplies to much of Europe. Its geopolitical situation is as the world's largest country, the biggest country in Europe, the biggest country in Asia, bordering fourteen states, and with legitimate interests across much of the northern hemisphere. Its public opinion and cultural values reflect these factors, and throw into the mix a sense of disappointment at national decline in the 1990s, of grievance – warranted or not – at perceived Western enmity, and of national pride built on notions of Russia as a great power, fated to lead and to guide lesser nations.

It is scarcely surprising, then, that contemporary Russia's interna-tional policies can appear on occasion to be contradictory, given that so much has to be held in check. Trade-offs have to be made between different priorities. In conclusion, though, to understand Russia's rela-tionship with the wider world, it is important to be able to pick out Russia's own priorities from among these countervailing factors. Among the twists and turns in relationships with different states that we have noted (and, for that matter, with the many states not covered here), and underpinning broader shifts in attitude towards concepts such as 'the West', contemporary Russia needs to be understood as a country that sees itself as a regional leader of global significance. We can argue over whether this self-perception is accurate, legitimate or delusional, but it is essential to acknowledge its hegemony within Russia. When trade-offs are made in Russia's international relations, regional leadership and 'great power' status are only tradable in extremis. And even then, as the history of post-Soviet Russia shows, every effort will be made to trade them back at the earliest opportunity.

9

Conclusion

The preceding chapters of this book have explored many aspects of Russia as it stands at the end of the first decade of the twenty-first century. There are different narratives within these chapters, stemming partly from the themes covered in each one, but also partly from differing notions of such questions as what constitutes progress, what makes a successful state, and against what standards we are considering contemporary Russia.

Perhaps the watchword for Russia, and the Russians, in this century so far has been stability. Compared to the twentieth century with its revolutions, world wars, civil war, famines, mass persecution, social upheaval, class warfare, dictatorships, Cold War, Soviet collapse, civil conflict, economic disaster and national decline, then the stability that coincided with the presidency of Vladimir Putin (2000–8) is particularly notable. Not only were these years of political and social stability, but also of economic growth and increasing presence on the international stage. It is this narrative which, as set out in Chapter 7, is promoted by the Putin–Medvedev regime.

When Russia emerged from the Soviet Union it was a country in shock, and the strikingly large number of excess deaths and decline in life expectancy of the 1990s stand witness to this fact. Old certainties were gone, a superpower disappeared, millions of people found themselves overnight waking up literally in a different country from the one in which they had gone to sleep. The so-called 'shock therapy' of economic reform was as much an experiment on the people as was the introduction of Communist ideas in the Soviet era, based on the theories of intellectuals but tried out to harmful effect on millions of Russians. Processes which in other countries took decades or even centuries were expected by many observers in these same countries to take place in Russia with unheard-of rapidity.

Many empires have decayed in the past, but few have simply been signed away in one fell swoop as was the Soviet Union by Boris Yeltsin, Leonid Kuchma and Stanislau Shushkevich (the leaders of Russia, Ukraine and Belarus) in the Belovezh Forest in December 1991. Democratic countries the world over have seen the gradual development of political parties winning representation incrementally over decades of fighting for concessions from the ruling elite. Few have been expected to complete this transition from dictatorship to democracy in a few years, at the same time as transforming their economy from a relatively closed, state-controlled system to a globally competitive market economy.

These gigantic and simultaneous system changes – empire, democracy, economy – occurred together in Russia. They were accompanied by a complete dismantling of the censorship and propaganda of the preceding decades, meaning that not only were Russians suddenly confronted with an array of ideas, religions and cultural experiences previously unavailable to them, but that this happened in the same decade that the internet was created. At the same time too, Russians were suddenly allowed to travel abroad freely.

If that is the 1990s in Russia, it is little wonder that we identify stability as the watchword of the following decade, nor that stability has been at the heart of the narrative that contemporary Russia's regime has promoted. To Putin and Medvedev, and indeed, opinion polls tell us, to most Russians, the 1990s were a 'time of troubles', after which the economy grew, living standards increased, and Russia regained something of its great-power status.

However, there are different narratives, which stem from different perspectives. A common view in the West is that the first decade of the twenty-first century has seen Russia go backwards, not forward. According to this narrative, the nascent democracy of the Yeltsin years has been stifled by a resurgent authoritarianism, even – in the most vehement version of this narrative – by a resurgent Soviet-style secret police once again seeking to control Russia. What we have seen since the turn of the millennium is the gradual, firm, and occasionally brutal, removal of plurality from politics, the media and even big business in Russia. Whereas elections in Russia in the 1990s were genuinely competitive and unpredictable, the election of Medvedev to the position of president and head of state in March 2008 was a done deal the moment Putin supported his candidacy. State control of the popular media has meant that the space for dissident voices to be heard has shrunk. The development of civil society has similarly been damped down by the state, and in many respects Russia appears to be reverting to authoritarian type.

Those who follow this line of argument do not have much truck with the view that Russia is being expected to cope with too much too quickly, and that democratization took much longer in the West. They point instead to other former Soviet countries that have succeeded in becoming fully fledged democracies and market economies with remarkable alacrity. They argue that the problem with Russia is not that it is moving too slowly towards democracy and the market, but that it has actually stopped moving in that direction at all and has turned back.

Most observers will grant that there is truth in both of these narratives. There is no doubt that the 1990s were, for most Russians, a decade of great upheaval and uncertainty. Jobs were lost, savings wiped out, and day-to-day existence became increasingly difficult. The privatization process resulted in a very few people becoming incredibly rich by gaining the nation's assets, and then in many cases using them for their own gain. The oligarchs used their wealth to buy power, and their power to become richer. The state, in contrast, lacked both power and wealth – taxes were not collected, wages were not paid, the provision of health care, education and defence was minimal, crime and corruption flourished, and the component parts of the Russian Federation dismissed the writ of the centre in sufficient numbers for there to be genuine concern that Russia itself might disappear.

A good case can be made, then, for the strengthening of the state under Putin from 2000 onwards. At the same time, though, a truly strong state is one whose strength is in its institutions and not dependent on the continuation in power of particular individuals. While Russia's Constitution and its leaders declare the existence of democracy, it is difficult to envisage contemporary Russia experiencing a democratic change of regime in the near future. Instead, Russia's ruling elite has a fear of political pluralism. They toy with the notion, many even believe that in the longer term it is the way to go, but then they persist in the view that the time is not yet right for Russia to risk a genuinely competitive election.

They persist too with the state paternalism that is rooted in Russia's history, with the idea that the state knows best and – as we noted in Chapter 2 – that opposition is a rather unnecessary diversion away from fulfilling the vital tasks standing before the country. Nor does this view simply seem to be one conveniently held by Russia's rulers in order to justify their own perpetuation in power. Public opinion has been remarkably approving of Russia's ruling regime in the twenty-first century, under both Putin and Medvedev. Approval ratings of 70–80 per cent for the president demonstrate satisfaction with stability and economic growth to be the key factors. Concerns over democracy and freedoms scarcely affect public approval at all in this respect.

We also noted in Chapter 2, however, that the flip-side of a political and popular culture that tends to venerate the capabilities of the state, is that disillusionment sets in rapidly when the state fails. Of course, this happens the world over, but in mature democracies there is an opposition waiting in the wings to replace the failing regime, and an established mechanism by which this process takes place. Russia lacks the sort of opposition that looks ready for power. And while it has a formal process for the transfer of power to an opposition by elections, this has never yet happened, and so that process must at best be judged as untried, and at the worst as unforeseeable.

What, then, of the coming decade in Russia? The tandem of President Medvedev and Prime Minister Putin was established in 2008 with a manifesto called 'Russia 2020'. This is made up of a sensible set of policy commitments centred on developing the Russian economy from its lucrative raw materials base to become diversified and technology-driven. As part of this process, Russia itself would become more widely developed, with investment in its physical infrastructure opening up more and more of its vast territory to the advantages of economic growth, and the continued implementation of plans to improve the provision of health care, education and housing across the country.

Implicit in the 'Russia 2020' plan is again the notion, backed up by the constitutional elongation of the presidential term to six years from 2012 onwards, that the state should not be distracted in its vital tasks by too much in the way of politicking, elections and democratic choice. This does not necessarily mean that democracy has been terminally junked in the regime's conceptualization of Russia 2020. The concept of democratic competition with two centrist parties vying for power can be read into current developments as a possible scenario in a decade or so. Overall, what 'Russia 2020' is about is another of those concentrated periods of modernization so familiar in Russian history (see Chapter 1).

Russian history, however, never runs as smoothly as the implementation of a plan to 2020 might imply. Alternative scenarios exist, and these stem from the problems facing contemporary Russia that we have identified throughout this book. The continuing global economic crisis that began in 2008 undermines the smooth development programme as planned. Prudent financial management by the Putin government in the boom years of 2000–8 meant that Russia had paid off debts and built up reserves by the time the economic slowdown hit. However, this slowdown has necessitated some of these reserves being spent on fending off the effects of the crisis, rather than on the development process as intended. Also, it may be that the impact of the economic downturn on the Russian people might create disillusionment with the state and its leaders. In the longer term, political disillusionment and growing poverty bring back on to the agenda potential outcomes widely discussed in the 1990s. Worst-case scenarios include the growth of extreme nationalism, or resurgent separatist movements prompted by increasing economic disparities between regions. Neither of these appear to be imminent from the perspective of 2009, but they remain as possible scenarios in the event of ever more severe economic collapse.

Equally, however, there is the possibility that Russia's position as a supplier of raw materials means that, even though terms of trade may decline, it none the less has a secure medium- to long-term resource to provide the basis for economic development. Whatever the precise outcome of the economic downturn for Russia, though, it will have to deal with demographic decline over the next fifty years or so. Related to this, the question of immigration – particularly with regard to the Far East and its proximity to populous China – will require political skill to deal with it effectively. Russia's national identity as a 'great power' both influences and depends on wise navigation through these problems.

These are the challenges that lie ahead for Russia, and, of course, the future is always uncertain. What is absolutely certain, though, is that these challenges will be addressed increasingly by a post-Soviet generation. The younger generation of Russians, of which President Medvedev is a forerunner, has grown up in a comparatively open country, indeed far more open in so many ways than that in which their parents lived. For all its many faults, Russia's first twenty-first century decade has been one of relative stability and increasing prosperity. The task for the coming generation is to let stability evolve into the change necessary to develop a modern twenty-first-century state, economically diverse, technologically advanced, securely pluralist, and yet still recognizably Russian.

Recommended Reading

There is a wide range of literature on Russia, though in comparative terms the pool of academics working on Russia-related topics is relatively small and so the constant need for updated material is not always met in every field of study covered in this book. Aside from academic writers, Russia is one of those countries that is sufficiently distinctive for it to make a keen impression on Western journalists and travellers, leading to a steady stream of memoirs, travel books and so on. This brief guide sets out a few key texts that will enable you to widen your knowledge of the themes covered in each chapter of this book.

1 The Historical Context

A good and recent overview of Russian history is provided by Hosking (2001), and an accessible overview of the past two centuries is available in Westwood (2002). The most up-to-date history, from Tsarism to contemporary Russia, is to be found in Service (2009). There is a vast amount to choose from in terms of histories of the Soviet era, from books covering the entire period, such as Volkogonov (1998), to those devoted to particular leaders. For Lenin and Stalin, recent comprehensive biographies are those written by Service (2000 and 2004, respectively). A definitive account of Khrushchev and his time in power is that by Taubman (2003). For the Brezhnev era, books by Bacon and Sandle (2002) and Tompson (2003) give useful introductions. The Gorbachev years are well-served by authors such as Brown (2007) and Sandle (2009), and by Gorbachev's own memoirs. Yeltsin, as well as the three volumes of his own memoirs, is the subject of useful biographies by Aron (2000) and Colton (2008). There are many accounts by participants and observers of the years around the collapse of the Soviet Union, and perhaps particularly engaging for Western readers are those by the British and US ambassadors of that time, respectively Braithwaite (2002) and Matlock (1995).

2 Land and People

A geographical overview of post-Soviet Russia is available in Shaw (1999). Environmental matters are dealt with by Oldfield (2005) and by Feshbach

(1992). Feshbach also deals with the demographic problem facing Russia. The story of the development of Moscow is provided by Colton (1996), and updated in a fascinating account of life in contemporary Moscow by Shevchenko (2009). Ross and Campbell (2007) present an assessment of the regional policy pursued by Vladimir Putin. A useful account of the Chechen conflict is available in Sakwa (2005). An up-to-date assessment of religious matters can be found in Knox (2005). For stories of travels into the Russian heartland in the post-Soviet years, Richards (2009) reaches aspects of the Russian land and people not touched by most academic accounts.

3   Social Structure and Social Policy

Compared with overviews of Russian politics, the number of book-length accounts of Russian society is relatively small. Health issues are covered well in Manning and Tikhonova (2009), and the same authors' 2004 book on poverty and social exclusion similarly provides a fine overview of its topic. An account of developments in the judicial sphere is available in Jordan (2000 and 2005) and Sharlet (2001). The Khodorkovsky case and its implications are covered in definitive detail by Sakwa (2009). For a harrowing, non-academic account of an Englishman caught up in Russia's judicial system during the Putin years, Tig Hague's *Zone 22* (2008) does not stint on graphic description. For an assessment of reforms in the higher education system in the post-Soviet era, see Bain (2003).

4   Politics and Government

A vast amount has been written about the politics and government of contemporary Russia, with the most comprehensive being Sakwa (2007). A critique of the Putin era is contained in Baker and Glasser (2005) whereas Michael Stuermer's (2008) readable account of the Putin years takes a less stringently critical line. Lilya Shevtsova (2005) gives more of an insider's view. Bacon and Renz (2006) consider the growing authoritarianism of Putin's Russia from a security perspective. Various aspects of Russian politics are succinctly and expertly covered in White *et al.* (2009).

5   The Economy

A fine guide to the workings of the Soviet economy is to be found in Hanson (2003). There are a number of assessments of the reform attempts in the 1990s, largely focused on a 'Where did it all go wrong?' theme. For coverage of this period, see Freeland (2000). An insight into the criminality and corruption of the early post-Soviet years is available in Brzezinski (2002). The economic developments of the Putin era are not so widely covered. None the less, an excellent and concise overview is given by Tompson (2004), and an assessment of Russia's global economic interaction is to be found in Letiche (2007).

6 Rights, Freedoms and Civil Society

The situation in the Soviet Union in relation to rights, freedoms and civil society is dealt with well in an account of the life of Sergei Kovalev, Boris Yeltsin's human rights commissioner in the 1990s; see Gilligan (2004). Howard (2003) sets out the legacy of communism in relation to civil society, though this book does not focus solely on Russia. The best book on Russian civil society is that edited by Evans *et al.* (2005). Belin (2002 and 2004) provides useful accounts of the development of the media under Yeltsin and into the Putin era. White (2008) covers civil society and the media in some depth.

7 Ideas and Culture

Concepts of the Russian Idea and the Russian approach to life are the subject of McDaniel (1996) and of Pesmen (2000). Alena Ledeneva (1998 and 2006) explains much about contemporary Russian political and economic life through her studies of social interaction. An excellent literary account of Russian perceptions of life on the threshold between the Soviet and post-Soviet eras is to be read in Hobson (2001). Russian identity in the post-Soviet era is surveyed in Billington (2004) and the place of death and memory in Russia is splendidly evoked in Merridale (2000). Literature in contemporary Russia forms the subject of Laird (1999).

8 Russia and the World

The legacy of the Soviet Union in foreign relations is dealt with well in Nogee and Donaldson (1992) and the development of relations in the Commonwealth of Independent States (CIS) forms the subject of Webber (1997). A good account of US–Russian relations for most of the Yeltsin era can be found in Talbott (2002), and on the decline in these relations, Tsygankov (2009) provides impressive clarity. Perspectives on Russian foreign policy towards Europe are available in Webber (2000) and Prozorov (2006). Bobo Lo (2008) concentrates expertly on the relationship between Russia and China. Lo (2003) also delivers the best account of Russia's foreign relations under Putin's first term. For analysis that goes up to the end of Putin's second term, Donaldson and Nogee (2009) are always reliable.

Russia Online in English

A small selection of useful websites covering various aspects of Russian affairs is listed below.

General

State Statistical Agency: www.fsgs.ru/wps/portal/english

Government and politics

President: www.president.kremlin.ru/eng/

You can watch the President's video blog, with English subtitles, at www.president.kremlin.ru/eng/sdocs/vappears.shtml

The official sites of the Russian government and parliament, as opposed to that of the president, do not put much effort into an English version.

The State Duma website (www.duma.ru) and the Federation Council website (www.council.gov.ru) are in Russian.

The government website (www.government.ru) has some English language content at: www.government.ru/content/governmentactivity/government_meetings

News

The Moscow Times: www.moscowtimes.ru

Russia Profile: www.russiaprofile.org

Radio Free Europe: www.rferl.org

CDI's Russia Weekly: www.cdi.org/russia

Blogs

Robert Amsterdam: www.robertamsterdam.com

Russia Other Points of View: www.russiaotherpointsofview.com

Academic analysis

Centre for Strategic and International Studies, Russia and Eurasia Program: http://cis.org/program/russia-and-eurasia-program/

Carnegie Moscow Centre: www.carnegie.ru/en

Royal Institute of International Affairs – Russia programme: www.chatham-house.org.uk/research/russia_eurasia

Russia Votes: www.russiavotes.org

Economics

Bank of Finland Institute for Economies in Transition: www.bof.fi/bofit_en/index.htm

Public opinion

The Levada Center: www.levada.ru/eng

Miscellaneous

The Moscow Metro: www.metro.ru

Russian religious news: www.stetson.edu/~psteeves/relnews

Forum 18 (religious freedom): www.forum18.org/index.php

Bibliography

Ahdieh, R. B. (1997) *Russia's Constitutional Revolution: Legal Consciousness and the Transition to Democracy 1985–1996* (Pennsylvania: Penn State University Press).

Alexander, James (2000) *Political Culture in Post-Communist Russia: Formlessness and Recreation in a Traumatic Transition* (Basingstoke: Macmillan).

Anderson, John (2003) *Religious Liberty in Transitional Societies: the Politics of Religion* (Cambridge: Cambridge University Press).

Antonenko, Oksana and Kathryn Pinnick (eds) (2005) *Russia and the European Union* (London: Routledge).

Aron, Leon (2000) *Boris Yeltsin: A Revolutionary Life* (London: HarperCollins).

Bacon, Edwin (1998) 'Party Formation in Russia', in Philip Davies and John White (eds), *Political Parties and the Collapse of Old Orders* (New York: SUNY Press).

Bacon, Edwin (2002) 'Church and State in Contemporary Russia: Conflicting Discourses', in Rick Fawn and Stephen White (eds), *Russia after Communism* (London: Frank Cass).

Bacon, Edwin (2004) 'Russia's Law on Political Parties: Democracy by Decree?', in Cameron Ross (ed.), *Russian Politics under Putin* (Manchester: Manchester University Press).

Bacon, Edwin and Mark Sandle (eds) (2002) *Brezhnev Reconsidered* (Basingstoke: Palgrave).

Bacon, Edwin and Bettina Renz, with Julian Cooper (2006) *Securitising Russia: The Domestic Politics of Vladimir Putin* (Manchester: Manchester University Press).

Bain, Olga (2003) *University Autonomy in the Russian Federation since Perestroika* (London: Routledge).

Baker, Peter and Susan Glasser (2005) *Kremlin Rising: Vladimir Putin's Russia and the End of Revolution* (London: Simon & Schuster).

Belin, Laura (2002) 'The Russian Media in the 1990s', in Rick Fawn and Stephen White (eds), *Russia after Communism* (London: Frank Cass).

Belin, Laura (2004) 'Politics and the Mass Media under Putin', in Cameron Ross (ed.), *Russian Politics under Putin* (Manchester: Manchester University Press).

Berliner, Joseph (1988) *Soviet Industry from Stalin to Gorbachev: Essays on Management and Innovation* (Aldershot: Elgar).

Billington, James H. (2004) *Russia: In Search of Itself* (Baltimore, Md.: Johns Hopkins University Press).

Bivens, Matt (2003) ' A Glum Report Card on Russia', *Moscow Times*, 2 June.

Bowker, Mike (2004) 'Conflict in Chechnya', in Cameron Ross (ed.), *Russian Politics under Putin* (Manchester: Manchester University Press).

Bowker, Mike and Cameron Ross (eds) (2000) *Russia after the Cold War* (Harlow: Longman).

Braithwaite, Rodric (2002) *Across the Moscow River: The World Turned Upside Down* (Newhaven, Conn.: Yale University Press).

Breslauer, George (2001) 'Personalism versus Proceduralism: Boris Yeltsin and the Institutional Fragility of the Russian System', in Victoria E. Bonnell and George W. Breslauer (eds), *Russia in the New Century: Stability or Disorder?* (Boulder, Col.: Westview Press).

Brown, Archie (ed.) (2001) *Contemporary Russian Politics: A Reader* (Oxford: Oxford University Press).

Brown, Archie (2007) *Seven Years that Changed the World: Perestroika in Perspective* (Oxford: Oxford University Press).

Brus, Wlodzimierz and Kazimierz Laski (1989) *From Marx to the Market: Socialism in Search of an Economic System* (Oxford: Clarendon Press).

Brzezinski, Matthew (2002) *Casino Moscow: A Tale of Greed and Adventure on Capitalism's Wildest Frontier* (New York: Free Press).

CIA (Central Intelligence Agency) (2008) *World Factbook* (Washington, DC: Potomac Books).

Cockerham, William (1999) *Health and Social Change in Russia and Eastern Europe* (London: Routledge).

Colton, Timothy J. (1996) *Moscow: Governing the Socialist Metropolis* (Cambridge, Mass.: Harvard University Press).

Colton, Timothy J. (2008) *Yeltsin: A Life* (New York: Basic Books).

Danks, Catherine (2009) *Politics Russia* (Harlow: Longman).

Donaldson, Robert H. and Joseph L. Nogee (2009) *The Foreign Policy of Russia: Changing Systems, Enduring Interests* (Armonk, NY: M. E. Sharpe).

Evans, Alfred B., Laura A. Henry and Lisa McIntosh Sundstrom (2005) *Russian Civil Society: A Critical Assessment* (Armonk, NY: M. E. Sharpe).

Feshbach, Murray (1992) *Ecocide in the USSR: Health and Nature under Siege* (London: Aurum Press).

Fish, M. Steven (2000) 'The Executive Deception: Superpresidentialism and the Degradation of Russian Politics', in Valerie Sperling (ed.), *Building the Russian State: Institutional Crisis and the Quest for Democratic Governance* (Boulder, Col.: Westview Press).

Fish, M. Steven (2005) *Democracy Derailed in Russia: The Failure of Open Politics* (Cambridge: Cambridge University Press).

Forbes Magazine (2009) www.forbes.com/2009/03/11/world-richest-people-billionaires-2009-billionairesland.html (last accessed 18 September 2009).

Freeland, Chrystia (2000) *Sale of the Century: Russia's Wild Ride from Communism to Capitalism* (New York: Random House).

Gill, Graeme and Roger D. Markwick (2000) *Russia's Stillborn Democracy? From Gorbachev to Yeltsin* (Oxford: Oxford University Press).

Gilligan, Emma (2004) *Defending Human Rights in Russia: Sergei Kovalyov, Dissident and Human Rights Commissioner, 1969–1996* (London: RoutledgeCurzon).

Goldman, Marshall I. (2003) *The Piratization of Russia: Russian Reform Goes Awry* (London: Routledge).

Gorbachev, Mikhail (1996) *Mikhail Gorbachev: Memoirs* (New York: Doubleday).

Hague, Tig (2008) *Zone 22* (London: Penguin) (also known as *The English Prisoner*; and in the United States as *Tomorrow You Go Home*).

Hahn, Gordon M. (2004) 'Managed Democracy? Building Stealth Authoritarianism in St. Petersburg', *Demokratizatsiya: The Journal of Post-Soviet Democratisation*, 12(2).

Hamilton, Alexander, James Madison and John Jay (2008) *The Federalist Papers*, Oxford World's Classics (Oxford: Oxford University Press).

Hanson, Philip (2003) *The Rise and Fall of the Soviet Economy* (Harlow: Longman).

Hare, Paul, Mark Schaffer and Anna Shabunina (2004) 'The Great Transformation: Russia's Return to the World Economy' (Edinburgh: Centre for Economic Reform and Transformation, Herriot-Watt University); available at: (www.sml.hw.ac.uk/cert/wpa/2004/dp0401.htm).

Harrison, Mark (2002) 'Economic Growth and Slowdown', in Edwin Bacon and Mark Sandle (eds), *Brezhnev Reconsidered* (Basingstoke: Palgrave Macmillan).

Herspring, Dale (ed.) (2006) *Putin's Russia: Past Imperfect, Future Uncertain* (Lanham, Md.: Rowman & Littlefield).

Hobson, Charlotte (2001) *Black Earth City: A Year in the Heart of Russia* (London: Granta).

Hoffman, David (2002) *The Oligarchs: Wealth and Power in the New Russia* (New York: PublicAffairs).

Hosking, Geoffrey (1998) *Russia: People and Empire, 1552–1917* (London: Fontana Press).

Hosking, Geoffrey (2001) *Russia and the Russians: A History* (London: Allen Lane).

Howard, Marc Morjé (2003) *The Weakness of Civil Society in Post-Communist Europe* (Cambridge: Cambridge University Press).

International Helsinki Federation for Human Rights (2003) *Torture and Inhuman or Degrading Treatment or Punishment in Selected OSCE Participating States,* Report by the IHF to the Special OSCE Meeting on the Prevention of Torture, Vienna, 6–7 November.

Jordan, Pamela (2000) 'Russian Courts: Enforcing the Rule of Law?', in Valerie Sperling (ed.), *Building the Russian State: Institutional Crisis and the Quest for Democratic Governance* (Boulder, Col.: Westview Press).

Jordan, Pamela (2005) *Defending Rights in Russia: Lawyers, the State and Legal Reforms in the Post-Soviet Era* (Vancouver: University of British Columbia Press).

Kahn, Jeffrey (2002) *Federalism, Democratization, and the Rule of Law in Russia* (Oxford: Oxford University Press).

Kings College London, International Centre for Prison Studies (2009) *World Prison Brief*), www.kcl.ac.uk/depsta/law/research/icps/worldbrief/ (last accessed 18 September 2009).

Knox, Zoe (2005) *Russian Society and the Russian Orthodox Church: Religion in Russia after communism* (Abingdon: RoutledgeCurzon).

Kornai, János (1992) *The Socialist System: The Political Economy of Communism* (Princeton NJ: Princeton University Press).

Laird, Sally (1999) *Voices of Russian Literature: Interviews with Ten Contemporary Writers* (Oxford: Clarendon Press).

Lane, David and Cameron Ross (1999) *The Transition from Communism to Capitalism: Ruling Elites from Gorbachev to Yeltsin* (Basingstoke: Macmillan).

Lean, Geoffrey (2006) 'The Dead Sea that Sprang to Life', *Independent on Sunday*, 28 May.

Ledeneva, Alena V. (1998) *Russia's Economy of Favours: Blat, Networking and Informal Exchanges* (Cambridge: Cambridge University Press).

Ledeneva, Alena V. (2006) *How Russia Really Works: The Informal Practices that Shaped Post-Soviet Politics and Business* (Ithaca, NY: Cornell University Press).

Letiche, James (2007) *Russia Moves into the Global Economy* (London: Routledge).

Lewis, David (2000) *After Atheism: Religion and Ethnicity in Russia and Central Asia* (London: Curzon).

Lieven, Dominic (1998) *Chechnya: Tombstone of Russian Power* (Newhaven, Conn.: Yale University Press).

Linz, Juan (1990) 'The Perils of Presidentialism', *Journal of Democracy*, Winter, pp. 50–69.

Lloyd, John (1999) 'The Russian Devolution', *The New York Times Magazine*, 15 August.

Lo, Bobo (2003) *Vladimir Putin and the Evolution of Russian Foreign Policy* (Oxford: Blackwell/Royal Institute of International Affairs).

Lo, Bobo (2008) *Axis of Convenience: Moscow, Beijing, and the New Geopolitics* (Washington, DC: Brookings Institution).

Manning, Nick and Nataliya Tikhonova (eds) (2004) *Poverty and Social Exclusion in the New Russia* (Aldershot: Ashgate).

Manning, Nick and Nataliya Tikhonova (eds) (2009) *Health and Healthcare in the New Russia* (Aldershot: Ashgate).

McCauley, Martin (1998) *Gorbachev* (Harlow: Longman).

McDaniel, Timothy (1996) *The Agony of the Russian Idea* (Princeton, NJ: Princeton University Press).

Maes, Francis (2002) *A History of Russian Music: From Kamarinskaya to Babi Yar* (Berkeley, Calif; University of California Press).

March, Luke (2002) *The Communist Party in Post-Soviet Russia* (Manchester: Manchester University Press).

Matlock, Jack (1995) *Autopsy on an Empire: The American Ambassador's Account of the Collapse of the Soviet Union* (New York: Random House).

Meier, Andrew (2004) *Black Earth: Russia after the Fall* (London: HarperCollins).

Merridale, Catherine (2000) *Night of Stone: Death and Memory in Russia* (London: Granta Books).

Midgley, Dominic and Chris Hutchins (2004) *Abramovich: The Billionaire from Nowhere* (London: HarperCollinsWillow).

Nogee, Joseph L. and Robert H. Donaldson (1992) *Soviet Foreign Policy since World War II* (London: Macmillan).

OECD (2004) *OECD Economic Survey of the Russian Federation* (Paris: OECD).

Oldfield, Jonathan (2005) *Russian Nature: Exploring the Environmental Consequences of Societal Change* (Aldershot: Ashgate).

Pesmen, Dale (2000) *Russia and Soul: An Exploration* (Ithaca, NY: Cornell University Press).

Pilkington Hilary (ed.) *et al.* (2002) *Looking West? Cultural Globalization and Russian Youth Cultures* (Pennsylvania: Penn State University Press).

Politkovskaya, Anna (2003) *Putin's Russia* (London: Harvill Press).

Prozorov, Sergei (2006) *Understanding Conflict between Russia and the EU: The Limits of Integration* (Basingstoke: Palgrave Macmillan).

Putin, Vladimir (2000) *First Person: An Astonishingly Frank Self Portrait by Russia's President* (London: Hutchison).

Rahr, Alexander (2000) *Wladimir Putin: Der 'Deutsche' im Kreml* (Munich: Universitas).

Read, Christopher (2001) *The Making and Breaking of the Soviet System* (Basingstoke: Palgrave Macmillan).

Reddaway, Peter and Robert W. Orttung (eds) (2004) *The Dynamics of Russian Politics: Putin's Reform of Federal–Regional Relations, Vol. I* (Lanham, Md.: Rowman & Littlefield).

Remington, Thomas F. (2000) *Politics of Russia* (London: Longman).

Remington, Thomas F. (2001) *The Russian Parliament: Institutional Evolution in a Transitional Regime, 1989–1999* (Newhaven, Conn.: Yale University Press).

Richards, Susan (2009) *Lost and Found in Russia: Encounters in a Deep Heartland* (London: I. B. Tauris).

Ross, Cameron (2004) 'Putin's Federal Reforms'. in Cameron Ross (ed.). *Russian Politics under Putin* (Manchester: Manchester University Press).

Ross, Cameron and Adrian Campbell (2007) *Federalism and Local Politics in Russia* (London: Routledge).

Sakwa, Richard (ed.) (2005) *Chechnya: From Past to Future* (London: Anthem Press).

Sakwa, Richard (2007) *Putin: Russia's Choice*, 2nd edn (London: Routledge).

Sakwa, Richard (2009) *The Quality of Freedom: Khodorkovsky, Putin and the Yukos Affair* (Oxford: Oxford University Press).

Sandle, Mark (1998) *A Short History of Soviet Socialism* (London: UCL Press).

Sandle, Mark (2009) *Gorbachev: Man of the Twentieth Century?* (London: Hodder Arnold).

Schumpeter, J. A. (1934) *The Theory of Economic Development* (Cambridge, Mass.: Harvard University Press).

Service, Robert (2000) *Lenin: A Biography* (Basingstoke: Palgrave Macmillan).

Service, Robert (2004) *Stalin: A Biography* (Basingstoke: Palgrave Macmillan).

Service, Robert (2003) *A History of Modern Russia: From Nicholas II to Putin* (London: Penguin).

Service, Robert (2009) *The Penguin History of Modern Russia: From Tsarism to the Twenty-first Century* (London: Penguin).

Sharlet, Robert (2001) 'Russia's Second Constitutional Court: Politics, Law, and Stability', in Victoria E. Bonnell and George W. Breslauer, *Russia in the New Century: Stability or Disorder?* (Boulder, Col.: Westview Press).

Shaw, Denis (1999) *Russia in the Modern World* (Oxford: Blackwell).

Shevchenko, Olga (2009) *Crisis and the Everyday in Post-Socialist Moscow* (Bloomington, Ind.: Indiana University Press).

Shevtsova, Lilya (1999) *Yeltsin's Russia: Myths and Realities* (Washington, DC: Carnegie Endowment for International Peace).

Shevtsova, Lilya (2005) *Putin's Russia* (Washington, DC: Carnegie Endowment for International Peace).

Stuermer, Michael (2008) *Putin and the Rise of Russia* (London: Weidenfeld & Nicolson).

Talbott, Strobe (2002) *The Russia Hand: A Memoir of Presidential Diplomacy* (New York: Random House).

Taubman, William (2003) *Krushchev: The Man and his Era* (New York: W.W. Norton).

Tompson, William (2003) *The Soviet Union under Brezhnev* (Harlow: Longman).

Tompson, William (2004) 'The Russian Economy under Vladimir Putin', in Cameron Ross (ed.), *Russian Politics under Putin* (Manchester: Manchester University Press).

Transparency International (2008) *Corruption Perceptions Index 2008* www.transparency.org/policyresearch/surveysindices/cpi/2008 (last accessed 17 September 2009).

Tsygankov, Andrei (2009) *Russophobia: Anti-Russian Lobby and American Foreign Policy* (Basingstoke: Palgrave Macmillan).

United Nations (2009) *UNData* http://dara.un.org/Data.aspx?d=Gender Stat&f=inID%3A12 (last accessed 18 September 2009).

Volkogonov, Dmitri and Harold Shukman (ed.) (1998) *The Rise and Fall of the Soviet Empire: Political Leaders from Lenin to Gorbachev* (London: HarperCollins).

Vujačič, Veljko (2001) 'Serving Mother Russia: The Communist Left and the Nationalist Right in the Struggle for Power, 1991–1998', in Victoria E. Bonnell and George W. Breslauer, *Russia in the New Century: Stability or Disorder?* (Boulder, Col.: Westview Press).

Webber, Mark (1996) *The International Politics of Russia and the Soviet Successor States* (Manchester: Manchester University Press).

Webber, Mark (1997) *CIS Integration Trends: Russia and the Former Soviet South* (London: Royal Institute of International Affairs).

Webber, Mark (2000) *Russia and Europe: Conflict or Cooperation?* (Basingstoke: Palgrave Macmillan).

Webber, Stephen (1999) *School, Reform and Society in the New Russia* (London: Macmillan).

Westwood, J..N. (2002) *Endurance and Endeavour: Russian History 1812–2001* (Oxford: Oxford University Press).

White, Stephen (2000) *Russia's New Politics* (Cambridge: Cambridge University Press).

White, Stephen (ed.) (2008) *Media, Culture and Society in Putin's Russia* (Basingstoke: Palgrave Macmillan).

White, Stephen, Richard Rose and Ian McAllister (1997) *How Russia Votes* (Chatham, NJ: Chatham House).

White, Stephen, Richard Sakwa and Henry Hale (2009) *Developments in Russian Politics 7* (Basingstoke: Palgrave Macmillan).

Wilson, Elizabeth (1994) *Shostakovich: A Life Remembered* (London: Faber &Faber).

Witte, John and Michael Bourdeaux (eds) (1999) *Proselytism and Orthodoxy in Russia: The New War for Souls* (Maryknoll, NY: Orbis).

World Health Organization (2000) *The World Health Report 2000 – Health Systems: Improving Performance* (Geneva: World Health Organization).

World Health Organization (2008) *WHO Report on the Global Tobacco Epidemic* (Geneva: World Health Organization).

Yeltsin, Boris (1990) *Against the Grain: An Autobiography* (London: Pan).

Yeltsin, Boris (1994) *The View From the Kremlin* (London: HarperCollins).

Yeltsin, Boris (2000) *Midnight Diaries* (London: Weidenfeld & Nicolson).

Index